# Handfasting
## and wedding rituals

# about the authors

**Raven Kaldera** has worked as a Pagan wedding consultant on and off for fifteen years, doing costuming, props, ritual design, theatrical production, and occasionally performing nonlegal handfastings.

**Tannin Schwartzstein** is the Archmage of Worcester, Massachusetts, where she runs the occult shop Bones and Flowers and is a licensed Pagan minister.

*Welcoming Hera's Blessing*

# Handfasting
## and
## Wedding Rituals

*Raven Kaldera & Tannin Schwartzstein*

Llewellyn Publications
Woodbury, Minnesota

FIRST EDITION
Eighteenth Printing, 2021

Book design by Rebecca Zins
Cover background image ©Digital Vision
Cover photo ©Doug Deutcher
Cover design by Lisa Novak
Editing and layout by Andrew Karre and Rebecca Zins

*Library of Congress Cataloging-in-Publication Data*
Kaldera, Raven.
    Handfasting and wedding rituals : welcoming Hera's blessing / Raven Kaldera & Tannin Schwartzstein.—1st ed.
          p.    cm.
    Includes bibliographical references and index.
    ISBN 13: 978-0-7387-0470-8
    ISBN 10: 0-7387-0470-9
    1. Marriage customs and rites. 2. Marriage—Religious aspects—Neopaganism. 3. Marriage—Religious aspects—Goddess religion. 4. Same-sex marriage. I. Schwartzstein, Tannin. II. Title.

GT2690.K35 2003
392.5—dc22

2003060797

Llewellyn Publications
A Division of Llewellyn Worldwide Ltd.
2143 Wooddale Drive
Woodbury, MN 55125-2989
www.llewellyn.com

Llewellyn is a registered trademark of Llewellyn Worldwide Ltd.

Printed in the United States of America

# Contents

# preface

Why ask the blessing of Hera, the Greek goddess of marriage, on this book? Most of us who studied classical mythology saw her as a jealous harridan rather than a sweet, positive goddess. And yet . . . even leaving aside the idea that her anger may be a later addition to her character (once she was deprived of most of her power and kept on solely as the consort of Zeus), Hera is still a power to be reckoned with. Every time someone weeps because they have no permanent partner, or desperately wishes to be married, or gnashes their teeth all night with jealousy because their mate is off with another, they invoke the energy of Hera into their lives. Conversely, every time people make commitments or dream about a wedding or wade into a counseling session with the clear faith that this can only make them stronger together, they are also invoking her power.

Marriage, like all things worth doing, is an ambivalent situation. It's not easy to make a commitment to someone, promising that you will hang in there, not run away, keep working and fighting and sharing, not give up until it seems hopeless, thinking of her every time you make a decision, putting her needs first yet not stinting your own. It's not easy at all. In fact, it can be grueling (though rewarding) work, and that's why half of all marriages end in divorce. Yet we still keep on doing it, again and again and again. The dream is too attractive, and the eventual reward down the road is nothing to be sneezed at. Marriage is a crucible within which people find out more about themselves, their upbringing, their brainwashing, their demons, their strengths, their challenges, and their true paths. It's almost impossible to commit yourself to that kind of close connection with another human being, even if only for a while, and not learn something deep about yourself.

Thus we come back to Hera. She is not an easy goddess, though her gifts are great. She demands attention, perhaps more than is convenient—like a marriage. She provokes arguments and questions entitlements—like a marriage. She does not want to let go, or be put second in any way, or be told to be quiet and decorative and supportive. She makes you work for her blessing, sometimes requiring truly heroic acts, which is the real secret of marriage. Thus we ask for her blessing on this book, even though it deals only with the positive part of wedded life—the beginning.

Hera traditionally was a triple goddess with three forms: bride, married woman, and widow. This book is dedicated to Hera the Bride, but we are always aware that the other two forms go with the package. It's the hardest thing about marriage, the part that no one talks about—no matter how much work you put into the relationship, sooner or later it is going to end, like all things. Either you will get divorced or someone will die. This bitter thought, hovering just outside of view at every wedding, simply makes the joy of the moment more intense. It's the way life works; you take the challenging with the harmonious. Hera understands this.

In September 1999, I married Bella, who is now my wife. I had just gotten a gender change from female to male, and I was getting legally married again, this time as the bridegroom and not the bride. It felt pretty strange, although we knew it was right—we'd been together for seven years and were still deeply in love. However, while we were planning the wedding, Hera kept calling me to talk to her. Since I'd reviled and rejected her while I lived as a woman, I felt even more uncomfortable about facing her now as a man, but she would not be denied. Strangely enough, she seemed less forbidding now that I was on the other side of the equation. I wrote this poem as tribute for her, and she approved in spite of the ambivalence that it expresses and blessed our union. Sometimes I think the gods are perfectly happy with any kind of tribute, even if it is suspicious, or fearful, or even negative. They just want acknowledgement of their power, whatever it inspires. Thank you, Lady.

## for hera

Lady, I am getting married

This autumn, we will stand

Before the people and swear oaths

And you will watch, and laugh at me

That I ever scorned you, ever thought

To flee your sphere. I followed wilder gods

Whose thoughts did not range past a day, a month,

Perhaps a year, for such bonds as you bank on

Seemed more chains to me than webs of love.


I'd seen how you'd treated my companions

Of childhood, sitting on your couch

With your prim pursed glance, your pride

In your stubborn faithfulness,

Your bitter vengeance wreaked on the wrong targets—

The battered wives, the hangdog husbands,

The obsessed and their restraining orders, the children

Cowering from the rage in the next room, these

I laid at your doorstep, horror in my heart—

I would not be loved for what I had sacrificed.

And yet here I am, reluctantly

Burning much-grudged incense at your altar

Glancing from side to side, as if afraid

That someone might see me kneeling for Hera,

Great Lady of Heaven, Queen of All the Gods,

Revered by all in ancient times,

Whose Juno lives in every woman—you deserve better,

Lady, than my awkward suspicion.

I ask you, choking out the words,

For that gift you give above reproach—

To live in love with one who loves you

All the days of your lives on the Earth.

Say you believe in Hera, you fool,

Say

I do.

—RAVEN KALDERA 1999

*chapter 1*

# pagan couples

As Pagan clergypeople, one of the great parts of our community service work is marrying people. It has been our pleasure and duty to bear witness to couples' commitment to one another, their faces shining with joy and love, before the gods and their community. However, the days or months leading up to that point had often been fraught with a good deal of trial and tribulation for Neopagan couples who wanted to write their own ceremonies and had very little to choose from.

There were certainly a number of handfasting rituals in the books of the Neopagan "old masters," and many of those had some truly beautiful lines, but they generally tended toward the same format. We found that the needs of modern Neopagan couples were too varied to resort to one-size-fits-all wedding ceremonies. Some were deep in the broom closet and wanted a "nondenominational" ritual that had Pagan overtones but could pass in front of intolerant non-Pagan family members. Some wanted it openly Pagan, but light—a ceremony that reasonably tolerant non-Pagan guests would find inoffensive and not uncomfortable. Others wanted it Pagan all the way, but with a theme other than the "traditional" format—combining it with semihistorical aesthetics, Tolkien elves, Native American words, science fiction, fantasy faeries, or any number of other interesting ideas.

In some cases, one partner was Pagan and the other practiced a different religion that they wanted incorporated into the ritual. These couples usually felt that it would be easier to incorporate Jewish or Christian imagery into a ceremony performed by a Pagan clergyperson than to attempt to push Pagan ritual into a more conservative church or temple structure, and they needed inspiration.

Then there was the problem of nontraditional marriages. Although queer weddings are certainly not disallowed in our faith, there was little attempt to create ceremonies for nonheterosexual couples (one exception to the former was Z. Budapest's lesbian wedding tryst in *The Holy Book of Women's Mysteries*), and none at all for polyamorous group-weddings.

We've found quite a few books on the market that contained build-your-own-wedding materials—pieces of texts and invocations—but they were all geared toward a Judeo-Christian world. It can feel unsatisfying for many couples to simply change "God" to "Goddess" half the time, and go from there. We have had couples turn to us confused and frustrated when they were told they would, in essence, have to choose from a few similarly formatted rituals or create their own from scratch. "I asked the High Priestess who was going to perform our ceremony if there was a reference book we could buy on the subject, and she laughed!" was one dejected groom-to-be's comment.

*Handfasting and Wedding Rituals* is that reference book. Even with all the rituals—whole and in pieces—that you'll find in here, nothing may suit you exactly. That's all right. Feel free to mix and match, pull out a vow here or a circle casting there. Maybe only a few lines may inspire you, but if they spark you to write the words that you really need, then this book has done its job.

You will find all the rituals and ritual segments in this book labeled with level 1, level 2, or level 3. This denotes the level of obvious Pagan content. A level 1 ritual can be performed in front of non-Pagans to whom you do not wish to explain your religion. These rituals are a way to incorporate subtle Pagan aesthetics into your wedding and still be "stealth," if that is what you require. No deity names are invoked in these rituals, and they can be passed off as fantasy or folk tradition. Level 2 rituals are "Pagan Lite"; they may invoke deities, but they do not require the guests to have any knowledge of Paganism, and they don't contain activities that might upset most non-Pagans. Level 3 rituals are for the hardcore Pagan couple who are not concerned with the shockability of their audience. Deities are invoked repeatedly, in all their glory, and no attempt is made to lighten the tone.

# getting started

Have your ceremony planned out as far ahead as possible. You, your clergyperson, and the participants may find it much less stressful to have copies of it months ahead of the wedding date so as to be familiar with it when the time comes. When Raven and Bella married, their complex ritual was put on paper literally two days before the wedding date, and poor Tannin, who was marrying them, only got handed the final copy an hour beforehand, and she stumbled through the complicated wording as best she could. Be kind to the people who are helping you make this day special, and give them plenty of time to get familiar with it and not make fools of themselves—or you.

You will also want to think about how long you actually want your rite to be. Once you've decided on the wording and plan of action, do a walk-through with people reading the parts and making the motions (this doesn't have to be the actual people who are in the ceremony; you can find friends for stand-ins) and see how long it takes. Take note of how your vows sound. The vows that seemed perfect on the page may be wrong or awkward when read aloud. Remember that juggling props like chalices and knives and scrolls and cords takes more time than you might think, and candles can suddenly refuse to light. Don't keep people standing in a circle for longer than half an hour, and provide chairs for the elderly or disabled and those with small children. Don't rush through it, either; slow is better. People are actually going to want to hear what's going on. With this in mind, if it reads as an hour in a simple rehearsal, it's going to be an hour and a half in real time, and you might want to shorten it.

We've found, by trial and error as Neopagan clergypeople, that anything under twenty minutes feels too short for people who may have come a long way to watch a ritual happen, and anything over an hour and a half can be too long for an audience to remain focused. Also, the more people present, the shorter the ceremony should be. (We've found that the more people in a crowd, the shorter the attention span of everyone in it.) Use the above time guideline for a crowd of fifty onlookers, and subtract a minute for each additional person until you get down to an hour, and then subtract a minute for each two additional people. If you have a really big crowd, keep it at about half an hour. If it's an elaborate ceremony, practice with props and restrictive costumes in advance. Don't overschedule things to do; for instance, one couple wanted to plant a tree as part of their ceremony, but someone pointed out to them that they would both be clad in flowing silks and probably didn't want to go digging holes and shoveling dirt in their expensive and fragile outfits.

Rehearsal also helps with estimating space. Sitting people take up more room than standing people but are less comfortable. Any kind of dancing, musicians, or even ritual walking about or gesticulating requires room. If you are going to use friends to call the quarters, make sure that they have four clear spaces to move to without pushing people aside. Also, make sure the props are appropriate for their users. We know of one very small priestess who was asked by the groom to cast a circle with his five-foot claymore, which she found in midritual was too heavy for her to lift and dangerously sharp, as well. She had to draft a helper to hold the tip up and walk around her in a circle while she staggered under the weight of the hilt.

You may also want think about the problem of volume. If there will be two hundred people present in an outdoor area, will everyone be able to hear you? If they can all hear you, will it be so loud that it disturbs the neighbors? In this day and age of portable sound equipment, it's easy to miscalculate the noise level, and, conversely, unamplified voices are not as loud and distinct in the open air as you think.

The religions of relatives are often a touchy subject in Pagan handfastings, especially legal ones. We strongly warn against using your wedding as your coming-out-of-the-broom-closet statement. It's akin to inviting your parents to a drag show you are starring in as your way of telling them that you're gay. It's far more respectful, and safer, to talk to them about it beforehand. One bride, the daughter of fundamentalist parents, sent them a very Pagan-oriented invitation, and then explained the situation over the phone. She said, "If you're not comfortable with this, I respect that, and I'll understand if you can't make it. If there's something that I can do to make you more comfortable, tell me, and I'll decide if it's workable."

Respect aside, you should never assume that the public nature of a wedding will keep people on their best behavior. We've seen terrible outbursts at weddings from disgruntled relatives. It's better to make sure that everyone knows everything beforehand and that there are no surprises. This also goes for relations who are currently feuding. If you just can't bring yourself to talk to your family about your religion (or any potentially explosive family situation), then maybe you should either talk to a therapist about it or else not invite them. Some people actually hold two weddings, a secular one and a spiritual one, or they hold weddings with different guests, in order to make everyone comfortable.

For that matter, if any of your guests may be uncomfortable with any part of your ceremony, let them know about any unusual activities on the invitation. If you're expecting people to participate in something (more actively than watching, anyway), let them know this as well. It's best not to surprise anyone with a ritual role on the day of the wedding; let them know well beforehand. And even if you have designed your ceremony for the maximum number of active participants, please make room for guests who are shy, uncomfortable, or don't feel well and only want to watch.

And speaking of respect, it's important also to respect the venue. Don't hold your handfasting on a site where you don't have permission to be. Even if it's a "deserted" space such as a quarry or overgrown lot, someone may own it. Public areas usually require permits of some sort; this includes cemeteries, parks, and the town green. It's a bad omen to have the police break up your handfasting. On the other hand, forewarned police officers (or forest rangers, etc.) can be allies in keeping interlopers out of your space, or reassuring neighbors that this is "only a wedding."

If you do get permission, make sure you understand the regulations set by the owners, and be prepared to follow them to the letter. Do not bring items to the ceremony that are illegal in certain public areas. Things like fire (including tobacco and incense), weapons (edged or otherwise), animals, video or flash cameras, alcohol, bloodletting, and food and beverages can all be illegal in public places. Certain types of entertainment may also be questionable, such as "fortunetellers," which includes any kind of diviner, since in some towns these activities are illegal under panhandling laws. When in doubt, check with the local authorities. If you must have these things at your ceremony, make arrangements with the owner of a private site. It's better to pay a little extra money than to be publicly humiliated.

Plan to bring a cleanup crew, and leave your site clean. In times of ecstatic celebration, it's easy to forget the rules of common courtesy. Plan for that cleanup period, even if it only consists of a site check. You might try designating one friend (preferably someone willing to stay sober) who will do a litter and lost-and-found patrol after the guests have left.

The "wonderful wedding experience" usually doesn't come about without a whole lot of careful planning. There are books available on general wedding etiquette, catering, reception issues, and so forth; we've touched on only those problems that are particular to Pagan handfastings. However, despite all the complexities of preparation and arrangements, the united efforts of the couple, the clergyperson, and assorted friends and family can result in the most wondrous and inspiring memory of a couple's life together. That's why we keep on performing them, time after time.

*chapter 2*

# handfasting history

We first find the word "handfasting" actually referring to a kind of marriage in the British Isles, something that we would consider the equivalent of common-law marriage. Unlike "official" weddings, which had some kind of officiant, and would be recorded solemnly by people whose job it was to record these things, handfasting was simply performed by a couple in front of a witness or two. It was generally no more complex than the couple joining hands (thus making "fast" their hands) and declaring themselves united, sealing it with a kiss.

Traditionally, the handfasting gesture made a figure-eight with the hands, right to right and left to left. Taking right hands was the common greeting of shaking hands; the handfasting merely went one step further and had participants join left hands as well, symbolizing that all parts of themselves were joined, left and right, female and male, solar and lunar. (It is interesting to note that during the Renaissance, a form of marriage was developed which allowed upper-class men to wed their lower-class mistresses, even if they were already legally married to their wives. This was called a Morganatic marriage, and the participants joined their left hands but not their right ones.) Another traditional handfasting gesture is still used at conventional weddings: drinking from two glasses, poured from the same jug, with arms interlinked.

Handfasting, as common-law marriage, was most often performed by the peasantry. Their estates did not need any paperwork to combine; indeed, many would have no more than the clothes on their backs and perhaps a sackful of belongings. It was finally made illegal in England in 1753, when marriages were proclaimed valid only when performed by a paid clergyman, but Scotland retained the handfasting custom up until 1939—so for nearly two centuries desperate couples often eloped over the border to marry.

Upper-class couples, on the other hand, often did have large estates that needed accounting for, not to mention dowries, dowers, bride-prices, and political annexations and consolidations. While every wedding was theoretically the joining of two families, the weddings of the rich and powerful might also join two villages or even kingdoms, and thus they required much more in the way of inarguable witnessing. For this social strata, the word *handfasting* came to mean a betrothal, when a couple were promised to each other, with the expectation that the next few months (or years) before the wedding would be filled with legal wrangling. Children could be handfasted with each other, and these betrothals could be broken later if better prospects arose.

With the advent of the church rather than the civil wedding, the term *handfasting* fell out of usage until the 1950s and the repeal of the witchcraft laws in England. This brought a number of hidden occultists out of the broom closet and began the Neopagan movement. Early witchcraft chroniclers and clergy, like Gerald Gardner and Doreen Valiente, needed a word for their wedding rite that was not associated with a legal marriage, as there were no legal Pagan clergy at that time, and the old term was dug up again.

In the original, hardcore Gardnerian tradition, you are supposed to handfast with your magical partner. Gerald Gardner supposedly believed that one could travel mentally in time along the Akashic records; because of this, the ideal handfasting was to vow to each other for "this life and all future lives to come." Theoretically, one would meet up with one's former soulmate again and again and renew these vows. It was also considered crucial that your magical partner be of the opposite sex, since this created the manifestation of the god-and-goddess polarity. Because of this, Gardnerian Wiccans were encouraged to handfast to their opposite-sex magical partner, regardless of sexual preference or with whom they were actually having sexual relations. On the other side, when Z. Budapest started the feminist Wiccan tradition on the 1960s, she used the word "tryst" instead of "handfasting" specifically to indicate same-sex (and usually female) marriage ceremonies.

In the early days of the Pagan movement, handfastings were supposed to be closed rituals, open only to the couple and their coven. Due to closeting, the couple might even have a church ceremony for their family and non-Pagan friends, which would have been considered a necessary evil. The handfasting rituals were also deliberately designed to be as different as possible from church weddings. Today, however, we are seeing a massive upsurge in Pagan weddings by couples who are in love with many of the traditional Judeo-Christian elements (for example, the white dress and veil and the rows of attendants in special matching costumes) and who want to invite everyone in their lives, regardless of religious faith. In some cases, they want to use the cultural wedding icons in order to make the wedding valid and believable in the eyes of the non-Pagan guests. This has led to a collage of cultural traditions, as each couple tries to choose symbols that are both meaningful to them and that will resonate with their audience.

*chapter 3*
# magical aesthetics

One of the most-asked questions when planning a Pagan handfasting is, "What stuff is
symbolic of love?" Actually, there are so
many things that have been used as being
symbolic of love that it would be impossible to list them all here, but we'll put down
a few. These are items or symbols that are
associated with love deities or with weddings in ancient times or that have taken
on such symbolism over the last century
for the modern Neopagan demographic.

Please also see appendix C, where
Allyson Chaple of Ritual Fantastique
Theme Weddings has provided an exhaustive list of appropriate flowers for wedding
bouquets around the theme of love.

# botanicals

## *flowers for friendship*

**Arbor Vitae**

**Boxwood**

**Fuschia**

**Galax**

**Gerbera daisy**

**Ivy**

**Alstromeria**

**Pansy**

**Periwinkle**

**Pine**

**Pussywillow**

**Rose, yellow**

**Wallflower**

**Willow**

**Zinnia** (thoughts of absent friends)

## *flowers for magical wreaths, bouquets, and decorations*

**Asphodel** (generally a flower of mourning, but symbolizing love that endures past death)

**Baby's Breath** (if children are wanted)

**Bleeding Heart**

**Bluebell** (symbolizes constancy)

**Columbine**

**Cupid's Dart**

**Honeysuckle**

Ivy (symbolizes bonds and inseparability)

**Kiss Me Over the Garden Gate**

**Love Lies Bleeding** (symbolizes love that endures difficulty)

**Love-in-a-Mist** (also known as Devil in a Bush)

**Mimosa** (the tree, not the sensitive plant)

**Myrtle**

**Orange Blossom** (traditional for bride's wreath, unlucky for anything else)

**Rose** (of course, the flower of Venus)

**Scarlet Runner Bean**

**Seaholly**

**Violet**

**White Clover** (the common clover that grows in your lawn)

**Wild Geranium**

**Yarrow** (traditionally presented to the bride in a small bouquet in the receiving line, as it represents knowledge and experience, which she would supposedly gain in the first days of her married life)

*essential oils (for anointing or scenting ritual items)*

**Ambergris**

**Apple Blossom**

**Bergamot**

**Honeysuckle**

**Jasmine**

**Musk, patchouli, and ginger** (for physical passion)

**Rose**

**Sweet Pea**

**Vanilla**

**Violet**

*herbs and incense components (for wreaths, bouquets, sachets, or incense)*

Basil

Cardamom

Coriander

Damiana

Elecampane

Honey

Lavender

Lemon Balm

Lemon Verbena

Lovage

Marjoram

Meadowsweet

Myrtle

Orris Root

Rose Petals

Rosemary (for remembrance)

Sugar Maple

Vetivert

Wine

Yohimbe *(Note: Damiana and yohimbe are aphrodisiacs, and it seems a shame to burn them and not just make them up into a potion for the happy couple on the wedding night! To make an infusion, combine one ounce of yohimbe bark, one ounce of damiana leaves, and 1,000 mg of vitamin C [for better absorption and to prevent nausea] in two cups of boiling water. Boil for five minutes, steep for twenty minutes, strain out all the plant matter, and decant to drink later. Be warned, however, that yohimbe can cause hallucinations in large quantities, so drink at your own risk, and preferably only under the tutelage of someone who is familiar with its use. Please treat the sacred plants of our ancestors with due respect!)*

# *colors*

In the Renaissance, every color had a specific meaning, even down to tiny shades and gradations. Many of the color names used then are now long gone, such as murrey (dark wine-red), watchet (light blue-green), Catherine pear (peachy-russet), or goose-turd (obnoxious greenish-yellow). A selection of colors, usually from two to eight, were carefully chosen by the bride and groom to symbolize the qualities that they wanted in their marriage.

Although we have not yet been able to find a comprehensive list of all the color meanings, modern wedding planners can use their intuition and ask themselves what different colors mean to them. Sometimes it's simply the favorite colors of the hand-fasting couple. At Raven and Bella's wedding, they looked at color meanings and decided that they were just going to retreat to using deep red (a version of her favorite scarlet that he could stand), malachite green (his second favorite, the first being orange, which she vetoed), and metallic gold for nobility. They decided that the red was passion and the green a commitment to the Earth. Another couple, much older, chose a combination of white, silver, turquoise blue, and amethyst. The blue and purple symbolized the couple's birthstones, and the traditional wedding white was paired with silver to symbolize their silver hairs of wisdom.

These days, red generally symbolizes passion (as well as anger and action). In China it means happiness and is the traditional wedding color. Pink is a muted version that suggests childhood and childlike joy. Green symbolizes new beginnings, springtime, the Earth, and fertility. It's probably hands down the most popular color for Pagan weddings. Both green and pink have been used for Venus, the planet of love, while Mars, her polar opposite and sometime mate, is red. On the other hand, green could link to the fertile Green Man and red is a women's menstrual color.

Colors like blue and purple have been used in handfastings to suggest serenity and bliss, as they are sky hues. Black is another favorite; this may seem odd, but black is traditionally the color of Saturn, planet of limits and laws, and the positive side of Saturn is the ability to make a commitment. Wearing or using black at a wedding suggests that the couple understand the depth of their commitment and take it seriously.

White is the most ambivalent color of all, it seems. As it's the traditional color of Judeo-Christian weddings, it's usually at least considered by Pagan couples—and usually discarded. With a few exceptions, the association of white with virginity has mixed and often negative meanings for Pagan brides, the great majority of whom will not be virgins and will be quite proud of that fact. In a sex-positive religion, virginity has no special status; it's just a transient and alterable commodity and another way of being in the world. Wearing white is far rarer among Pagan brides than among the general population, largely because of these mixed feelings about the Christian judgment of the white wedding; but, on the other hand, some Pagan brides decide to use white because they simply love the color. Symbolically, it can stand for newness of spirit or the Maiden Goddess, rather than just physical intactness.

# candles and candle etiquette

Candles are a traditional part of many weddings, not just those of Pagans. The first people to use candles for weddings were the ancient Greeks, who actually used dozens of them, mimicking the stars in the sky as being witnesses to the wedding vows. (See the Grecian Wedding on page 248.) Good candle colors for weddings are white, red, pink, green, and pastel colors, and they can be anointed and consecrated before the ritual with any of the above oils. If you are going to use them, however, there are a few good rules of thumb to keep in mind:

- If there are a lot of candles, put them in jars or use hurricanes, those glass cylinders that can be placed over candles. It's too easy for someone to brush against an unguarded candle and knock it off.

- If you intend to have walls full of candles, with or without jars, set up special shelving if there's none available. Try to get the shelves at face height or above, so that the candles burn high and are less likely to get jostled off. Don't put them on tables or near the edge of any shelf. If you do set up special shelving (we did, at one wedding) build it with a horizontal rail at the edge of each shelf, at about midcandle height, like what you find on many spice racks or old-fashioned plate display shelves. This lessens the candle-dumping possibility even further.

- If there are small children around who cannot be trusted around flames, make sure that they are placed higher than those children can reach. Children who must actually carry candles should practice with them well beforehand, so you know they are capable. Have an adult ride herd on them and take the candles away as soon as the ceremony is over. If there are cats or dogs around, confine them in another room.

- If you have attendants carrying candles, make sure that there is an adequate wax protector around the base to prevent wax splashing onto people's hands or the floor. Candle holders with wide bases, cardboard "ruffs" or collars, or candles in jars are considerate of your attendants. Also, make sure that everyone knows where to put their candles after the ritual, so no one stashes still-burning candles in some corner somewhere.

- Make sure that everyone, even the adults, understands that they can't wave their arms around while carrying candles. Give candle carriers plenty of room so they won't jostle each other and set each other's clothing or long hair on fire accidentally. Don't keep them holding lit candles for too long; they are tiring and you can't put them down like you can a bouquet.

- Beeswax candles are beautiful and smell great, but they burn at a much higher temperature than stearin candles, so they are a poor choice for people to carry. Splashing beeswax will cause bad burns.

- Ventilate. Candles produce smoke, and stearin candles are full of chemicals that can bother people. Preperfumed candles can irritate people with allergies to perfume; use essential oils rubbed on an unscented candle instead.

- At the feast table, be careful that the candles don't have a smell that might interfere with the appetites of the diners. Unscented or beeswax candles are best here.

- Candelabras should have trays under them to catch drips, especially if it isn't your property. Candles with wreaths and decorations around the base should be protected so that when they burn down, they don't set anything on fire. This is especially important with dried flowers.

- For outdoor rituals, jars are best. The wind will be sure to blow unprotected candles out. If you line a path with candles in jars, make sure that it's very wide to account for staggering partygoers. Lighting candles outside, as in a lighting-type ritual, can be pretty darn difficult and take up way too much time as people struggle to keep things lit long enough. Create some sort of windscreen—a few people surrounding the altar and spreading their arms in a great cloak, for example—to protect the flames.

- Lovely as it is, it's very hard to read small lines by candlelight. If your officiant needs enough light to read, and it's dark with only lit candles going, give him or her a small flashlight or booklight, and make sure the words are printed in very large type. A small clip-on snake-light type attached to a clipboard works especially well.

- It goes without saying that no candle should be left alone in a room, even for a few minutes. Assign someone to go around and make sure that all candles are out after the ceremony. People have lost their entire houses to candle accidents.

- Please make sure that you ask the facility where you're getting married if candles are allowed. There's nothing worse than lighting a candle in the middle of the ceremony, hearing a beep, and then being drenched in water from the sprinkler system.

# bonfire etiquette

Many Pagan weddings are held outside, often on private property, and the celebrating may go on into the night. There's nothing like having a bonfire for people to gather around during the reception (or possibly even the ceremony); it's a traditional part of too many Pagan rituals to be ignored. However, like all things having to do with fire, it can cause problems or get out of control if you're not careful. Make sure that you have permission before you start any fire on someone else's property, and go over this checklist beforehand.

- Make sure you have the fire laid beforehand, and someone who is very good at starting fires designated. You don't want to stand around while someone fusses for half an hour trying to get it lit. In the old days, sacred fires were supposed to be lit with flint and steel, without matches. Other methods might use a glass lens. However, don't make your wedding ceremony the first time you try this out.

- Make sure that piled-up logs are stable. Tall, teetery piles are dangerous even unlit.

- It's a bad idea to start fires with accelerants, as the fire may get out of control. Sacred fires are best started the traditional way, with tinder, kindling, and fuel.

- Never burn plastic in the bonfire. If you intend to burn paper trash, it probably shouldn't be in the sacred bonfire. Don't put firecrackers or other explosives into the fire. Don't put aerosol cans into the fire. Even an unopened beer can might explode in the fire. Don't chuck lighters into the fire. Don't let drunken people urinate in the fire: it causes a stink. (These problems may seem unlikely, but we've seen them happen at weddings.)

- No horseplay around the fire. Children should be monitored.

- Generally, one sober person should be designated fire-tender. This person should know where the fire-control equipment is, and should have the authority to delegate others to fetch firewood when necessary. They should stay awake and sober until the fire is completely doused.

- You should have the following tools on hand: a long-handled shovel, tongs or heavy welding gloves, buckets with water and/or sand for fire control, a fire extinguisher, a flashlight, a sharp axe, and a bow saw or other handsaw.

# Wedding incense

Incense can be used as part of the ceremony (to cast the element of air, for example), or to create scent in the air before the ritual. Make sure the area is well ventilated before lighting any. It's useful to make sure that whoever has charge of lighting and dousing candles is also in charge of lighting and dousing incense. They should have a lighter in their pocket, and a water spritzer at hand in case the incense has to be doused quickly for someone's breathing comfort. Also remember that if you're using charcoal in a metal container, it can make the container too hot to pick up, so place it on something heat-resistant, like a slab of stone, in case it needs to be quickly moved.

### Hera's Incense

2 parts lavender

1 part lovage

1 part thyme

1 part rosemary

1 part orris root

### Aphrodite's Incense

2 parts rose petals

1 part violet

1 part lavender

1 part myrtle

1 part lemon verbena

1 drop musk oil

### Frigga's Incense

1 part juniper

1 part lemon balm

1 part marjoram

1 part meadowsweet

1 part pine needles

5 drops mead

### Parvati's Incense

1 part cardamom

1 part coriander

1 part cinnamon

2 parts vetivert

1 drop ylang ylang oil

## Sun, Shine on My Wedding Incense

1 part bay

2 parts heliotrope

1 part ground sunflower seeds

1 part ambergris

1 part marigold petals

1 pinch saffron

5 drops olive oil

## Wedding Night Incense

2 parts basil

1 part cinnamon

1 part elecampane

1 part damiana

6 drops jasmine oil

# incense alternatives

Many public and private venues won't allow any fire or smoke, as it may trigger fire alarms or do property damage. Some people are also uncomfortable with or allergic to smoke, so especially if you are doing your ceremony in a small and poorly ventilated place, you might want to use alternatives. If you can light candles but not have lots of smoke, you can put the incense ingredients in a potpourri pot of the sort that comes with a votive candle beneath them to warm the water and spread the scent. If you can't have any flame, use large open bowls of water (in safe places where no one can stagger into them and dump them). Add rose water, lavender water, or essential oils (see list on page 13), or a small amount of cologne. Use only a few drops for essential oils, and a couple of teaspoonfuls for scented waters. Float the petals of fragrant flowers on top. It's best to experiment with this beforehand by leaving a batch of your mixture in an empty room for a few hours, and then testing the strength of the scent with your nose. Another possibility is taking this mixture and decanting it into a spray-bottle, squirting the floor and ceiling (not furniture) with the scent.

## *woods for the broom*

Many handfastings end with the traditional jumping of the broom, and many couples enjoy making their own as a magical talisman to hang around the house afterwards. (In chapter 8 there are several varieties of broom-jumping introductions, including one that involves making a specifically magical broom; see pages 89–91.) If you want to make your own broom, we suggest choosing the wood for the handle like you would choose wood for a magical wand, only with the elements of love in mind. Here's a list of woods that would be appropriate for a wedding broom:

**Any fruit tree**—apple, cherry, peach, apricot, plum, orange, lemon, etc.—
   is especially good.

**Birch.** Symbolizes beginnings.

**Flowering trees** such as mimosa, lilac, or crape myrtle.

**Hawthorn.** The May tree, sacred to the Love Goddess of Beltane.

**Linden.** Symbolizes bonding and peace.

**Maple.** The best of all, a traditional love-oriented wood.

**Rowan.** Sacred to Brigid or Bride.

Traditionally, the broom brush is made from the broom plant, which is botanically *Cytisus scoparius*, known in medieval Europe as *Planta Genista*. Other traditional ritual broom ends are made from sheaves of grain, or you may use any long grasses. An herbal broom is a nice thing to have as well, but be warned that anything leafy will shed when dry. You can wind a vine or wreath of flowers around the handle and tie ribbons of your wedding colors to it. If you don't have designated wedding colors, try green for fertility, pink for love, red for passion, white for forgiveness, blue for peace, and gold for joy.

# *favors & decorations*

Wedding favors are a great thing for you and your spouse to bless before the wedding, as a partner activity; they are the gift of your love that you are giving out to the community. Allyson Chaple, a Pagan wedding consultant for Ritual Fantastique Theme Weddings, suggests the following:

*allyson's ritual fantastique pagan wedding favor list*

- Make Green Man faces, made of clay or hardened and shellacked. Put masking tape over the eyes, spray them with green stone-flecked spray paint, and then pull the tape off and paint the eyes to look alive. Attach silk or real sprigs of ivy and green leaves in a spray behind the face and hang up.

- Make or buy small brooms. They're available in craft stores or you can bundle dried herbs together and tie them to sticks with rough twine. Decorate with a sprig of silk, dry, or fresh flowers; wrap bright ribbons around the handle, and hang.

- Evergreen tree plugs, symbolizing eternity and sacred to the forest gods, are available to order through tree nurseries. Easily rooting plants such as spider plants, aloe, or ivy also work well.

- Packets of seeds make good favors, as do flower bulbs and tubers. You can also make your invitations or placecards out of hand-pressed paper in which you have embedded wildflower seeds. Tear paper into small pieces, wet down thoroughly, and leave it in the water until it becomes mushy; add flower seeds and immediately spread it thin between metal window screens and press down. Put the paper in a well-ventilated area to dry, and then cut it into shapes. Print your words on it, and your guests can then plant the invitation or placecard as is and watch it bloom. This has the added benefit of magically creating many sets of "roots" for your relationship.

- Jars of specialty honey (sacred to Aphrodite) or extra virgin olive oil in colored bottles (for consecration or cooking purposes, depending on the guest), possibly with edible herbs or spices sacred to love. (See page 14.)

- Many vineyards sell single-serving size bottles of wine that you can have labeled with your names, wedding date, and perhaps a verse or blessing.

- Bells, traditionally used to keep evil spirits away, can be fastened onto small hoops or attached to doorknob hangers, tassels, light-pulls, or other items to hang up around the house. Include a tag saying something like, "May the blessing of love keep evil spirits away from your community."

- Stained glass suncatchers come in many mystical patterns such as suns, moons, stars, etc. The plastic bake-in-your-oven types are available at craft stores and can be created en masse cheaply.

- Magical soaps or floor washes, scented with special herbs or oils and tied with a ribbon or wrapped in homemade paper, can be accompanied with a note as to how this can cleanse your house with the power of love. Another option is bath salts or bath lotion.

- Birdseed packets can be given out to propitiate the forest spirits. Please advise your guests that it will not keep more than a month or two, so use it soon.

- You can gear your favors to the closest Pagan holiday. For example, flower seeds for Beltane, small cauldrons or Brigid crosses for Imbolc, specially anointed and blessed candles at Samhain, decorated wedding eggs a la Fabergé for Ostara. For a wedding in the Lammas/Harvest time, bottles of specialty whole grains or flours are nice; you can grind the grain yourself to give it a special touch. For Yule, try origami stars or tree ornament. For Mabon, give out jars of love-herb jelly or small garlands of dried nuts and berries.

- Symbols that are important to the bride and groom can be interwoven into a hanging ornament, napkin ring, or other item.

- Magical ink in a bottle with a cut quill and a ribbon-tied roll of parchment. If you aren't sure of your guests' familiarity with such things, wrap the parchment in a paper with directions.

- Magical love-herb potpourri in a sachet, pomander, or bottle. Make sure to include orris root, as it is both a fixative and a love plant.

- Tie together dried *bouquet garni* herbs in a bouquet for cooks to take home and add to dishes. Another option is bags of ritual salt. In ancient times, salt was so valuable that it was used to pay taxes. You can give out coarsely ground salt, sea salt, or special Japanese "moon salt," which is harvested from the ocean on the night of the full moon.

- Gris-gris or medicine bags with small stones, feathers, shells, herbs, perhaps a votive candle.

- Specialty incense, bag or stick. Some incense companies will sell unscented sticks, which you can douse with your own special oil combination.

- Crystals or tumbled stones, perhaps of the couple's favorite type. You could engrave a stone, or just write on it with a permanent marker, and inscribe the couple's bind rune (the combination of their rune initials).

- You could also pass out small magical charms. Another twist to this is to make a cake (possibly separate from the regular wedding cake) with two or more layers. Attach strings to the charms and embed them between the layers in frosting or filling, with the strings coming out the sides. Each guests gets the chance to pull out one charm, so this can be a divinatory activity as well as a blessing. This is a variation of the Victorian tradition of the cake pull, which was originally limited to the bridesmaids.

  Suggested charms might be: a few coins tied together for wealth, a piece of candy for sweetness, a tiny plastic baby figure for the next person to conceive or sire a child, a tiny ship for adventure, a dove for a peaceful time, a tiny pistol for a "shotgun wedding," a house for moving one's home, a mouth for arguments, a painted flower for a new-blossoming love, a cracked or broken heart, a harp or guitar for romance and love songs, a tiny mask for deception, a shoe for having an affair (for "leaving one's shoes under someone else's bed"!), and of course a gold ring for the next person to get married.

- Tiny magical or ritual wands made of a special wood (see above), decorated with feathers, stones, or other embellishments appropriate to the wedding.

- Keys have magical significance, meaning the unlocking of the mysteries, so keychains can be magical charms. You could even include a tiny ornate key on the chain.

### the wedding banner

Among some of the Pagan couples we know, the wedding banner has become a tradition. This consists of a large (usually three feet by three feet) fabric banner with the symbols of the couple's wedding, in the wedding colors, appliquéd on. Some of the banners bear things like roses, a blade in a chalice, a golden ship, two cups, or a sun and moon. Whenever anyone gets handfasted and invites one of these couples (assuming that their marriage is still intact), their wedding banner is also invited and hangs in a place of honor with any other wedding banners, including that of the current bridal couple. These banners bring the energy of steady, enduring unions to the new coupling.

*chapter 4*
# the prenuptial ritual

In traditional wedding plans, the night before the wedding is a time when the bride and groom separate with groups of their friends, usually segregated by gender, and do silly things that they theoretically shouldn't be doing after they're married. This tradition is supposed release tension and fear about the upcoming mess the following day, but it always made me vaguely uncomfortable. Certainly there will be a lot of little fears about the party itself, such as: Will the cake fall? Will it rain? Will my little sister trip over her train and fall headfirst onto elderly Aunt Julia? Will my divorced parents and their new spouses start a fistfight in the middle of the reception? Will born-again Aunt Madge storm out of the VFW hall in a snit? Will all the participants show up sober? Will the food burn and the car stall? Will anyone actually show up for this fiasco?

It's all right to have these feelings, and it's all right to want to do something that helps you forget about them, but all too often the implication is that you're nervous about an entirely different feeling. What you're really doing is distracting yourself from getting cold feet—from not showing up at the altar at all—and we're profoundly uncomfortable with that. If, after all this, you are less than 95 percent sure that this is the absolutely, positively right thing for you to be doing, then you shouldn't be getting married. I don't care how much the caterers cost. These are things to be dealt with long before the bachelor party. It's okay to feel excited, because it is a big deal, but it should feel more like the excitement before your graduation and less like a going-away party after having been drafted.

Anyway, assuming that you have resolved these feelings and you've decided (as some of us do) that you don't feel like going to a sex-segregated party and getting plastered, and you'd like to do something different, here's a suggestion. It's a ritual celebrating love, in all its forms, that can be performed by a friend or the elder of your spiritual group with anyone you like present. It will set the tone for the next day, and both bride and groom can be there.

# love ritual

*This ritual was first presented by our queer Pagan group, Q-Moon, as part of a series of "L" rituals that we thought up when we were at a loss for regular themes—Love, Lust, Lingam, Labia, Laughter, Liberty, Leather, Lace, and so forth. Our coven/ritual group was scheduled to do a ritual to honor love, and at the last moment the priestess of Aphrodite who was supposed to run it called me, Raven, in a panic and bowed out. She had been having marital problems and couldn't do the ritual with a whole heart (even priestesses of Aphrodite have marital problems). But to ask me—the priest dedicated to the Dark Goddess and Lord of the Dead—to do the love ritual? Come on! I could handle a Samhain ritual fine, but. . . . When I told my wife in confusion, she wasn't at all surprised. "But dear," she said sanguinely, "you're very good at love." I guess she'd know. Anyway, I wrote these quarter calls and this invocation. Feel free to use them.*

*Drape the altar with pastels and set it with many flowers and shells, including a small figure of Aphrodite and some small pictures of people embracing, valentines, candies, peaches and cherries, etc.*

*You will also need a tray of cookies or sweet bread, a bowl of honey,*
*and a chalice of juice or wine cooler. Have on hand a small bowl of*
*"kissing stones," small tumbled stones with hearts painted on them,*
*usually with nail polish.*
   *The circle is cast using the following invocations:*

**east:** Spirits of the east,
   Venus of air!
   Love high-flying
   Light and free as a butterfly
   Love without boundaries,
   Love that speaks and sings
      like a sweet choir
      of angel harmonies
   First love, young love,
      Springtime love
   Long distance love
   Circle of friends
   Letters perfumed in roses
      scented in vanilla
   Whirlwind love, rainbow love
   Sing us your sweet song

**south:** Spirits of the south,
   Venus of fire!
   Love like the hot flame
      that rises within us
   The dance of passion
   The electric spark of touch
   The kiss of life,
      the hot blushes rising
   Love that can't wait,

the strategy of attraction,

the tactics of pursuit

Love that burns, consumes,

singes our wings!

Like a moth to your flame,

Teach us to hold up our heads

in pride!

**west:** Spirits of the west,

Venus of water!

Love like the tides,

ebbing and flowing,

crashing on the rocks,

sweeping all before you

Deep and unknowable

Love sweet as wine

as mother's milk

Love of parent and child

Love jealous, love possessive,

Stormy tears at sea,

Whirlpool that drags you down.

Love like the river

that flows along forever,

Let us drink of you!

**north:** Spirits of the north,

Venus of earth!

Love rooted deep like mountains

in the bedrock of commitment

Love bound in metal rings

Love tied to hearth of stone

where walls mean a safe place

where we are welcome, we are kin

Tended like the farmer

lovingly works the land

Love that knows how to grow

and yet remain steady

Love that marks its boundaries

Love you can depend on

Love like new-baked bread and honey,

sustain us!

**officiant:** Pink and red and green and blue and gold

Love comes in many colors.

Love Goddess pink

Baby pink

Newborn infants' newborn love

Rose pink, tentative, hesitant

First blush of dawn—hail Hathor

Love comes in many colors.

Love God red

Passion red

Apples and valentines

Arrows struck to the heart

Rose red—hail Cupid

Love comes in many colors.

Love Goddess green

Sea green

Malachite green of many waters

Springing from the foam

Green of new life—hail Aphrodite

Love comes in many colors.

Love God blue

Sky blue

Piping the music of love

To many longing ears

Deva blue—hail Krishna

Love comes in many colors.

Love Goddess gold

Honey gold

Golden glow of life

True color of love

Sun gold, ornament gold,

Hail Oshun, hail Freya,

Love comes in many colors.

*Next the officiant speaks. At our ritual the priest spoke about how we are not taught, in this society, to really love another human being as an equal; we are just given a lot of general social programming and left to figure out the implementation by ourselves.*

officiant: *(cuts some sweet bread or lays some cookies in a bowl of honey and passes it around)* This is the honey of love. As you taste it, give thanks to the Love Goddess for everything she has given you. *(the chalice is passed around with the following instruction:)* Ask the Love Goddess to give you something you want, no matter how outrageous or unattainable it may seem.

*Then the kissing stones are distributed, and everyone is shown how to use them. If you give a kissing stone to someone, they have to give you a kiss, although it need not be on the lips, the hand or foot or shoulder is all right; you can even kiss your own fingers and touch them in blessing. Traditionally, at this point, most Pagans would thank the gods and goddesses, release the quarters, and open the circle. To do this, first have the individuals who did the deity invocation stand and thank each deity mentioned by name, asking them to always bless the love lives of the participants. Then the individuals who did the quarter invocations stand, call upon their element by name, thank the spirits of that element for their gifts, and tell them that they can go on to their chosen tasks. The officiant declares the circle "open" and everyone can get to partying.*

*chapter 5*

# quarter castings

ot all handfastings will invoke the
traditional four elements in the traditional four directions, and that's all right.
Although it does provide a useful symbolic
formula, it doesn't work for some people,
who would rather create something else.
The idea behind circle casting of any kind
is to delineate a space, and then make it
sacred and special through visual or spoken means. This can be done as simply as
having someone walk all the way around
the space, waving a sword or wand, sprinkling water, smudging, or tinkling wind
chimes, beating a drum, or sprinkling glitter. We've seen a beautiful and entirely
wordless elemental invocation done once
that involved half a dozen people walking
in each direction, armed with musical
instruments. Earth was invoked with deep,
booming drums and fire with light, patter-
ing ones such as doumbeks. Air was

invoked with bells and chimes and wind instruments, all playing without discernable rhythm; and water was invoked with rattles and a harp. A simple wordless tune was sung by one person in each group. To an outsider, it would have seemed merely a musical performance, but to the folks in the circle, its meaning was unmistakable.

Another way to keep it simple is just to have someone perform a simple action in each direction—lighting a candle, pouring water in a cup, sprinkling salt, lighting a stick of incense, or waving a fan. Or you can be more elaborate and use lines and scripts, some of which are provided below. Most of these quarter castings deal with the traditional directions and elements, but feel free to swap them about if you like. You can also use the quarter castings in the Prenuptial Ritual; we'd grade them at about level 2.

# "call to the beloved" quarter casting
### (level 1)

*This is a simple casting meant for a ceremony where the bride and groom want to call the elements themselves. Because it invokes the elements symbolically but not directly, it's acceptable for weddings that are only slightly or subtly Pagan. The bride and groom go from direction to direction, starting in the east and circling around to south, west, and north.*

**groom:** I went to the east, the direction of dawn, and I heard my beloved calling my name. Her voice was like the singing of birds in the morning.

**bride:** I went to the east, the direction of beginnings, and I called out for my beloved, and he answered. His voice was like the touch of a spring breeze.

**groom:** I went to the south, the direction of noon, and a shining light appeared, and I saw my beloved clearly. Her spirit was like a bright flame that guided me home.

**bride:** I went to the south, the direction of heat and passion, and a great light shone down, and I saw my beloved clearly. His spirit was like the light of the sun itself, warming my path.

**groom:** I went to the west, the direction of evening, and I found my beloved waiting for me by a cool river. I took her hand, and in it placed my heart.

**bride:** I went to the west, the direction of the ocean, and I found my beloved waiting for me by a deep well. I took his heart, and gave him my own in exchange.

**groom:** I went to the north, the direction of midnight, and I made a place for my beloved and I to put down roots like a great tree and live together bound to the Earth. And I waited for her there.

**bride:** I went to the north, the direction of high mountains, and I found the place where my beloved waited for me. And I took his hand and entwined with him from my roots to my topmost branches, to live together bound to the Earth.

**groom:** And I knew perfect love and perfect trust.

**bride:** And I knew perfect love and perfect trust.

# musical element quarter casting
### (level 1)

*This casting is meant to be done by five people, each with musical instruments. The caster in the direction of air has a flute, penny whistle or horn; the fire caster has a tambourine; the water caster has a set of wind chimes; the earth caster has a drum, and the fifth person should stand in the middle with a bell and invoke Spirit.*

**air:** *(plays a string of notes on flute or horn to get people's attentions)* For behold! We gather here with words of blessing to celebrate the joining of _____ and _____. We sing their happiness to the heavens, to be carried on the winds all over the world.

**fire:** *(beats the tambourine)* For behold! We gather here with warm hearts to celebrate their passion for each other. We rejoice in the glow of their love.

**water:** *(jingles the wind chimes)* For behold! We gather here with tears of joy in our eyes to celebrate the force that makes two separate people flow onto one path. We shower them with an ocean of our delight.

**earth:** *(beats the drum)* For behold! We gather here to watch their commitment grow like trees reaching for the sky. We honor their persistence and wish them hope for the future.

**spirit:** *(rings the bell)* For behold! We gather here to witness the union of two bright and powerful spirits joining their lives together. May you never hunger nor ever thirst.

36

# poetic quarter casting
### *(level 1)*

*If the the couple wants to choose special people to read each of these quarter castings, it should ideally be an adolescent boy or girl for the east (perhaps a sibling of the bride or groom); a newly married friend for the south; a long-married friend for the west; a parent of the bride or groom for the north; and a person that both respect as a mentor for the center.*

**east:** The scent of love is roses on the wind,

The spring day dawns, and we rise and begin.

**south:** The sight of love is two pairs of flashing eyes

That lock onto each other and reflect summer skies.

**west:** The taste of love is kisses like wine,

As we share the cup that is yours and mine.

**north:** The feel of love is a warm embrace,

Held like a babe in our safest place.

**center:** The sound of love is a silent song

That runs through our souls, resounding and strong.

# animal totem quarter casting
## (level 1)

*Many people work with animal totems for spiritual purposes; perhaps as many as work with deities. Some may prefer to use animal figures to specific gods, as they have a more tribal and less religious feel to them, and can camouflage divine natures within animal symbolism. This is also a good ritual if you have at least eight friends who like to dress up in animal masks.*

*The eight individuals doing the circle casting should be costumed as follows: The element of air is invoked by two people. One should wear feathers and large wings of any natural bird color. One should wear an insectoid mask—or at least antennae—and butterfly or moth wings. The element of fire is invoked by two people. One wears a feline mask (lion, panther, etc) and furs. One wears a canine mask (dog, wolf, jackal, etc.) and furs. The element of water is invoked by two people. One wears a bodysuit of sleek grey spandex. (Note: This person need not be thin, and it is actually more appropriate if he or she is not.) One wears robes that resemble fish scales. The element of earth is invoked by two people. One wears tight fabric in a snakeskin design. One wears horns or antlers and hoofed sandals.*

**air 1:** Living spirit of the winds! You who are the soul of all birds, come to us! Eagle and hawk, raven and cormorant, sparrow and kestrel, robin and crow, swallow and hummingbird! Sing to us of the ecstasy of far flight!

**air 2:** Living spirit of the winds! You who are the mother of the dragonfly, bear us up! Moth and butterfly, bee and wasp, all who fly on gossamer wings! Speak to us of hive and tribe!

**fire 1:** Living spirit of the flame! You who prowl with us, sharp of fang and claw, give us the spark of life! Lion and leopard, tiger and lynx, predator who walks alone, make us keen of vision!

**fire 2:** Living spirit of the flame! You who hunt with the pack, strong of limb and jaw, give us courage to chase what we desire! Wolf and hyena, fox and jackal, predator who runs with his brothers, make us keen of scent!

37

**water 1**: Living spirit of the water! You who warm the seas with your blood and milk, give us comfort! Whale and dolphin, manatee and sea cow, seal and otter, sing to us of the deep music!

**water 2**: Living spirit of the water! You who rule the sea in swarms, glimmer like hope in our sight! Salmon and shark, herring and barracuda, swordfish and angelfish, teach us survival!

**earth 1**: Living spirit of the earth! You who are closest to the Mother's breast, teach us to reverence her. Serpent and lizard, worm and beetle, toad and salamander, show us that to be humble is to be raised up in glory.

**earth 2**: Living spirit of the earth! You who are the heart of the herd, protect us! Deer and elk, cattle and goat, antelope and wild sheep of the mountain! Strike the fond Earth with your hooves and know you are beloved of the Mother.

*The animal spirits all leave a token in each direction—a claw, a feather, a scale, the wing of an insect, a snakeskin.*

**all**: *(turn to the center and say in unison)* We bless this circle and all within it, and we celebrate your wild joy in the taking of a mate, for such is the energy of life itself, the beginning point of the cycle of life.

# magical avatar quarter casting
## (level 2)

*This quarter casting uses the imagery of mythical beasts and divine creatures. It's nice to have the callers wearing flowing cloaks of appropriate colors, perhaps with symbols of the creatures represented. If you can find pendants or other sorts of jewelry or charms with those figures on them, give them out as gifts to your ritual helpers.*

**east**: Spirits of the east, powers of air!
Laughing sylphs that ride the winds,

Faery dancers laughing on the breeze,

Pixies in the morning's meadow,

Sprites that fly on gossamer wings!

Devas of the realms of air,

Be with us!

**south:** Spirits of the south, powers of fire!

Flaming phoenix of rebirth,

Salamander walking unharmed through flames,

Dragon sleeping on riches and breathing fire,

Faery horses striking sparks from your hooves!

Devas of the realms of fire,

Be with us!

**west:** Spirits of the west, powers of water!

Naiads of the flowing rivers,

Undines of the oceans deep,

Mermaids singing sirens' songs,

Tritons swimming with the dolphins!

Devas of the realms of water,

Be with us!

**north:** Spirits of the north, powers of earth!

Dryads who safeguard the great trees,

Gnomes who mine the depths underground,

Elves of the forests, walking silent trails,

Deep faeries of the hidden caves!

Devas of the realms of earth,

Be with us!

# astrological quarter casting
### (level 2)

*This quarter casting uses astrological symbolism. Ideally, it should be performed by twelve people, each of whom has a strong influence of that particular sign in their astrological chart. This can be used with the Astrological Challenge Handfasting Rite in the Full Rites chapter (page 214). Since many people can accept astrology—if only as an amusing hobby or pastime—more easily than they can accept openly Pagan ritual, it classifies as a level 2.*

**first person:** *(comes forward dressed in red and bearing a flaming torch, and stands in the south)* Aries, great ram of the springtime, whose gift is bravery, bless us with the courage to speak our love loudly and proudly and never walk ashamed.

**second person:** *(comes forward dressed in green and bearing a large stone, and stands in the north)* Taurus, bull of the green fields, whose gift is strength, bless us with the ability to endure all hardships without crumbling and never break no matter how hard the burden.

**third person:** *(comes forward dressed in light blue and bearing a knife or sword in each hand, and stands in the east)* Gemini, twin riders of the wind, whose gift is thought, bless us with the ability to think sharply as a razor and to separate the true from the false.

**fourth person:** *(comes forward dressed in grey and silver and bearing a large seashell, and stands in the west)* Cancer, child of the ebbing and flowing tide, whose gift is feeling, bless us with the ability to know our own hearts and to gather our loved ones about our hearth in love and safety.

**fifth person:** *(comes forward dressed in yellow and gold and bearing a sparkler, and stands in the south)* Leo, great lion of the sun, whose gift is will, bless us with the ability to act on our joy, and to bare our souls to others without fear.

40

**sixth person:** *(comes forward dressed in brown and carrying a basket of grain, and stands in the north)* Virgo, pure maiden of perfection, whose gift is mending, bless us with the ability to work hard at that greatest of tasks, the repair of the world, and to see God in all the details.

**seventh person:** *(comes forward dressed in pink and lavender and carrying incense or smudging smoke, and stands in the east)* Libra, child of harmony, whose gift is justice, bless us with fairness in every debate, and help us balance our views with those of others.

**eighth person:** *(comes forward dressed in dark red and carrying a goblet of wine, and stands in the west)* Scorpio, stinging scorpion and high-flying eagle, whose gift is desire, bless us with the ability to follow our true passions and to start over again from the beginning when it is needed.

**ninth person:** *(comes forward dressed in orange and carrying a large candle or lantern, and stands in the south)* Sagittarius, mystical centaur archer, whose gift is clear sight, bless us with the ability to see truth wherever it is found, and to speak it aloud without fear of censure.

**tenth person:** *(comes forward dressed in black and carrying a wooden bowl of salt, and stands in the north)* Capricorn, climbing goat of the high mountains, whose gift is persistence, bless us with the ability to keep climbing even when the way is hard and to never lose sight of our goals.

**eleventh person:** *(comes forward dressed in purple and carrying a large fan, and stands in the east)* Aquarius, bearer of the waters of knowledge, whose gift is newness, bless us with the ability to be ready for the future and all it brings and not to fear change.

**twelfth person:** *(comes forward, dressed in deep blue and carrying a chalice of water, and stands in the west)* Pisces, fish of the deep sea, whose gift is faith, bless us with the ability to step beyond our own wants and needs and to learn compassion for all beings.

# elemental banner quarter casting
## (level 3)

*This casting was created for Raven and Bella's wedding. Banners with elemental symbols are set on poles and given to each of four people representing the elements. The people thrust the banners high as they speak their lines.*

**air:** Spirits of the east, powers of air! Bless these lovers with every breath they take. Spring maiden of the dawn, Lady of all new beginnings, lend us your presence.

**fire:** Spirits of the south, powers of fire! Warm their days and nights with passion and adoration! Brigid of the bright spark, Shiva of the transforming flame, and Hestia of the welcoming hearth, lend us your presence!

**water:** Spirits of the west, powers of water! May their love run deep and strong as the rivers of all the world. Aphrodite Urania, the builder of bridges; Oshun, daughter of the river, lend us your presence!

**earth:** Spirits of the north, powers of earth! Give them a strong foundation on which to stand. Great Pan of the wild forests, Mother Gaea beneath our feet, lend us your presence!

# circle closings

Circle closing can be accomplished in many ways. Most people are used to weddings that end with the kiss and the recessional, and then everyone trails out to do the receiving line and to party. If you don't want to mess around with an audible or symbolic circle closing, you can have the clergy, or the individuals who cast the quarters, go to each direction silently after everyone has left and mentally dismiss the elements (or audibly dismiss them, if the room is empty). If you want an audible uncasting, simply have them thank the element, bow or raise their arms, gesture, and step back, preferably in the reverse order that they were invoked.

## stone ritual circle closing

You can create closure of the sacred space in an entirely different way than it was begun. For example, some weddings have used the Stone Ritual, which goes as follows: The bride and groom should provide a number of polished tumbled stones. One couple we know used rose quartz, and another used stones of different types. These are passed around to the onlookers in a basket, and they are encouraged to take one apiece. The clergyperson instructs them to hold the stones and project into them all the good wishes that they have for the couple. Then the stones are gathered back together and kept in a special jar for good wishes forever.

43

## divinatory deck circle closing

Another closing ceremony we have seen started before the ritual opened, with a member of the wedding party passing around handmade cards and pens. The guests were instructed to write one word or phrase on each card, denoting a quality they hoped would bless the newlyweds—e.g., trust, laughter, or perseverance. These cards were later collected and combined into a special divinatory deck for that couple and their relationship; if they were having problems, they could draw one card to find out what needed to be stimulated between them.

# the receiving line

Receiving lines are a tradition carried over from medieval times. Somewhere along the line, the bride's garters were seen as good luck—probably because they were worn under her skirts near the rarely seen thighs and thus were associated with sex and fertility. The greed for the bride's garters became, for a while, so strong that hapless peasant brides were assaulted mere minutes after their vows by male onlookers, who often flung them down, pulled up their skirts, and ripped the garters off of their bodies, apparently to the laughter of the crowd. The two garters would be fought over by the men until two of them managed to get away with the stolen booty, or the garters were torn to shreds. This violence, not to mention the problem of brides being kidnapped right out of the wedding procession by disgruntled rejected suitors, added to the need for a large wedding party for the purpose of bridal protection.

Upper-class brides, unlike their peasant sisters, were determined not to have anything so barbaric occur at their expensive nuptials. Heavily guarded wealthy brides started two interlocking customs: first, that the garters would be removed by the groom and flung to the crowd, and second, that small "knots" or bows of ribbon would be sewn to the hem of the bride's dress and passed out one by one to the guests (and occasionally flung to the crowd), as sort of a consolation prize. This guaranteed that everyone would get some good-luck piece of fabric to take with them, without needing to do violence to the bride or each other. These knots of decorative ribbon, sewn by the hundreds around the hem of the gown, were usually in the bride and groom's colors. The colors started out as the heraldic colors of the two uniting families, but by the early Renaissance they were chosen by the couple for their esoteric meanings—saffron meant virginity, straw-color meant abundance, "murrey" or mulberry color meant steadfastness, "horse flesh" or bright bronze meant gallantry, "carnation" or bright salmon-pink meant carnal love, "maiden's blush" or light pink meant modesty, grass green meant joyous youth, deep sky-blue meant staunch servitude, ivory or milk white meant innocence, and tawny orange meant merriment.

The need for clipping off all those bows right after the ceremony and hurling them at the onlookers created a tradition of the bride wearing a small pair of scissors on her belt, which led to a custom that the small scissors, usually in a case, should be a gift from the groom's parents to their future daughter-in-law, given to her the night before the wedding. This had a double meaning, as scissors were often called "wedding knives" because they were two opposite-edged "knives" that had been "wedded together" with a rivet. The receiving line started out as a way that guests at more genteel weddings got their good-luck bows. As indicated by the wording, you were originally supposed to actually "receive" something.

In modern times, most couples simply use the receiving line according to the Victorian custom of "receiving" congratulations and thanking the guests. When Raven and Bella got married, they reenacted the older custom of the bows, which had been made and basted onto Bella's skirts at the bridal shower. Raven's mother gave her a pair of fancy embroidery scissors, and Raven and Bella cut and handed out bows in their chosen colors of burgundy and malachite green. At a handfasting some years later for a friend who had been a bridesmaid in Raven and Bella's wedding, the favors were small brooms decorated with little ribbon bows. Raven and Bella were given one with a bow kept from their own wedding to preserve continuity.

*chapter 6*
# deities and invocations

lthough we now think of most non-Pagan
weddings as taking place in churches,
marriage went from being a sacred affair in
ancient times to a completely secular affair
in Christian medieval times. Weddings
were not allowed to be performed in
churches, as they had to do with sex and
thus were technically impure. The marriage
ritual also subtly invoked the Goddess in
many ways, including its very name (from
the Latin *maritare*, which came from the
goddess name Mari/Mariamne/Marah/
Marina/Mary), and was therefore even
more profane. Instead, they might be performed before the church door or, more
likely, in a wood, field, town green, or
home. Martin Luther concurred with the
contemporary view of marriage as a secular institution and insisted on keeping it
out of his new reformed faith, but as soon

as he was safely dead his late-sixteenth-century followers promptly created the solemn wedding ceremony that is used today. Jumping on the bandwagon, the Roman Catholic Church also formalized the sacrament of marriage at the Council of Trent, making it a church-sanctioned activity. Most cultures had a deity that oversaw marriage, and to whom marriage was sacred. Overwhelmingly, that deity was female, and to this day, weddings are often seen as something that the bride does, with the bridegroom merely a necessary prop in the theatrical display. Until recently—and probably still in some cases—attitudes were quite different for men and women. At the bridal shower and the prewedding party the mood was one of excitement and anticipation; at the bachelor party, though, the implication was dread and regret, as if marriage were more a loss than a gain. These attitudes are more cultural than personal; we expect that many a bridegroom went through the bachelor party motions more because he and his friends felt that it was expected of them than because he was really perceiving it as a last fling before imprisonment.

Finding a male deity related to marriage was a harder dig than we thought. There was the Greek demigod Hymen, "Guardian of the Marriage Bed," but his only role seemed to be that of guarding the bride's virginity until the wedding, a role which most modern couples, with access to birth control, may have no use for.

# Bes

Another exception is the Egyptian god Bes. He is pictured as a small, dwarfish man with the large head, broad torso, and short, bowed legs and arms of an achondroplastic. His eyes are large and oversized, and alone among Egyptian gods, he wore a long, curly beard. Starting out as a local god of good fortune from Punt, he became more and more popular as time went on and became especially associated, strangely enough, with marriage and women's beauty. The image of his squat form often decorated rouge-boxes and the handles of mirrors, and he was said to be able to grant beauty and a happy marriage. His head was also carved on bedsteads, as he was the guardian of sleep.

## hymn to bes

*Recite the following hymn to Bes the night before your wedding day;
his blessing will ensure that you and your beloved will be rested and
calm for the big event.*

O little dancer from the Land of Punt

Guardian of sweet dreams

Giver of beauty both inside and out

Tonight I sleep singly for the last time,

And tomorrow I will sleep as one of two.

Bless these bonds I soon shall don,

Bless the bed in which we shall sleep,

Bless the mirror into which I will look

Tomorrow morning when I awake.

Bring us laughter, dancing Bes,

And protect us from all disasters

For all our lives together.

47

## hera

Among the Greek pantheon, Hera reigned supreme as goddess of marriage. She was
an ambivalent goddess at best, although some research has been done suggesting that
her older form was less harridan-like, and that this metamorphosis came about
through patriarchal conquest. At any rate, the Hera of classical Greece was both a
generous, benevolent matriarch who blessed all happy couples, and a violent, vengeful shrew who was quite likely to attack and kill her husband's mistresses. Her name
is most likely connected to the Indo-European word for "sky," as, like her husband
Zeus, she was a heavenly goddess.

Hera had three forms, symbolizing the three stages of a married woman's life. Hera Parthenia was the bride, getting ready to be married; Hera Teleia, meaning "fulfilled," was the married woman; and Hera Chera was the widow. Unlike the later Hera who was always seen as simply married, this triplicate echoes an earlier Hera who embodied all three stages, both turning toward and turning away from coupleness and acknowledging that eventually one partner must die and leave the other one alone. She was invoked at the borders of each stage: at the betrothal, when a young girl went from single maiden to bride-to-be; at the wedding; and at widowhood. Only divorce was not in Hera's milieu, that being more the sort of thing for gods of death and war.

Her symbol was the peacock, and a good item to use for invoking her is a peacock feather. Another of her symbols is the Milky Way, as she is the Heavenly Mother rather than the Earthly Mother, so a sprinkling of milk tossed into the air is another possible accompaniment to invocation.

## hymn to hera

*This can be used on the program or wedding announcement; directly after the quarter casting in order to invoke her presence; or as a blessing on the couple at a later point in the ceremony. Ideally, it should be read by someone who is happily married.*

Keeper of promises,

Maker of vows,

Queen of the Heavens,

Queen of clasped hands

And clasped hearts,

Look down on us with benevolence.

Bless this our union

And teach us that a binding

Can mean freedom.

# juno

The Romans absorbed many of the Greek gods, and many of their deities were similar, but not exactly the same, as Greek ones. The Roman counterpart of Hera was Juno, consort of Jupiter the king. She, too, had many titles, delineating in a fairly detailed manner her various duties. As Juno Pronuba she arranged marriages; as Juno Moneta she advised the prospective couple on marital wisdom; as Juno Domiduca she escorted the bride and bridegroom over the threshold of their new home; as Juno Nuxia she coated the lintel and doorposts with protective scented oils; as Juno Cinxia she unknotted their girdles at the marriage bed; as Juno Regina she aided the new wife in the responsibilities of the household; as Juno Ossipago she protected pregnant wives and strengthened the baby's bones; as Juno Rumina she assured the mother's supply of milk; as Juno Sospita she aided delivery; and as Juno Lucina, goddess of light, she brought light into the world and brought about the infant's first view of the brightness outside the womb.

Juno was considered a goddess of wise counsel, whom Jupiter called on frequently for advice, and her name, *juno*, was the feminine form of the masculine *genius*, or wise indwelling spirit. Her festival, the Matronalia, was celebrated on the Kalends of March. It was a family festival where the lady of the house received presents from her husband and children. As well as the peacock, which she inherited from Hera, her animal is the goose, and a goosefeather can be used to invoke her blessing.

## hymn to juno

*This can be used on the program or wedding announcement; directly after the quarter casting in order to invoke her presence; or as a blessing on the couple at a later point in the ceremony. This should also be read by someone who is happily married.*

| | |
|---|---|
| Juno Pronuba[1], bless this our commitment, | pro-*noo*-bah |
| Juno Moneta[1], give us wise counsel, | mo-*nay*-tah |
| Juno Domiduca[1], bless our feet upon the threshold, | do-mee-*doo*-cah |
| Juno Nuxia[1], protect the home we share, | *nooks*-ee-ah |
| Juno Cinxia[1], bless our two bodies entwined, | *sinks*-ee-ah |

49

Juno Regina, help us through the daily chores,

Juno Lucina[1], Lady of Light,               loo-*see*-nah

Matron All-Mighty, Incomparable Queen,

Bring light of joy to this new beginning.

# aphrodite/venus

Although not specifically a goddess of marriage, Aphrodite/Venus, the Greco-Roman goddess of love and beauty, is often called upon at modern Pagan weddings. Among her many different titles that correspond to her matronage of some type of sexual activity, there is the little-known title Aphrodite Genetrix, the matron of marital sex, the one who brings spark back into the marriage bed. This particular aspect is especially useful to invoke at a wedding, although any aspect of Aphrodite that a couple feels close to can be invoked. There is a ritual dedicated to Aphrodite Urania, the androgynous Bearded Aphrodite, in the Nontraditionalists chapter (page 140).

## hymn to aphrodite

*This can be used on the program or wedding announcement; directly after the quarter casting in order to invoke her presence; or as a blessing on the couple at a later point in the ceremony. Ideally, this should be read by someone who has, in the couple's opinion, at least some of the qualities of Aphrodite: feminine, attractive, highly sensuous, charming, and sexually experienced.*

Aphrodite Foam-Born, green as the sea,

Open the arms of these lovers

As the sea rushes to greet the shore.

Aphrodite Honey-Gold,

Give them sweetness at every morning's table.

Aphrodite Flowering One,

Let their bodies learn each other's language

And never forget this silent speech.

# eros/cupid

Another deity that can be invoked is Eros, the archer son of Aphrodite. Eros, or Cupid as the Romans called him, has been stereotyped as the small, fat, petulant winged boy seen on valentines, but he was traditionally shown in ancient times as a slender, beautiful youth. The story of his own marriage to Psyche is a tale of love and union achieved against all odds, of both partners overcoming fears and illusions through ordeal. His lover, Psyche, can also be invoked.

51

## hymn to eros & psyche

*This can be used directly after the quarter casting in order to invoke the presence of this divine couple, or it can be read as a blessing on the bride and groom at a later point in the ceremony. The Eros part is read by man and the Psyche part by a woman; ideally they should be in a relationship together, but that's not a dire necessity.*

I. Eros, Incarnation of Love,

Archer whose swift arrows pierce the heart,

We stand here wounded with joy

Pierced with ecstasy

Bleeding happiness from our hearts.

Bless this our love

And may tenderness forever lie between us.

II. Psyche, Incarnation of Soul,

Seeker on the eternal quest,

We stand here touching souls

Seeking the future together

On a journey where we come home to love.

Bless this our connection

And carry us over all obstacles in our road.

# frigga

In the Norse mythos, marriage and the household were ruled over by the goddess Frigga (*free*-gah), wife of Odhinn/Odin. Frigga is the orderer of relationships, be they household, family, tribe, or community. She is both goddess of hearth and home and of the family relationship to the community; she is the loving wife and the leader's wise consort. She rules from the Fensalir hall in Asgard and is associated with spinning; it is said that she spins clothing out of the clouds. The best symbol for invoking her is a spindle twined with handspun wool, which may also be used for binding hands.

Frigga is considered the guardian of *frith*, which translates roughly as "peace between all social groups." As such, she is an excellent goddess to invoke at a wedding where there is tension between in-laws, divorced parents, or the parents and the couple themselves. To Frigga, the bonds of family are very important, and if they are likewise important to a worried couple-to-be, perhaps Frigga could be invoked before the wedding day and asked to make peace among all present.

Although Frigga is thought of as being utterly faithful, and indeed the keepers of vows and oaths are among her handmaidens, she is sometimes seen pleasuring herself with other men, including Odhinn's brothers and the occasional guest. Rather than seeming contradictory, this is a reflection of the ancient Teutonic/Nordic customs of hospitality and polyandry. It was not uncommon for a woman to marry a set of brothers for reasons of tribal harmony, nor was it considered wrong of her to offer bed-companionship to an honored guest in the name of hospitality, although it was not required. Frigga keeps the ancient Norse model of fidelity: all her children are Odhinn's, and she is fiercely loyal to him and is at his side for any need of his that she can fulfill. Had monogamy been the rule during the time and place when she was most popular (like the classical Hera), she would likely have been considered monogamous, as she is a guardian of the tribal and social rules. However, this association with nonmonogamy means that she can be invoked appropriately at polyamorous weddings as well as monogamous ones, as long as the polyamorous wedding includes overtones of family and tribe building within a loving community rather than an emphasis on sex.

Frigga had a long list of handmaidens, many of whom were directly involved in the business of marriage and others who were secondarily involved, as their spheres included household wealth and harmony. The invocation for them is also included below.

# hymn to frigga

*This can be used on the program or wedding announcement; directly after the quarter casting in order to invoke Frigga's presence; or as a blessing on the couple at a later point in the ceremony. This should also be read by someone who is happily married.*

Lady of Asgard[1], cloaked in stars,                                    *az*-gard

Spinner of clouds and weaver of peace,

Finest treasure of Odhinn[1],                                          *oh*-din

Orderer of all people, frith-maker,

You who set things right

And join all hands in fairness,

Giver of counsel, keeper of hospitality,

First at the hearth and threshold,

Hamingja[1] of the Aesir[2],                          ha-*ming*-ya / *ay*-seer

Give us your blessing on this day,

A blessing not only of these folk who love

And come to be joined by your silken-spun threads,

But on their kin, and their kind, and their tribe,

And all of us who hear watch and witness their vow

And seal it with our love.

53

# hymn to frigga's maidens

In the name of Vara, may this couple take on this geas in full heart.

In the name of Syn[1], may they keep their boundaries strong.            *sin*

In the name of Lofn[1], may they reach always for reconciliation.       *loaf*-en

In the name of Gna[1], we proclaim this promise to all.                 *g'na*

In the name of Gefjon[1], may they be an example.                       *geff*-yon

In the name of Eir[1], may they tend each other's wounds.               *air*

In the name of Snotra[1], may they learn to work together.              *snow*-tra

In the name of Sjofn[1], may their affection be strong.                           *syoaf*-en

In the name of Huldra[1], may wealth flow through their hands.          *hool*-dra

In the name of Hlin[1], may their love survive even death.                  ha-*leen*

In the name of Fulla[1], dear sister of Frigga,                                      *fool*-ah

    may they have always abundance.

In the name of Vor, we will hear and witness this oath.

54

# hermaphrodeity

Some couples may also wish to invoke the Hermaphrodeity, the two-in-one God/dess, in all Hir forms. There are a variety of reasons for this. Some may be transgendered themselves, and want to invoke a form of Spirit which more closely resembles them. Alternately, the Hermaphrodeity can symbolize man and woman as one being, one unit, and thus be appropriate for two single-gendered people of opposite gender who are being symbolically bound together. In India, even to this day, the transgendered priestesses referred to as *hijras* are considered good luck to stand by at a couple's wedding, as they symbolize within themselves the *Hieros Gamos* (*heer*-os *gahm*-os), the Sacred Marriage.

Of course, the modern Pagan community has its own versions of the sacred hijra, and the gods are always pleased when you call upon them for their traditional duties. This prayer should be spoken by someone who considers themselves to be somewhere between male and female—transgendered, or simply spiritually androgynous. It is appropriate for them to cross-dress, if they have not modified the gender of their bodies, or to dress androgynously.

# hymn to hermaphrodeity

*This can be used on the program or wedding announcement; directly after the quarter casting in order to invoke her presence; or as a blessing on the couple at a later point in the ceremony.*

Hermaphrodeity,

Spirit Two-As-One,

You who have many names and forms,

We call you to bless Two

Who wish to be as One.

Aphrodite Urania[1], bearded love goddess,     yer-*ah*-nee-ah

Lilith, hairy goddess of the desert,

Shiva, Lord Who Is Half Woman,

Dionysus, dancer, womanly one,

Agdistis[1], betrayed one,     ag-*diss*-tiss

Baphomet[1], lord of ecstasy,     *baff*-oh-met

Obatala[1], Creator of the human race,     oh-*bah*-tah-lah

Zurvan[1], sage and crone in one,     *zoor*-van

Shapeshifter, trickster,

One who encompasses all,

Bless this joining as you bless all joinings,

Bless this threshold as you bless all transitions,

Bless this moment in your wonderful eyes.

55

*chapter 7*

## Vows

*P*ersonal note from Raven:
The vows are actually the most important
part of the entire ritual, as they are the public affirmation of the couple's intent, spoken in their own voices. Without the vows,
there is no surety that the marriage is real. I
know that for myself, actually speaking the
vow—making the promise in front of all
those people—was a belly-dropping experience. This is it, this is for real, my body
responded, and the blood roared in my
ears. We had done it; we had pledged in
front of all those people and it was Done.
It is a magical promise, made in front of
the gods, with all the weight of a geas (a
magically binding oath-spell). Even those
who are not religious and don't see marriage as anything other than a secular
arrangement sometimes find themselves
having a spiritual experience in the middle
of their weddings.

# selecting vows

Vows can be loosely grouped into two varieties: spoken and repeated. Spoken vows involve the couple facing each other and making those vows to each other directly, without the aid of clergy. Repeated vows, on the other hand, usually involve the clergyperson reading off the vows while the couple repeats them back. In some modern secular weddings, the vows have been so condensed and repeated that the couple only ends up saying "I do." In past centuries, long spoken vows were more common, and people had to do a lot more talking as part of their ceremony. We admit to being a little annoyed by the abbreviated nature of modern wedding rituals.

There's something to be said, however, for both sorts. Spoken vows are more personal; two individuals look each other in the eyes and speak directly, intimately; they have control over the space and the energy and the ritual. The circle becomes, just for a moment, a private space in which they can speak their hearts and have their feelings witnessed. On the other hand, people getting married often have stage fright and forget their lines, or are in such a flurry of activity beforehand that they don't get a chance to memorize them properly, or are just nervous and lousy at remembering long pieces of poetic text. They may prefer to go easier on their harassed memories and just repeat back what a clergyperson says rather than muff lines on this important day. Many couples do both, first speaking to each other and then doing a repeated vow. This is what Raven and Bella settled on, and you can read those vows below.

One of the sensitive parts of any vow is the mention of time. In the traditional non-Pagan ceremony, there's the "till death do us part" line that gives some people a case of the willies just to hear it, to the point where some modern non-Pagan couples drop it entirely. In certain Neopagan traditions, couples are encouraged to create "term handfastings," usually first in an interval of a year and a day, and then in intervals of five years, ten years, life, and the rather extreme "life and all lives to come." We have performed handfastings for all those intervals, including for couples who insisted on "forever," and ones who insisted on no mention of time limits at all. One of the most popular for short-term no-limit handfastings is "so long as love shall last."

This is a personal issue and couples should work it out together carefully. On the one hand, vows that are taken seriously can actually help buoy up a relationship during hard times, and "forever" may give a couple the strength that they need to hang on. On the other hand, sometimes it is right and necessary to split up, and there's no reason to have vows hanging on your past that create guilt and feelings of failure. Each couple has to make this decision themselves, and no clergyperson should push one time limit over another or even push for having one at all. If you are the clergy in question and you honestly do not think that the couple you're facing will make it together for a year and a day, much less forever, please read chapter 15, A Note to Pagan Clergy (page 283) to get some advice on that subject.

For couples, it's good to select your vows carefully. Read every word and decide if you truly understand them, and if they say what you want to say. It's better to reject an elegant-sounding vow that you find somewhat ambiguous or ambivalent than to say the wrong thing in front of all the gods and your community. It's not that you'll be struck by lightning if you make the promise in the name of what gods you like and then break it, but there is a certain amount of karma to breaking any vow, even if it only results in the mess you have to clean up later.

Discuss the meaning of the words with your partner, and make sure that he or she has the same idea of what those words mean. For example, Raven and Bella chose to use the vows from the Book of Common Prayer of the Anglican Church: "With this ring, I thee wed, and with my body I thee worship, and with all my worldly goods I thee endow." Some people at the wedding found the last line materialistic, reeking of premarital contracts and other nonromantic monetary issues. To Raven and Bella, it was important, because it said to them, "We recognize the power that shared material resources have in a relationship, and we trust each other not to get nasty over them." A vow may be written that promises a partner the sun, moon, and stars, but the partner it is said to may not find that specific enough to be meaningful. It is imperative to make sure that everyone involved agrees on the meanings of the words, especially the flowery ones.

# binding hands

The most important (and traditional) part of most modern Neopagan handfastings is the binding together of hands. Traditionally, it goes like this: The bride and groom face each other and hold right hands and left hands together, so that their clasped hands cross. This creates a figure eight, the sign of infinity, when seen from the top down. The clergyperson or some other honored individual (often a child, stepchild, or the maid of honor and best man) ties the cord around one person's left wrist and the other person's right wrist. In the infinity position, this is easy to do as they are next to each other, and all the officiant has to do is figure-eight around the two closest arms. The traditional numbers of knots are three, six, and nine.

Then, ideally, the couple should stay bound together throughout the entire reception until such time as they can pop off and consummate the marriage. Raven and Bella opted to do this for their wedding, as it was held on their own property and the bed wasn't far away. On the other hand, if the two of you are going to be involved in some post-reception activity such as dishwashing, cleanup, or driving home, it's perhaps better to slip your hands out of the cord as soon as the receiving line is finished. If this is going to be the case, make sure that you inform the cord-tyer so that they can tie it loosely enough for both parties to slip out of. The knots themselves should never be untied, unless a divorce ritual is needed some time in the future. Put your cord somewhere safe, where it won't be disturbed or lost.

If the couple doesn't want to actually bind their hands together or would prefer to be apart during the reception in order to greet people, dance with friends, etc., another option is to borrow the idea of one couple we know and make two separate cords. Her cord was braided out of white, red, and black silk cord to represent the Maiden, Mother, and Crone; his was braided out of green, gold, and grey for the youthful Green Man, the Sun King in all his power and maturity, and the wise Sage. After they had spoken their vows, they tied the two cords together with six knots (six being the number of love) and stated that this symbolized their willingness to love each other through youth, maturity, and old age. The cord was then placed in a special box and taken with them to the reception, where it was placed on their table and eventually on their home altar.

If you use a single cord, it should be at least six feet long in order to go several times around both people's wrists. It should be thick enough to be tied easily—thick yarn or silk rattail cord should be the smallest diameter—and thin enough so as not to be unwieldy. You can braid several cords together—one couple used both triple Goddess/God colors mentioned above braided into a single band—or pick a single cord in a color important to both couples. Raven and Bella realized the day before the wedding that they had neglected to bother with acquiring a cord, but just then a friend pulled into the driveway with a length of white satin cord wrapped with tiny seed pearls that was left over from her wedding gown. She wanted to know if it might be useful; Bella told her happily that her wedding gown was red, but that the cord was perfect for playing a much more important part.

One sort of cord that is strongly associated with Pagan history is the witches' measure. It is said that medieval covens would take a cord the height of each of their members, knot them in three places (the length from fingertip to outstretched fingertip; the diameter of the chest at heart level; and the diameter of the head), and touch them with the bodily fluids of each individual. These would then be kept in a safe place to insure the good behavior of the members—in a time when a single careless word could kill, using spells to bind people for the safety of their coven-mates was considered good policy. However, the measure can quite effectively be used as a wedding cord. One cord can be used for both people, with the knots of both sets of measurements tied in (and the shorter person's height knotted in as well), or two cords can be made separately and knotted together.

The color of the cord(s) is an intensely personal thing, and can only be chosen by the bride and bridegroom in question. It can be their favorite colors, or their wedding colors, or colors that are personally symbolic to them. The colors can also symbolize the qualities that they most wish to bring to the relationship. For example, red could symbolize passion, orange could be for energy, yellow for joy, green for growth, blue for truth, purple for nobility, brown for hard work and loyalty, black for eternal commitment, white for newness, grey for quietness, silver for communication, and gold for warmth.

The vows that follow were created for real people, for their real handfastings. We thank them for allowing us to use them. The cord-tying can be added before or after any of these vows.

# simple repeated vows
### (level 1)

*This vow was written for the clergyperson to read in short lines, for the couple to repeat. The first two paragraphs are switchable; either the bride or the bridegroom can be addressed first, as they choose. Traditionally the bride is always addressed first, but in this era of (hopefully) sexual equality, we feel that the couple should choose this themselves.*

**officiant:** *(to first partner)* _____, do you choose to take _____ as your wife, to care for her above all others, to provide for her happiness before even your own, and to treat her with honor and respect, both publicly and in private, so long as your love shall last? *(he answers)*

*(to second partner)*: _____, do you choose to take _____ as your husband, to care for him above all others, to provide for his happiness before even your own, and to treat him with honor and respect, both publicly and in private, so long as your love shall last? *(she answers)*

Give me your hands. The tying together of the hands symbolizes that you are no longer two separate people but a new unit, a family, bound together in mutual love.

Repeat after me: I, _____, *(bride repeats)* promise you, _____, *(r)* that I will stand by you in sunshine and in storm, *(r)* in darkness and in light, *(r)* through good times and bad. *(r)* Will you accept me as your wife? *(r)*

Repeat after me: I, _____, *(groom repeats)* promise you, _____, *(r)* that I will stand by you in sunshine and in storm, *(r)* in darkness and in light, *(r)* through good times and bad. *(r)* Will you accept me as your husband? *(r)*

# heart-binding vows
## (level 1)

*This vow adapts to being either spoken or repeated. It was written by our friends Jezanna and David for their handfasting. Each line was read off by the bride and repeated back by the bridegroom. On the last line, the bridegroom said, "I will," and then repeated the line to the bride, who said also, "I will."*

I wish to join my life with yours.

To stand by your side and sleep in your arms

To be joy to your heart and food to your soul

To work as partners and live as a family

While we grow old together.

I vow to love, honor, and respect you

To hold you to my heart

But not bind you to my will.

I promise to listen carefully and to speak the truth

To stay with you through struggles and pleasures

All the days of my life.

Will you accept me and all that I am?

# raven and bella's vows
## (level 2)

*These vows were performed at Bella and Raven's wedding in September of 1999. They have two parts, spoken and repeated. The first section was personalized to each individual; Bella chose to write something of her own, and Raven, being a musician, chose to sing. Bella's personal vow is included as an inspiration for others to write their own. The second part of the vow is repeated; the clergyperson (in this case, Tannin Schwartzstein, the co-author) gives the vow to them line by line.*

**bride:** When first I met you, I was gripped by intrigue and fascination. Your voice jogged forth wisps of memory of former days and times, and I knew that you were the one. With this certainty came also remembrance of another older dream, so absurd and impossible when first I dreamed it that I dared tell no one; I kept the dream like a treasure in a casket for fear of the mockery airing it might entail. This dream was so powerful and so wonderful that it would not pass away, but only grew stronger and more demanding until it could not be denied or even resisted.

The dream was like a love charm coin, incomplete without its other half, demanding wholeness. Then we came together, and even the stars and planets proclaimed the rightness of the union from the horoscopes we cast. When your dream met my dream, the fusion generated a potential with possibilities much, much greater than the sum of the originating ingredients. So here we are, on the blessed earth, making our commitments to each other legal and binding, not merely demonstrating our already existing covenant, but claiming all the rights and responsibilities of a married couple before witnesses and demonstrating that our shared dream, so absurd and impossible, is as real and durable as the rocks below your feet. Love built the dream, and love will make it last forever.

*Raven, instead of a spoken vow, took up his guitar and sang Bella a sere-
nade: Bob Franke's "Beggars to God." Another groom might pick a similarly
meaningful song or write his or her own statement. When the groom has spoken or played, the repeated vows are made.*

**officiant:** *(to bride)* Repeat after me. I,_____, *(bride repeats)* do come here of my
own free will to seek the partnership of my beloved. *(r)* I come with all love,
honor, and sincerity, wishing to become one with he whom I love. *(r)* Always
will I strive for his happiness and welfare. *(r)* His life will I defend before mine
own, *(r)* and I will always be his truest friend. *(r)* All this I swear in the names
of the gods, *(r)* and may they give me the strength to keep my vows. *(r)*

**officiant:** *(to groom)* Repeat after me: I, _____, *(groom repeats)* do come here of
my own free will to seek the partnership of my beloved. *(r)* I come with all
love, honor, and sincerity, wishing to become one with she whom I love. *(r)*
Always will I strive for her happiness and welfare. *(r)* Her life will I defend
before mine own, *(r)* and I will always be her truest friend. *(r)* All this I swear
in the names of the gods, *(r)* and may they give me the strength to keep my
vows. *(r)*

*Raven and Bella took a classic line from the Anglican Book of Common
Prayer, which isn't Pagan but is very old, and it spoke strongly to us.*

**bride:** *(placing ring on groom's finger)* With this ring I thee wed, and with my body
I thee worship, and with all my worldly goods I thee endow.

**groom:** *(placing ring on bride's finger)* With this ring I thee wed, and with my body
I thee worship, and with all my worldly goods I thee endow.

# earth vows
### (level 2)

*Ideally, these vows should be spoken out of doors while standing under a tree or near a lot of vegetation. If indoors, large potted plants and/or potted trees should be brought in to frame the couple as they speak. The vows can be repeated back to a clergyperson, or spoken back and forth to each other by the couple.*

By seeds of all beginnings, I make this oath.

By roots of all depths, I swear to love you with all my might.

By stem and trunk that reach for the sky, I swear to respect your soaring spirit.

By bud that grows, I swear never to crush your dreams.

By leaf that kisses the sun and rain, I swear to share my joys and sorrows
   with you.

By flower that opens to the dawn, I swear that I do trust you.

By fruit that gives forth sweetness, I swear to nourish and support you.

By seed within the fruit that grows the tree anew,

I swear to begin anew with you, again and again,

As many times as the gods shall decree.

By life and death, by Lord and Lady, by hand and eye, by heart and spirit,

This I do swear to you here before the Fates

And mark my soul forever with your touch.

As all green things grow, so shall our love,

And its memory be carried forever beneath the feet

Of a thousand generations to come.

# *sacred trust vows*
### (level 2)

*This vow was written by Corbie Petulengro for her handfasting. It should ideally be spoken back and forth, with each member of the couple trading off on the lines. It can also be spoken as one-half of a personal vow by one member of a couple.*

I have loved many

But I have trusted few

And I trust only one enough to stand here today and pledge my love.

I trust you with my life like I trust my own destiny

Of which you are a part.

I trust you not to hurt me save by accident

And I trust you to make amends for those accidents.

I trust you to respect me, in places seen and unseen,

And to make your words reflect that respect.

I trust you to fight with me, yet never lose faith in our love,

And to fight by my side for those things that I value.

I trust you to be considerate of my heart before you act.

I trust you to see things in me that I cannot,

And to speak clearly and truthfully and not hold back your thoughts.

I trust you to accept that dance that I am given

By my gods and goddesses,

And support me on that path as I serve them.

I trust you to believe that I will give back

Everything you give to me

Three times over.

# vows to the divine within
### (level 3)

*In Paganism, we are not entirely separate from our deities. Their nature is found within us, and these vows reflect that fact. They can be either repeated or spoken, and switched so that either the bride or the bridegroom goes first.*

**bride:** I see in you the face of the God

And I promise to honor you as I honor him.

You light my life like Lugh and Apollo light the sky

And I promise never to take that light for granted.

Your body's wildness is like unto Pan's sacred dance

And I promise never to chain it.

Your generosity is as deep as the Corn King who is cut down

And I promise always to appreciate it.

Your judgment is as keen as the Lord of the Dead

And I promise never to bring dishonesty to it.

You instincts are as sharp as those of the Horned Hunter

And I promise always to listen to them.

You defend our home and our love with the strength of Mars

And I promise never to cease to respect you.

Your arms wrap me like the Green Man wraps the Earth

And I promise to turn to you when I am in need.

Your love is as precious to me as the air I breathe,

The blood in my veins, the work of my hands,

And the Earth from which I sprang and to which I will someday fall,

And I promise to hold you in my heart forever.

**groom:** I see in you the face of the Goddess

And I promise to honor you as I honor her.

You light my way in the dark like the Moon Goddess

And I promise always to find my way back to you.

Your body's sensuality is like the sea from which Aphrodite rose

And I promise that I will never seek to confine your charm.

You nourish my life as the Earth Mother sustains all life

And I promise never to take your caring for granted.

Your sight is as clear and deadly as that of the Death Goddess

And I promise never to deceive it.

Your senses are as fine as that of the Lady of the Animals

And I promise always to take them seriously.

Your strength is as certain as that of Athena,

And I promise never to cease to respect you.

Your laughter is like that of the Spring Maiden

And I promise always to return it, joy for joy.

Your love is as precious to me as the air I breathe,

The blood in my veins, the work of my hands,

And the Earth from which I sprang and to which I will someday fall,

And I promise to hold you in my heart forever.

69

# Winter Vows
## (level 3)

*These vows were written for a couple who had a very long courtship of several years, which they saw as the "seasons" of their love affair. They did get married in the winter, and it likely doesn't make sense to use these unless you are doing so as well. The vow can either be repeated or spoken back and forth, with the couple trading off lines so that each one gets to say both calls and responses.*

When we met, it was spring, and we danced with the Maiden.

By her bright mind, I swear to you my love.

When we loved it was summer, and we dallied with the Nymph.

By her warm thighs, I take you to my hand.

When we told each other our stories, it was autumn,

    and we gathered in our blessings with the Mother.

By her everlasting love, I hold you to my heart.

Now it is winter, and we will build a home together at the Crone's secret hearth.

By her ancient wisdom, I promise to grow old with you.

By all the mysteries of the Earth below, I hold my ground and see you eye to eye.

By all the mysteries of the stars above, I take your dreams as my own.

By all the mysteries of the cosmos, I pledge myself to you.

# year-and-a-day vow
*(level 3)*

*We've chosen to consider this year-and-a-day vow as a level 3 ceremony item, as trial marriages are still very much a Pagan-only phenomenon, and it is unlikely that you would be trying to pass it off as part of a non-Pagan ceremony. It is also assumed that this is a non-legal handfasting. It is a repeated vow, and either the bride or the bridegroom can go first.*

**officiant:** *(to either the bride or groom)* _____, for the next year and a day _____ shall be the light of your life and the fire in your heart. She *(he)* shall be the face you see upon awakening and the kiss that sends you to sleep at night. Hers *(his)* will be the needs that you will struggle to fulfill and the heart whose feelings you must take into consideration before taking any action. She *(he)* will slowly grow into the center of your world, the polestar of your dreams. You will dance with each other among the spring's new greenery, rejoice together in the summer's heat, nourish each other with the autumn fruits, and warm each other through the cold winter. *(Note: These seasonal phrases can be reordered to represent the time of year when the couple is actually doing the handfasting.)* Do you swear to pledge yourself to her *(him)* for one turn of the green Earth around the great sun?

**bride/groom:** I do.

**officiant:** If you do not choose to renew your vows together after your time for loving has passed, do you swear to treat each other with respect and kindness and do everything in your power to part friends?

**bride/groom:** I do.

**officiant:** Then I pronounce you handfast. As your hands shall be bound, so shall your lives be bound together, for as long as love shall last.

# Vow for minors
## (level 3)

*Teenagers often fall in love and want to do something to mark their
(probably temporary but likely quite passionate) commitment to each
other. By giving them a nonlegal handfasting option, you reduce the
possibility of elopements and other foolishness, as well as showing
them that you take their love seriously . . . and if you don't, you
should, for their protection. These vows are specifically structured to
remind them how crucial such a commitment is. If the minor couple
is not heterosexual, you can remove the line about childbearing. For
further discussion of the ethics on handfasting minors, please read
chapter 15, A Note to Pagan Clergy. The vow is repeated for both
parties, and either one can go first.*

**officiant:** Repeat after me: I, _____, *(groom repeats)* promise you, _____, *(r)* that
for the next year and a day, *(r)* I will be with you as your partner and your
helpmate. *(r)* I will teach you what I know of love, *(r)* and learn from you as
well. *(r)* I will treat you with respect and care, in public and in private. *(r)* You
will be first in my heart and first in my free time. *(r)*

I will not abandon you nor slander you nor be dishonest to you. *(r)* When
there are tears and troubles, *(r)* I will take the time to listen and work things
out. *(r)* If you decide that we must part, *(r)* I will let you go without vengeful-
ness. *(r)*

I furthermore promise to do everything in my power *(r)* and make whatever sacrifices are necessary *(r)* to refrain from burdening you with a child of
our union *(r)* until such time as we are legally of age *(r)* and have the resources
to support a family. *(r)*

All this I swear before the gods, *(r)* with only love in my heart and only
truth on my lips. *(r)*

**officiant:** May the Lord and Lady bless you both.

*chapter 8*
# words of spirit

One of the things that varies the most among handfastings is the complexity of the clergyperson's task. Some couples will approach the officiant of their choice with an elaborate and well-thought-out ceremony, perhaps with the clergyperson only reading from their script or playing only the token role of signing the certificate. If you're the officiant in this situation, you should avoid the temptation of making your role bigger or insisting on adding long monologues that weren't in the couple's original plan. They are the stars; you are there to sign off on their fantasy. Their vision of how the wedding should go is most important.

On the other hand, some couples will have absolutely no idea of what they want done. Even being shown books of ritual may not help their indecision. Some may simply want a quick, Paganish ceremony where they don't have to do a lot of work and planning; in these cases, you're free to put something together for them, including whatever monologues you may want. It's best to run a copy of the program past them before the wedding, though, including everything that you plan to say. They might have an objection to a particular phrasing, or they may want things shorter or longer. Some people may have come out of a tradition where they're used to sermonizing; others may not have this background and may feel uncomfortable with long discourses or litanies. In this chapter, we've given a number of examples of things to say that we as clergy have come up with.

Another thing that you may have to be ready for is when the couple announces that they have anywhere from one to four people who want to take part in the ceremony in some way, perhaps reading something appropriate. You'll need to have a ready list of poems, prose pieces, quotations, and perhaps songs to hand out and let them look over. If you're the bride and bridegroom and you need to find something for the stuttering little sister to say, something for Mom to recite, and something for the talented friend to sing, this chapter also contains suggestions for those.

# blessings and invocations

## raven's blessing song

May the earth welcome your footsteps,

May the wind sing your tale,

May fire dance from your fingertips,

May the ocean speed your sail.

May your courage never fail you,

May your words be blessed with grace;

May the spirit of inspiration light your way.


May you be a friend to your destiny

May you always know your name.

May you learn to dance with lightning

When life brings storm and rain.

May you never be far from family

Whether kin by blood or heart;

May you never feel completely set apart.


May you walk through life like a balance beam

And never stumble and fall.

May you walk through a hundred angry glares

And may it not matter at all.

May you never cease to teach

And never cease to learn;

May the spark of hope inside you always burn.


May you walk with light through your underworld

May you never fear your dark.

May you learn to love the monsters

That populate your heart.

May you be healed of your deepest wounds

And wear the scars with pride,

And may your soul never have to hide.


May the earth welcome your footsteps,

May the wind sing your tale,

May fire dance from your fingertips,

May the ocean speed your sail.

May your courage never fail you,

May your words be blessed with grace,

May the spirit of inspiration light your way.

## communal blessing

Blessed be the earth we stand upon

And blessed be these two who stand before us.

Blessed be the eyes of the witnesses

And blessed be the two upon who they gaze.

Blessed be the arms of family and friends who embrace them

And blessed be their hands that entwine in love.

Blessed be our many loving memories

And blessed be their hearts that join together.

Blessed be the circle of community

And may our blessings be upon these lovers forever.

## eternal blessing

In the many names of the God of Love

Whose love began the universe,

Whose touch sparked all beginnings,

I bless this circle and all within it.

In the many names of the Goddess of Love

Whose love holds all things together,

Whose body encircles eternity,

I bless this circle and all within it.

In the many names of all who have ever loved

Whose stories are stars in the night sky,

Whose paths light our lives,

I bless this circle and all within it.

May only love enter

And only love depart.

## seasonal round silent blessing

A silent blessing is good for people who get stage fright and choke up during public theatrics. This ritual can be done indoors or outdoors. The priest or officiant in this rite actually symbolizes time. The scene is set by four stations, which can be tables inside or altars outside. The tables are set up to represent the seasons; as an example winter could be bare branches covered in white lace, spring could be set with flowers and so on. On each table is a stack of cards with keywords on them that name either a benefit or a difficulty of the season. Winter, for example, could have "cold" or "barren" as a difficulty; "stillness" or "sleep" as a benefit. Spring could have "blooming" or "rain." The couple both select two cards at each table and read them. They then mime how they will share the benefit with the other partner or protect them from the difficulty.

After they have drawn their cards and done their mimes, the officiant takes one of each of their hands and joins them. They then move their free hands so that one points earthward and one heavenward, symbolizing the "As above, so below" maxim.

## the labyrinth silent blessing

Make a simple labyrinth on the ground. You can just scratch one in the dirt or you can use chalk. If you're indoors, masking tape is a good choice. Several guests or members of the wedding party, representing deities, can stand along the path bearing small gifts, and as the couple passes by them, they receive the gifts and a quick touch on the forehead. The gifts should represent some appropriate gift to both the deity and the couple; for instance, someone dressed as Saturn could hand over a clock to represent patience, or someone dressed as Demeter could give them a sheaf of wheat for fertility, or someone dressed as Hathor could give them a glass of milk for mutual nourishment. It is fine to label the gifts with their meanings. Gifts that require some actual action to deal with are best; even the carry-along gifts should present the couple with the immediate issue of where to put and carry them. Returning the gifts is not an option.

# opening words for the ceremony

The most important thing about the opening words for a wedding ceremony is that there shouldn't be too many of them. The audience, and the couple, will be waiting nervously for the big moment that everyone's waiting for. They should pack a lot of meaning into a couple of paragraphs, get everyone's attention, and set the atmosphere for the important parts. It should also make the audience understand the importance of their role as witnesses to this oath, if possible, and make them feel included and not merely talked down to.

## universal opening (level 1)

officiant: Love is the energy that holds the universe together. Every electron in every atom does a dance with its partner, the proton, under the watchful eye of the neutron. If one partner leaves the embrace, the atom is unstable and may fall apart, causing terrible cataclysms. Today we stand here as neutrons, watching you both give your promises to do this dance wisely and well, and if one of you must leap out of it, to minimize the damage done. As individuals, you are strong; as a couple, nothing should stand in your way. Support each other, as the earth supports the tree and gives it nourishment, as the tree supports the vine and holds it up to the sun, as the vine supports the nest and gives it shelter, as the nest supports the eggs and gives them a place for life to begin.

## communal opening (level 1)

officiant: Friends and family, tribe and community, we are gathered here to celebrate love in all its forms, but especially the love that makes a commitment between two people. This kind of love is not afraid to make promises. It is not afraid to work and to struggle. It seeks not only to be but to continue. It is based not only on the pleasures of the present but on the hopes of the future. This is the kind of love that creates an anchor between two people, one that they can float away from and then find their way back safely. It also anchors a home and a family and along with other such great loves creates the bonds of a community. We celebrate and applaud the love and the promises of _____ and _____. May they always be a living hope for the future and for all of us.

*grecian deity opening (level 2)*

> officiant: In the name of Aphrodite, Lady of Love, we gather here today to witness
> and bless the love of _____ and _____. In the name of Eros, Lord of Love,
> we celebrate and applaud them. In the name of Themis, Lady of the Commu-
> nal Will, we send them forth as two and welcome them back as one. In the
> name of Apollo of the Sun, we shower them with joy. In the name of Artemis
> of the Moon, we wish them a thousand blissful nights. In the name of Hera,
> Lady of Marriage, we hear and respect their vows. In the name of Gaea, the
> Earth beneath our feet, we link their union to those of thousands of genera-
> tions of ancestors and forward to thousands of descendants yet to come.
> Praise them with great praise!

# presenting the rings

It's no accident that the symbol of marriage is the ring: the circle that never ends,
includes everything, and is penetrated by the finger that cannot stand alone. Although
some couples don't use rings, most still prefer that part of the ritual for its permanent,
tactile symbolism.

Some Pagans have rings specially commissioned, often with Celtic knotwork to
represent eternity, or wreaths of leaves to represent the link with nature, or even traditional claddaugh rings with hands clasping hearts. One couple that we know who
each had several body piercings decided to create a unique twist on the ring tradition:
each of them pierced their nipples with a piercing ring the size of their partner's ring
finger, wore it in their flesh for several months, and then had them replaced the day
before the wedding. The rings were exchanged the next day. It was meaningful to
them to know that the ring on their finger had once been worn in the body of their
beloved.

*rings as cycles (level 1)*

> officiant: All things turn in circles. The Earth spins in a circle and turns around the
> sun, and the sun turns around the galaxy. Time turns in circles of birth and
> death and rebirth yet again, and the planets do also spin in this way. And, like
> all things, marriages move in cycles as well. Sometimes the fires will burn

brightly, and sometimes they will die down to coals and then spring up again in bright flames. Sometimes love is warm as the spring, and sometimes it becomes winter cold with troubles and disruption. By taking on the symbol of the circle, you make a promise to remember always that all things come around; to keep faith in spring while enduring winter, to never lose hope that the ashes will flame again, and that your love will be renewed.

### rings as promises (level 1)

officiant: Take hands, both of you. And all of you who love each other in this circle, please take each others' hands as well. We all understand the gesture that you are now making. To reach out to someone and be acknowledged, held, and loved is what we all want. Taking the hand of one who loves you is the symbol of that unspoken bond.

Your hands are also the part of you that you use the most. Every day you look down at your hands as they do their job, and this is also why we wear a token of our wedding vows there. Every day, as you look down, you will see a brief flash of light, a sparkle as the ring placed on you finger today will shine. It will remind you, again and again, over and over, of your promise to your loved one. Every time you take hands, you will feel that wedding ring on your partner's hand and you will both be reminded again in turn. It will always be with you, visible, worn openly and with pride. It will say to the world that someone loves me enough to make me a promise to share a life.

### rings as communal blessings (level 1)

officiant: We will now pass the rings around, carried by *(name of ringbearer)* in this dish *(or pillow or whatever)*, and we ask that each of you hold your hand over them and wish something good for the couple, who are to wear them on their fingers from now on. You may speak your wish aloud or simply make it silently. Your positive thoughts and energies will imbue these simple objects of metal with more than just the hopes and dreams of these two lovers. These wishes will show that they have a place in the community, and that it is blessing and supporting their union.

*rings connected to earth (level 2)*

**officiant:** These rings have hung on the branch of a living tree for three days and three nights. *(Note: If you do this magic spell, please make sure that the tree you leave them on is on the property of the bride and/or groom or clergyperson, and tie a cloth over the rings on the branch to protect them.)* They have sung with the living devas of the Earth, felt the branches humming above them, greeted the sky and wind, touched the energy of the Mother. When you don them, you too will be bound not only to each other but to that green, living energy which is the source of all life. This energy will sing to each other through these magical rings that you wear, breathing life into your relationship even when all seems barren, until such time as you remove them forever. They are more than a token; they are a spell of binding that will last as long as the life of that tree, outlasting even your own lives, so respect them and use them well!

81

# songs and poetry

These are just a few songs our couples have used in the past.

- "Give Yourself to Love" by Kate Wolf
- "Fashioned in the Clay" by Elmer Beal
- "Beggars to God" by Bob Franke
- "Weather Report" *(parts I and II)* by the Grateful Dead
- "Power of Two" by the Indigo Girls

# from "on love"

From *The Prophet* by Kahlil Gibran *(level 1)*

Love has no other desire but to fulfill itself.

But if you love and must needs have desires, let these be your desires:

To melt and be like a running brook that sings its melody to the night.

To know the pain of too much tenderness.

To be wounded by your own understanding of love;

And to bleed willingly and joyfully.

To wake at dawn with a winged heart and give thanks for another day of loving;

To rest at the noon hour and meditate love's ecstasy;

To return home at eventide with gratitude;

And then to sleep with a prayer for the beloved in your heart and a song of praise
on your lips.

## sonnet 116

By William Shakespeare *(level 1)*

Let me not to the marriage of true minds

Admit impediments; love is not love

Which alters when it alteration finds,

Or bends with the remover to remove.

O no, it is an ever-fixed mark

That looks on tempests and is never shaken;

It is the star to every wand'ring bark

Whose worth's unknown, although his highth be taken.

Love's not Time's fool, though rosy lips and cheeks

Within his bending sickle's compass come;

Love alters not with his brief hours and weeks,

But bears it out even to the edge of doom.

If this be error and upon me proved,

I never writ, nor no man ever loved.

# sappho's wedding song

The stars about the fair moon in their turn

Hide their bright face when she at her full

Lights up all earth with silver.

And round about the breeze

Murmurs cool through apple-boughs,

And slumber streams from quivering leaves.

And there the bowl of ambrosia was mixed,

And Hermes took the ladle to pour out for the gods;

And then they all held goblets, and made libation,

And wished the bridegroom all good luck.

Hail, bride! noble bridegroom, all hail!

Sing Hymenaeus!

Ah for Adonis!

Raise high the roof-beam, carpenters. *(Sing Hymenaeus!)*

Like Ares comes the bridegroom. *(Sing Hymenaeus!)*

Taller far than a tall man. *(Sing Hymenaeus!)*

Whereunto may I well liken thee, dear bridegroom?

To a soft shoot may I best liken thee.

Happy bridegroom, now is thy wedding come,

And thou hast the maiden of thy desire.

For there was no other girl, O bridegroom, like her.

The bride comes rejoicing; let the bridegroom rejoice.

Bride, teeming with rosy loves,

Bride, fairest image of the goddess of Paphos,

Go to the couch, go to the bed,

Softly sporting, sweet to the bridegroom.

May Hesperus lead thee rejoicing,

Honoring Hera of the silver throne, goddess of marriage.

Come, Aphrodite, goddess of Cyprus,

And in golden cups serve nectar

Delicately mixed with delights.

For love is far sweeter of tone than harp,

And more golden than gold.

84

## directions of love
By Corbie Petulengro *(level 2)*

When I was six we made paper hearts in school

And I sat turning paper doily lace in my hands with fascination—

Perhaps confused by the meaning of the holiday

I pasted them down in the likeness of a Santa Claus

And drew a rabbit too

Just for good measure.

The storm of invective from my harried first grade teacher

—not following directions, not listening, silly girl—

Might have charred the ceiling above my desk

And then she moved on to the next small anxious face.

As the ashes of her scorn rained down on my stunned

Six-year-old head

I felt they had blackened the neat braids

My mother had so carefully crafted.


When I was seven we made paper hearts in school

And I was proud—mine was cut even

And pasted most neatly with lace

Just like the one the teacher had made

Primly perfect

A symmetry of precision
And although my hair has not been confined in braids for years
I can still feel her pat of approval.

What fragile things we base our self-esteem on—
We who drift in and and out of compliance and rebellion
Outreach and withdrawal
Like the pathetic results
Of some unsuccessful Pavlovian experiment
Never to be sure whose voice
Orders each action we take.
What fragile things we have become
Treating our hearts like delicate china
Liable to be smashed by love's blithe, carefree dance.

We make our beloveds into gods, it is true—
But why are they always the vengeful ones
With the power to make a bored shrug into a hammer blow
An unthinking word into a razor blade
A choked-off snicker into strangling hands about your throat.

I want us to be the kind of gods they sing to at Beltane—
Bored only by our self-defenses
Chuckling only at our mistrust of surrender
Stamping gaily on the firm warm earth
Without worrying about what that joy might break open
I want to see those gods every time we touch.

I used to wish love had a set of directions

As easy to follow as the steps for making a valentine—

Cut it down to the right size and shape

Line the lace up neatly

Write "I love you" across the front

And don't forget to use enough glue.

But now that I know the price I paid

For following directions

I am glad that I am being forced to trust my own instincts,

Which tell me that you are the first step

On the path which is the rest of my life.

## child's wedding blessing
*(level 1)*

May the sun shine on all your days,

May the moon bless all your nights.

May you always remember to say something nice,

And forgive each other when you fight.

May the dark be warm and welcoming,

And always give way to the light.

## parental love blessing
*(level 1)*

Long ago, love made you,

And laid you in our arms.

Through the years love grew you

Until you came into your own.

Today, love joins you together

As you willingly take on this bond.

And the love you grew from will always bless you

As you begin the cycle anew.

## roman parental blessing
*(level 1)*

Juno, Lady of Marriage, bless my child.

Venus, Lady of Love, bless my child's beloved.

Ceres, Lady of the Fields, may their fortune grow.

Jupiter, Lord Thunderer, may luck always be with them.

Mars, Lord Protector, defend their vow.

Mercury, Lord of Words, bless their promise.

Sun above, witness our joy.

Moon riding the sky, light their nights.

Earth below, mark this day forever blessed.

# the symbolic great rite

The symbolic Great Rite is definitely a level-3 activity, as it is particular to Pagan and ceremonial magic rituals. (We refer to it as the symbolic Great Rite in order to differentiate it from the actual Great Rite, which involves ritual sex in a witnessed group situation.) In the classic symbolic Great Rite, the male half of the couple holds a knife of some sort and the female holds a cup of some sort, and the knife is lowered into the cup with the utterance of various sorts of words. In case anyone wants to add this classic rite to their wedding, we give some appropriate pledges below.

*classic version*

**groom:** As the athame is to the male . . .

**bride:** So the chalice is to the female.

**both:** And the two are joined in holy union, as the Lady with the Lord.

*romantic version*

**groom:** This blade that cuts through all obstacles hath found its way to you, my beloved. It is the sigil of my manhood and my soul.

**bride:** This cup that holds all the waters of the world hath drawn you to my side, my beloved. It is the sigil of my womanhood and my soul.

**both:** Blade into cup, man into woman, from woman springeth life. Thunderbolt into ocean, God into Goddess, from Goddess springeth life. And so the two are joined in everlasting holy union.

*non-gender-specific version*

**partner a:** Blade of the wind, breath of the sky, thunder that strikes deep with all the passion of the heavens, sacred moment of clouds and rain, bless our union.

**partner b:** Cup of the sea, life-giver of many waters, cauldron of all beginnings that awaits the spark of fire, salt of blood and tears, bless our union.

**both:** May we be one together.

*men's version, for two male partners*

*The two men use two wands instead of blades, one for each partner, and a third party kneels before them, holding up a chalice. They bind their wands together using a cord—perhaps a short piece of the same cord that will bind their hands, or perhaps the central part of the actual handfasting cord, so that if a hand-binding is done it can their hands and the two bound wands all together. The idea is for the wands to stay bound throughout the life of the relationship. On the third line, they place them both together into the chalice.*

**partner a:** Soul of the tree who springs from the flesh of the Green Man, hold all my good wishes for my beloved and bind me to his heart for all time.

**partner b:** Soul of the tree who springs from the flesh of the Green Man, hold all my good wishes for my beloved and bind me to his heart for all time.

**both:** May our love dwell forever in the deep and everlasting love of the Goddess, and may she bless our union.

### women's version, for two female partners

*The two women use two chalices, one filled with red wine and one with white. Alternately, any two different liquids can be used, but they should be chosen carefully to symbolize the nature of each partner. The first partner pours some of her liquid into the second partner's chalice, and she pours some back, and they keep mixing together in this way. On the last line, they pour the mixed liquids out onto the earth as a libation.*

**partner a:** Beloved, I share with you the ocean of my heart, the rivers of my woman's body, and the sweetness of my dreams. This is my wedding gift to you.

**partner b:** Beloved, I share with you the ocean of my heart, the rivers of my woman's body, and the sweetness of my dreams. This is my wedding gift to you.

**both:** May our love be bound and witnessed by she who is all eternal in the body of Mother Earth beneath our feet.

# that broom thing

Jumping over the broom is a common—and fun—way to end a Pagan ceremony. Usually the broom is held level a little above the ground by two members of the wedding party or two honored guests. Make sure that they don't hold it too high or suddenly raise it as you're about to jump; for the bridal couple to trip and fall over the broom is very bad luck as well as painful and awkward, and anyone who thinks it's a good idea to so sabotage your wedding shouldn't be given such an honor. In the case of physically disabled individuals, it is perfectly acceptable to lay the broom on the ground and step over it together, or to lay it below the ledge of a doorframe to step down over, or even slide under a hollow wheelchair ramp. Here are three ways for an officiant to announce the broom-jumping:

### broom-jumping (level 1)

**officiant:** In the old days, the broom was a symbol of fertility as well as a household object. It was the first thing brought into the home of a newlywed couple after bread and salt, and it was used to sweep their path so as to symbolize the sweeping away of obstacles. Both ancient European traditions and African-American traditions had newly wedded couples jump over the broom for luck, fortune, fertility of family and lands, and also to show that they would accept the ordinary domestic tasks of the house together, which as a daily household tool the broom represents. Are you ready?

### broom-jumping (level 2)

**officiant:** In ancient times, the broom was a symbol of fertility as well as a household object. Gathered from the broom plant, which was considered sacred, it was the first thing brought into the home of a newlywed couple after bread and salt, which represented comfort and wealth. Both ancient European traditions and African-American traditions had newly wedded couples jump over the broom for luck, fortune, and fertility of family and lands. Today, it has also come to symbolize the union of male and female, with the long handle, which symbolizes the masculine, fitting into the brush, which symbolizes the feminine *(skip this part for a nonheterosexual union)*. Since the broom is also an ordinary household tool, it symbolizes the couple's willingness to take on the ordinary tasks of a shared household together. Are you ready?

90

## broom-jumping (level 3)

*This requires a broom made specially for the handfasting ceremony in question. Its handle should be made from a wood that the couple finds especially meaningful. See the chapter on Magical Aesthetics for appropriate charts. The brush should be made either from the broom plant genista or from bound sheaves of any kind of grass grain such as wheat, rye, barley, or grasses gathered in a place special to the couple.*

**officiant:** Behold the broom! Ordinary household tool though it might be, it has a long and fascinating history. It has represented luck, fortune, and fertility of family and lands. Its handle of *(wood of your choice)* represents *(meaning of that wood)*, and today has come to symbolize the masculine energies. It brings the blessings of Herne and the forest spirits and all their wild cousins. Its brush, made of the sacred broom plant after whom kings were named *(or made of the grains of the field which sustain us, or made of grasses gathered from _____, a sacred place to _____ and _____ )*, has come today to symbolize the feminine energies. It brings the blessings of Mother Demeter and the Corn King and all their domestic cousins. As you jump it, it will symbolize your willingness to jump together over all obstacles, be they wild and unanticipated or mundane and expected. Since the broom is also an ordinary household tool, it symbolizes your willingness to take on the ordinary tasks of a shared household. Are you ready?

*chapter 9*
# mytheatrics

*I*n some homegrown weddings where the bride and groom are particularly theatrical sorts of people, dramatic scenes are acted out as part of the ceremony. These can be short and simple, like the abduction-of-the-bride scenario below or full-length plays with parts and scripts where the wedding party enacts some folktale or myth. Obviously, the latter are somewhat more elaborate and require more organization and preparation, not to mention having people who can actually act, but they are impressive and fun when they are pulled off well.

In this section, you'll find many scripts with stage directions. When preparing to perform these rites, there are two basic options: memorization and cue cards. Proper memorization of lines tends to give a much more professional quality to a performance. It takes a good deal of effort and time for longer scripts, but the results are often well worthwhile. The problems of getting the participants to memorize lines (besides traveling long distances to rehearse) may be too daunting; in this case, cue cards may be the best option. We strongly suggest multiple walk-throughs in order to be familiar with all the lines beforehand.

# wedding abductions

A surprising number of couples put mock abductions into their wedding rituals, and that includes Raven and Bella. We've known quite a few who have done this, although it is still a bit unusual and sensitive guests should be warned ahead of time. Why stage a mock abduction? One reason, given by couples whose weddings have a historical-period flair, is that many ancient and medieval weddings staged pseudo (or not-so-pseudo) abductions of the bride, and modern couples like the idea of connecting with their ancestors in this way. Ancient Greek brides in some city-states expected the mock abduction as part of the ceremony. In fact, there is some research to suggest that the "rape" of Persephone by Hades was actually a retelling of a perfectly normal "mock-rape" Greek wedding that we have misinterpreted; an ordinary Greek maiden may have expected her groom to sweep her off her feet and carry her away.

Early medieval bridegrooms often staged mock abductions as well, which were actually meant to publicly show the bride's consent: if she really had been being taken against her will, her family would have responded violently, but their good-natured laughter at her token, feeble, giggling struggles showed to all witnesses that this was a consenting match. It also allowed the groom to look good in front of all his new in-laws, as there was often a staged mock swordfight between him and another compatriot. Although some modern folks turn up their nose, the idea of wedding-as-entertainment for guests was par for the course in medieval times. In fact, it was bad form not to make your wedding into a spectacle to delight the public—thus jugglers, minstrels, singing maidens, staged abductions, and sword fighting. It was not until weddings were made a religious sacrament in the sixteenth century that they became the somber rituals that they sometimes are today.

Among the nomads of Afghanistan (a separate tribal group culturally unrelated to the Afghani nation), when a young man woos a girl, it is first settled between the families. Then both lad and lass are put on the tribe's fastest horses, taken to a long, empty stretch of desert, and the girl is given a whip and a hundred-yard head start. The boy's task is to chase her down and pull her unharmed from her saddle to his while she whips at him to keep him away. This tricky maneuver is impossible to pull off without her aid, so the mock abduction is transparently a measure of her consent. If she really doesn't want him, he'll get off with lashes across the face (assuming he can even catch her), and she is free to spurn his courtship. If she approves of him, her flailing will be token at best, and she will slow down and allow him to pull her across to his saddle.

Another reason that some couples stage a playful abduction is to work with the frequent last-minute fear that many couples have when facing a wedding. No matter how much you love each other, making a serious commitment like a handfasting or wedding can be nerve-wracking. By satirizing it and making it into a playful game, the fear can be faced and lessened. There's also no reason why the abduction has to be of the bride; we know at least one handfasting where the groom was abducted away from his mock-protesting crowd of groomsmen by the bride and her cadre of beautiful Amazon bridesmaids.

Of course, if you are going to stage an abduction, you will need a large area to work in, sturdy shoes for everyone involved, and plenty of rehearsal. Bella decided that the best way for her to be "snatched" without messing up her wreath, veil, hairdressing, and silk gown was for the two strongest groomsmen to come up behind her with their hands clasped into a human chair and scoop her up from behind, carrying her off. The maneuver had to be practiced a few times before it went off smoothly. Do be careful of everyone's fancy clothing; it's best to actually rehearse in the outfits or something of that same length and unwieldiness. Staged sword fights should be practiced several times and kept far away from guests who might blunder in and get hurt accidentally. It's best if this sort of thing is done only at fairly informal weddings and preferably outside where there is lots of room.

Keep in mind, however, that many modern guests may be horrified and even upset at a playful mock abduction. Some may see it as symbolically continuing or condoning the ancient tradition of woman-as-property, or they may be uncomfortable with a satirization of a nonconsenting marriage and be unable to see it as an actual proof of consent. If you are concerned about how well certain guests will take it, try to speak to them beforehand and allay their fears if possible. In the end, though, it's your wedding and your day, and you should do it the way you want.

When Raven and Bella got married, Bella was charmed by the abduction idea and Raven liked the thought of being able to stage a mock battle. On the other hand, neither of them liked the idea that the wedding might characterize men as strong, scary abductors and women as helpless, screaming, vulnerable victims. To address this, they armed all the bridesmaids with spears and polearms (decorated with colorful ribbons and tassels to match their dresses), and armed the groomsmen with blunt swords. When the groomsmen rushed out, scooped up the bride from behind the line of bridesmaids, and made off with her, Raven drew his sword and cried, "To me!" and led the bridesmaids in a charge against the abductors. One of the groomsmen (Raven's little brother) squared off in a quick staged sword fight, which the groom was allowed to win smashingly, while the bridesmaids fought the rest of the pack into submission and made them promise to behave. Then the wedding party were all escorted back to the altar area. At the end of the ritual, the same swords and polearms were used to make an arch for the couple to exit beneath. Everyone had a great deal of fun, and the handfasting was talked about for years afterward.



## full-length performances

Listed below are some mythical or folktale performances that have been enacted as part of handfastings or weddings we've been involved with or heard of. There are many more, of course, as many as there have been fictional weddings, and we're sure you can come up with them, but here's some inspiration to get you started.

# the legend of tam lin
## (level 1)

The ancient Scottish legend of Tam Lin goes like this: Fair Janet is a brave maiden who meets a strange and handsome man at a well surrounded by roses in the forbidden forest of Carterhaugh. He comes out of nowhere, speaks to her with romantic words, and they become lovers. Janet's father discovers that she is with child by him, and she returns to the well in despair. She meets Tam Lin again, and he confesses to her that he is a human captive of the Faery Queen, whom he had met and fallen in love with many years ago. He can only visit Fair Janet when the Queen is not watching, and he longs for escape.

Janet agrees to help him escape, and he explains that on that very evening, Halloween, she could save him—if she truly loved him. Here's how: The Fey Folk would ride by at a certain time, and he would be on one of the horses. She must leap out and pull him of his horse and hold onto him as tight as she could. The furious Faery Queen would attempt to enchant him in order to make her let go, but as long as she could hold on, she could win him away.

That night Janet does pull Tam Lin from his horse, and as she does, he begins to transform magically into many fierce shapes. She holds, though on, no matter what, and finally the Faery Queen gives up and lets Tam Lin go, and he and Janet are married and live happily ever after.

The Tam Lin legend works well as part of a Neopagan wedding with a Scottish Renaissance theme. The groom plays Tam Lin and wears a green tartan kilt and a ruffled white Renaissance shirt, a velvet laced vest, a tartan beret, and a tartan cloth thrown over his left shoulder and fastened at the belt on his right side. The bride plays Janet and wears a green tartan skirt, a Renaissance blouse and velvet laced bodice, and a green tartan "plaidie"—a long cloth folded in half and pinned by the fold to her shoulders; the outer fold hangs loosely while the inner fold is drawn around her and belted.

*When we saw this wedding done, half the wedding party was dressed similarly, as her attendants, while the other half dressed as faeries.*

*One member of the wedding party should play the Faery Queen and dress in rich, fluttery clothing with lots of silvery glitter, a crown of silver leaves, and leafy face paint. All her faeries should have leafy face paint and wear various surreal outfits of leaves and vines and cloth wings and feathers and fluttery stuff. They can "gallop" on hobbyhorses with horns and glittery manes.*

*Instead of an altar, set up an arch with a wishing well and two pots of roses trained over it. More roses can be tied to the arch to assist in the effect. If a clergyperson is present, he or she acts as the first of three choruses, narrating the story, the text of which is based on traditional Scottish ballads.*

*First the clergyperson, Chorus 1, comes out and stands before the celebrants.*

chorus 1: Oh, I forbid you, maidens all that wear gold in your hair,

To come or go by Carterhaugh[1], for young Tam Lin is there.    *car*-ter-haw

There's none that goes by Carterhaugh but must leave him a gift;

Either gold ring, or green mantles, or else their maidenhead.

chorus 2: Now gold rings may ye buy, maidens; green mantles may ye spin,

But if ye lose your maidenhead, ye'll ne'er get that again.

Yet up spoke our Fair Janet, the finest of all her kin,

*Janet comes forth and stands before the celebrants.*

janet: I'll come and go to Carterhaugh and ask no leave of him.

I'll wager, I'll wager, I'll wager with you five hundred marks and ten,

I'll maiden go to Carterhaugh and maiden come again.

chorus 3: Janet has belted her green kirtle a little above her knee,

And Janet has braided her yellow hair a little above her bree,

And she's ridden away to Carterhaugh as fast as she can be.

chorus 1: When Janet came to Carterhaugh, Tam Lin was at the well,

   And he left his steed a-standing there, but he did hide himself.

*Tam Lin crouches down behind the wishing well. Janet goes to the well and begins to pluck roses from the trellis.*

   She had not plucked a red, red rose, had plucked but two or three

   When up then started young Tam Lin at Lady Janet's knee.

*Tam Lin stands up and takes Janet's hand; she acts startled.*

   tam lin: And why plucks thou the roses, Janet, and why breaks thou the tree?

   Or why come ye to Carterhaugh without asking leave of me?

   janet: *(flirtatiously)* Carterhaugh it is my own; my da gave it to me,

   And I'll come and go by Carterhaugh and ask no leave of thee.

*They smile at each other; then he tugs her behind the well, where they embrace and sink out of sight.*

   chorus 2: He took her by the milk-white hand and by the grass-green sleeve,

   And he led her to the faery ground and begged her not to leave.

   He took her by the milk-white hand among the leaves so green,

   And what they did I cannot tell—the leaves were thick between.

   He took her by the milk-white hand among the roses red,

   And what they did I cannot say, but she ne'er returned a maid.

   chorus 3: Janet has kilted her green kirtle a little above her knee,

   And Janet has braided her yellow hair a little above her bree,

   And now she's off to her father's hall as fast as she can be.

*Janet comes out from behind the well, adjusting her clothing, and walks proudly to another area, where her bridal party and her "father"—can be the actual father or a stand-in—come up and surround her. The other female attendants take her hand and begin to dance in a circle dance.*

99

**chorus 1**: When she came to her father's hall, she looked so pale and wan

They thought she had some strange sickness, or been with some leman[1].  leh-*mahn*

She did not comb her yellow hair, nor make much of her head;

An ill thing that the lady took was like to be her death.

Four and twenty ladies fair were playing at the chess,

And out then came fair Janet, as green as any glass.

*Janet breaks away from the others and swoons to her knees.*

**chorus 2**: There were four and twenty ladies a-playin' at the hall,

And some were red and some were white, but Janet was like the snow.

Out then spoke an old grey knight laying o'er the castle wall, and said—

**male attendant**: Alas! For thee, fair Janet, your da will blame us all!

**janet**: *(standing defiantly)* Hold your tongue, ye old grey knight;

or else thee take ill too;

Father my bairn on who I will; I'll father none on you.

**chorus 3**: Out then spoke her father, and he spoke meek and mild—

**father**: And ever alas, my sweet Janet, I think thou art with child!

**janet**: If that I am with child, father, myself must bear the blame;

There's not a lord about your hall shall get the bairnie's name.

And if I be with child, father, 'twill prove a wondrous birth,

For I will swear I'm not with child to any man of Earth.

**father**: Is it a man o' might, Janet, or is it a man o' mean?

Or is it unto young Tam Lin that's with the faeries gone?

**janet**: If my love were an earthly knight as he's an elfin grey,

I would not give my own true love for any lord you say.

The steed that my true love rides on is lighter than the wind;

With silver he is shod before, with burning gold behind.

chorus 3: Janet has kilted her green kirtle a little above her knee,

And she has braided her yellow hair a little above her bree,

And she's away to Carterhaugh as fast as she can be.

*Janet goes back to the wishing well.*

And she's away to Carterhaugh and walked beside the wood,

And there was sleeping young Tam Lin, and his steed beside him stood.

She had not plucked a red, red rose; had plucked but two or three

When up then started young Tam Lin at Lady Janet's knee.

*Tam Lin comes out behind the well and takes her hand.*

tam lin: Why plucks thou the rose, Janet, among the leaves so green?

And all to kill the bonny babe that we got us between?

janet: The truth you'll tell to me, Tam Lin, and swear by root and tree,

If ever you were a mortal man, and mortal life did see?

tam lin: The truth I'll tell to thee, Janet; a lie I will not breathe;

A knight me got, a lady me bore, as well as they did thee.

Randolph, Earl Murray, is my sire; Dunbar, Earl March, is thine;

We loved when we were children small, which yet you well may mind.

When I was a boy just turned of nine my uncle sent for me,

To hunt, to hawk, and ride with him, and keep him company.

There came a wind out of the north, a sharp wind and a snell;

A dead sleep overcame me then, and from my horse I fell.

The Queen of Faeries caught me, and took me to herself,

And ever since, in yon green hill, with her I'm bound to dwell.

She set me on a milk-white steed, of noble faery kind,

His feet were shod with beaten gold, and fleeter than the wind.

And we that live in Faeryland no sickness know, nor pain;

I quit my body when I will and take to it again.

I quit my body when I please or unto it repair,

We can inhabit at our ease in either earth or air.

Our shapes and sizes we can convert to either large or small;

An old nutshell's the same to us as is the lofty hall.

We sleep in rosebuds soft and sweet, we revel in the stream,

We wanton lightly on the wind or glide on a sunbeam.

And all our wants are well supplied from every rich man's store,

Who thankless sins the gifts he gets and vainly grasps for more.

And it is such a bonny place and I like it so well

That I would never tire, Janet, in faeryland to dwell.

But aye, at every seven years they pay the teind to hell;

I'm so fair and full of flesh, I fear 'twill be myself!

And now's the time, at Hallowmass, late on the morrow even

And if you miss me then, Janet, I'm lost for long years seven.

**chorus 1**: The night is Hallowe'en, Janet, the morn is Hallowday,

And if you dare your true love win, you haven't time to stay.

The night it is good Hallowe'en, when the Seelie[1] Court will ride,　　　*see*-lee

Through Scotland and through Ireland both, and all the world wide.

And she that would her true love win, at Miles Cross she must bide.

**janet**: And how shall thee I ken, Tam Lin, and how shall thee I know,

Among so many faery folk, the like I never saw?

**tam lin**: The first company that passes by, stand still and let them go;

The next company that passes by, stand still and do right so.

The third company that passes by all clad in robes of green,

It is the head one of them all, for in it rides the Queen.

I'll ride then on a blood-red steed with a gold star in my crown,

Because I was an earthly knight, they give me that renown.

**chorus 2**: First let pass the black, Janet, and then let pass the brown,

But grip ye to the blood-red steed and pull the rider down.

**tam lin**: My right hand will be gloved, Janet, my left hand will be bare,

And these the tokens I give to thee if you would win me there.

**chorus 3**: You'll take the horse head in your hands and grip the bridle fast;

The Queen of Elfland will give a cry, and then a wicked laugh.

**tam lin**: They'll turn me in your arms, lady, into an eel and adder,

But hold me fast, don't let me pass; I am your bairn's true father.

I'll grow into your arms so cold like ice on frozen lake,

But hold me fast, let me not go, or from your firm grasp I'll break.

Again they'll turn me in your arms to a red-hot brand of iron,

But hold me fast, let me not pass, I'll do to you no harm.

I will wax in your two hands as hot as any coal,

But if you love me as you say, you'll think of me and hold.

They'll shape me in your arms, Janet, a dove and then a swan,

At last they'll fail, and I'll be in your arms a mother-naked man.

Cast your green mantle over me, I'll be myself again,

Cast your green mantle over me, and so I will be won.

**chorus 1**: Gloomy, gloomy was the night and eerie was the road

As fair Janet, in her green mantle, to Miles Cross she did go.

*Janet leaves Tam Lin, throws a large green piece of wool around her shoulders, and goes to a third area, where the faeries are starting to process from a distance. She hides behind a makeshift fence, wall, or signpost.*

The heavens were black, the night was dark, and dreary was the place,

But Janet stood with eager wish, her lover to embrace.

chorus 2: Betwixt the hours of twelve and one, a north wind tore the bent,

And straight she heard the elvish sounds upon that wind that went.

About that dreaded hour of night she heard the bridles ring,

And Janet was as glad of that as any earthly thing.

There's yarrow and rosemary in her hand, she casts a circle round,

And presently a faery band comes riding o'er the mound.

104

*Janet takes a bunch of herbs from her bodice, turns in a circle, and sprinkles them around. At this point the faeries draw closer, riding their hobbyhorses. Some play on penny whistles and pipes, running alongside. Tam Lin and the Queen are among them, at the end.*

chorus 3: Their oaten pipes blew wondrous shrill, the hemlock did blow clear,

And louder notes from hemlocks large, and bog-reed struck the ear.

Fair Janet stood with mind unmoved the dreary heath upon,

And louder, louder waxed the sound as they came riding on.

chorus 1: They sing, inspired with love and joy, like skylarks in the air,

Of solid sense, or thought that's grave, you'll find no traces there.

Will o' the Wisp before them went, sent forth a twinkling light,

And soon she saw the faery bands all riding in her sight.

Chorus 2: First she let the black pass by and then she let the brown,

But fast she gripped the blood-red steed and pulled the rider down.

*Janet runs out and pulls Tam Lin off of the hobbyhorse and out of the line. The faeries grab for him, but miss. He goes to his knees and she holds him fast and wraps her green cloth around him. The green cloth is lined with masks, which he pulls out and puts on, all while thrashing about.*

She pulled him from the blood-red steed and let the bridle fall,

And up there went an eldritch[1] cry—                        *el*-drich

faeries in chorus: He's gone among us all!

chorus 3: They shaped him in fair Janet's arms as an eel and then an adder;

    She held him fast in every shape to be her bairn's father.

*Tam Lin puts on first an eel mask and squirms about, then throws that down and puts on a snake mask and squirms further. Janet holds on.*

chorus 1: They turned him to an icicle that freezes in the cold,

    But fair Janet was never moved, and still she kept her hold.

chorus 2: They turned him to a burning brand that near set her alight,

    But Janet did not give in to fear, and so she won the fight.

*Tam Lin puts on first a mask of ice, and then one of fire. Then they are dropped aside.*

chorus 3: Then there he was in her arms at last a mother-naked man,

    She wrapped him in her mantle green and so her true love won!

chorus 1: Up then spoke the Faery Queen out of a bush of broom—

faery queen: She that has stolen young Tam Lin has gotten a stately groom.

chorus 2: Up then spoke the Faery Queen out of a bush of wheat—

faery queen: She that has stolen young Tam Lin has gotten my heart's delight.

chorus 3: Up then spoke the Faery Queen out of a bush of rye—

faery queen: She has taken away the bonniest knight in all my company!

    But had I known Tam Lin, thou knave, what now this night I see,

    I would have taken thy two grey eyes and turned thee to a tree.

    Oh, had I known, Tam Lin, thou rogue, before ye came from home,

    I would have taken your heart of flesh and put in a heart of stone.

    Had I but the wit on yestereve that I have bought today,

    I'd pay my teind seven times to hell ere you'd been won away,

    My love, ere you'd been won away!

chorus 1: Fair Janet, in her green clothing, returned upon the morn,

And there she met her father, the laird of Abercorn.

janet: For I have won young Tam Lin, as fair as fair to see,

For I have fought the faeries this night and he has come to me.

tam lin: For I have come to my true love, as brave as she can be,

And no other one shall I to have, save thee, Janet, save thee!

*They go to the wishing well, where the tone changes and Chorus 1 steps forth as clergyperson.*

chorus 1: *(to the bride)* Do ye take this man to be your lawful wedded husband, that you have snatched from danger and trouble and taken into your heart? Will ye love him and honor him and stand by his sides all the days of your life?

bride: I do indeed. *(places a ring on groom's finger)* With this ring I thee wed, and with my body I thee worship, and with all my worldly goods I thee endow.

chorus 1: *(to the groom)* Do ye take this woman to be your lawful wedded wife, who has saved you from a life of eternal wandering and fear, and take her into your heart? Will ye love her and honor her and stand by her all the days of your life?

groom: I do indeed. *(places a ring on bride's finger)* With this ring I thee wed, and with my body I thee worship, and with all my worldly goods I thee endow.

chorus 1: Then I now pronounce you husband and wife.

*They kiss. All cheer. Both faeries and human attendants begin a circle dance that spirals into the center and out again, circling the couple at its heart, and then the rite is ended.*

# the wedding of ariadne and dionysus
### (level 3)

*Dionysus was the Greek god of wine, a shamanic, altered-state, effeminate god. He was the youngest son of Zeus, called "Twice-Born" because of his near-death as a fetus. Ariadne was a goddess/princess of Crete who was supposedly promised to Dionysus when they were both infants, in a kind of political betrothal. The wedding was delayed for years while Dionysus fought madness and won, coming into his own as the god of wine and ecstatic states, dressed in women's chitons with long, flowing hair. By the time he got around to claiming her, she had eloped with the mortal hero Theseus, who, upon discovering her divine nature, abandoned her on the island of Naxos, where Dionysus found and rescued her. Their mythical wedding day takes place on September 4, and one couple we know decided to portray them as part of their handfasting.*

*The bride plays Ariadne, wearing a classic ancient Cretan gown with a skirt of many tiered ruffles, a tight bodice cut below the breasts (the bride we know decided not to go bare breasted, as the handfasting was held in a public park, but covered her breasts with a scarf), and soft-sculpture snakes twined around her arms and waist. She should wear a crown of stars. The groom dresses as Dionysus, in a purple chiton edged with Greek key trim, a fake pantherskin draped over the shoulders, and a thyrsus (a long wand tipped with a pine cone).*

*The wedding party has a choice of three themes: maenads, satyrs, and Cretans. Cretan bridesmaids wear a simpler version of Ariadne's dress; male Cretan attendants wore a white loincloth and fancy belt; maenads wear torn chitons and wreaths of grapevines on their heads (the cheapest costume). They can also wear the traditional fawnskin loincloth. Satyrs wear loincloths and vests made of animal skins and horns on their heads. Large homemade phalli make great accessories for satyrs.*

*The feast can be a traditional ancient Greek spread. The couple we know included a leg of goat roasted on a bed of lentils, stuffed grape leaves, olives, feta cheese, grapes and pomegranates, apple-grape-pomegranate sangria, and two cakes made with honey and barley flour. Instead of frosting, the cakes were decorated with marzipan (almond paste) mixed with various colors of food coloring and made into shapes applied to the top. The shapes included grapes and grape leaves, ivy, and serpents.*

*Set the site up with two areas: The first should be an area of brambles and trees, with a path cleared in it to an inner sanctum, where Ariadne and her attendants await. The second area includes an altar laid with a horn, a chalice of wine, a knife, and a candle, and a great table laid with the feast and twined with ivy and grapevines.*

*Dionysus comes forth and calls all the people together, reading from* The Bacchae *by Euripides.*

dionysus: Run on, run on, my Bacchae!

Like a stream of gold from the lavish east

Sing, sing, sing!

Let the drum stamp loud,

Stamp for him,

Throat, tongue, breath,

Blaze for him,

Let the leaping flute

Lure and tempt,

Calling out the powers of life

To join us, and play in the hills,

Then freedom!

Joy of a foal in the meadows with its mother.

Bacchae, dart!

Bacchae, run!

Bacchae, dance!

*The maenads and satyrs (and anyone else who wishes to join in) run in a mad race, waving tree branches, around the perimeter of the area; if there are woods, they should run off into the woods and then come back. Shouting, chanting, screaming, and leaping is encouraged. While this is going on, Ariadne and her group are in their area singing single long notes in harmony, like a low drone. This area should be surrounded by sticks of incense stuck into the ground, burning like a ring of smoke. A brazier with yet more incense stands in the middle, and around the edge of the incense circle Ariadne's Cretan attendants stand with staves, entwined with artificial snakes if possible.*

ariadne: I have fled the labyrinth,

   untwined the spiral,

   and come up into the upper air.

   I have walked the underworld,

   and now emerged into the sun.

   I have chased fickle mortal lovers

   as a hawk may chase a mouse

   and lost them in the underbrush,

   but now I long for the touch of a divine lover

   who will be my mate and my match.

   Now I wait for the wind that smells half of salt

   and half sweet wine

   for the one who left me a crown of stars

   as a promise of his return.

*Dionysus and his maenads approach and slow to a halt. He hails the circle of Cretans.*

dionysus: Hail, fellow travelers from the fallen city!

   Wilt thou welcome us to Naxos?

cretan: *(male or female)* Why come you this way, Lord of the Vine?

dionysus: For reasons three.

   First, and least, because the wind blew me here.

Second, because Fate directed my footsteps.

And third, and greatest, to woo she to whom I was promised so many years ago.

cretan: What bring you as a bride-price, Lord of Madness?

dionysus: I bring ecstasy of the body and soul.

I bring the taste of sweet wine, and the smell of autumn cider.

I bring knowledge of the veil between the worlds.

I bring rebirth and joy.

I bring my hands, and my heart, and a love to last a thousand years.

ariadne: *(standing forth)* My beloved, I have waited for you for time out of mind.

Yet the waiting was worth it, for my future stands before me now.

maenad or satyr: What bring you as a dowry, Lady of the Labyrinth?

ariadne: I bring courage of the soul and the serpent's tongue.

I bring the scent of frankincense and sandalwood.

I bring knowledge of the ancient mysteries of the dark places.

I bring the ability to shed one's skin and become renewed.

I bring my hands, and my heart, and a love to last a thousand years.

dionysus: My beloved, I come to fulfill my promise. Will you come to me?

ariadne: Gladly and willingly.

*She comes forth out of the circle, and her attendants follow her in a line. They approach the altar/feast table and stand before it. A maenad approaches with a bowl of grapes.*

maenad: Taste the sweetness of life.

dionysus: *(feeding Ariadne a grape)* Like the vine I am bound to your embrace.

ariadne: *(feeding Dionysus a grape)* Like the fruit I melt on your tongue.

**female cretan:** *(bringing forth a barley cake)* Taste the power of earth.

**dionysus:** *(feeding Ariadne a bit of cake)* Like earth I nourish our love.

**ariadne:** *(feeding Dionysus a bit of cake)* Like earth I am steadfast and constant.

**satyr:** *(bringing forth a horn of wine)* Taste the blood of delight.

**dionysus:** *(giving Ariadne a sip of wine)* You are in my blood and my eyes.

**ariadne:** *(giving Dionysus a sip of wine)* You are in my body like the nectar of the gods.

**male cretan:** *(bringing the knife from the altar)* Taste inevitability.

*Dionysus and Ariadne hold the knife with one hand on the hilt and the other pressing the blade, so that their palms touch with the blade between them.*

**dionysus:** I pledge myself to you, and I will love you even beyond death.

**ariadne:** I pledge myself to you, and I embrace our fate and all that it may bring.

**dionysus:** And this is the mystery.

**ariadne:** And this, too, is the mystery.

*They kiss, and all whoop and cheer. Ariadne takes the crown from her head and gives it to Dionysus, and he throws it into the air as hard and high as he can. In the original myths, he flung it into the air and it became the Corona Borealis, a constellation.*

**dionysus:** This crown of stars I set into the sky as a sign of my oath: that our love will live forever.

**ariadne:** May it be a beacon of light for all to see, and guide them in the night by the sign of our love.

*All cheer, and descend on the feast.*

111

# the tale of shiva and parvati
### (level 2)

*This ritual requires no attendants, and it may be added to or embedded into the middle of a different ritual. It is acted by the groom, who plays the god Shiva; the bride, who plays the goddess Parvati, and the clergyperson (or someone else), who narrates. When we saw this rite performed, both participants had very long hair, which was used as part of the rite. For short-haired individuals who aren't partial to the idea of wigs, the ritual can be altered.*

*Shiva wears a simple white loincloth and a long, open white robe. Three horizontal lines were painted on his forehead with ashes. He holds a skull in each hand and sits on a high place, above the rest of the audience. Parvati wears Indian dancer's clothing in many bright colors with a lotus painted on her forehead and much jingling jewelry and veils full of coins. The narrator can simply wear black. A second high place, above the crowd and directly facing Shiva, should be piled with cushions and left empty.*

**narrator**: Long, long ago, when the world was much younger, and the Age of Bronze was upon the Earth, Shiva the Great Destroyer, Mahadeva, Isvara, Lord of the Dance, clothed in space itself, went up onto the top of a mountain to meditate. He renounced the world, and all things in it, and became an ascetic. He meditated for a hundred years, seeing the past and the present and a million possible futures. Yet one thing he could not see, and this was his own future.

**shiva**: Why am I blind? What is missing from my life? Why is my future a mystery? Spirits of Karma and Dharma, speak to me!

**narrator**: But nothing came to Shiva, and he searched in vain. Meanwhile, Parvati the Lady of Generation, beautiful and terrible, sensuous and implacable, came upon Shiva as he meditated, and fell in love with him. *(Parvati dances out, sees Shiva, and falls to her knees, arms uplifted)* But in vain did she call out to him to notice her, for he was deep in his meditations, and her cries of love were nothing more to him than the buzzing of flies over his head.

**parvati:** Shiva, beloved, why are you cruel to me? Will you not hear me? You are my love and my light, my destined one, that the Lords of Karma have sent me to find. Will you not take my love? *(Shiva ignores her and "ohms")*

**narrator:** So Parvati danced a great dance of love and power and sensuality. Her dance made every animal on the earth seek out its mate; birds fell from the sky to find each other; flowers bloomed; and trees sprouted from the earth. No one could ignore her power—except Shiva. *(Indian music plays. Parvati dances a highly suggestive belly dance. Shiva continues to ohm. When it becomes clear that he is still ignoring her, she slumps in despair, turns away, and climbs up to the other high platform.)* But all was to no avail. When Parvati saw that nothing she could do would move Shiva, she fled in sorrow to the top of another high mountain, renouncing all the world, since she could not have the one she loved. *(Parvati settles herself onto the platform in a lotus position and begins to ohm herself)* A year went by, and then ten. Shiva was suddenly interrupted out of his meditations by the presence of another mind— a mind so bright and powerful that he had never seen anything like it. *(Shiva stops ohm-ing and looks surprised)* In that moment, Great Shiva fell deeply in love, and swore to find this beacon of light. *(he climbs down from his place to kneel in front of Parvati's platform, an awed look on his face)*

**shiva:** O Goddess of Enlightenment! I have traveled far to find you! Return to the world, and I will love you with all my heart!

**parvati:** Is it you, my beloved? Do you speak to me at last?

**shiva:** I have been the greatest of fools. What I was missing was you, the keeper of my female side. If you will come to me, I swear to uphold you as the crown of my existence, without which I am as nothing.

**parvati:** I come to you, beloved!

*She climbs down and takes his hand. They place wreaths of flowers about each other's neck.*

**shiva:** I am the principle of the lingam, rising high, and I say that I worship your body and soul.

113

parvati: I am Uma, the principle of the yoni, and I worship your body and soul.

shiva: I am the Destroyer of Illusions, and we see each other now for who we are.

parvati: And I am Durga, warrior of demons, and I say let there be no fear between us.

shiva: I am the Tandava Dancer, who destroys the universe and recreates it again, and I shall be with you through a thousand incarnations.

parvati: And I am Kali Ma, who creates and destroys all things in the universe, and I shall be with you to the end of time and beyond.

shiva: You are my Shakti, my female side; you are a part of me.

*She takes a ribbon and ties up the hair on one half of his head, so half is up and half is down, symbolizing the union of male and female.*

parvati: You are my male side as well, a part of me.

*He takes a ribbon and does the same for her.*

together: We are one. *(they kiss)*

narrator: And Shiva and Parvati lived for a million years of bliss.

# the story of hades and persephone
## (level 3)

*Since the wedding day of Hades and Persephone is the autumnal equinox, ideally the wedding should be as close to that day as possible. Deck the altar with autumn leaves and baskets of harvested grain. A basket of pomegranates should be displayed prominently, one of them partly peeled.*

*Persephone wears a simple white dress. Hades is dressed entirely in black. Demeter wears red or gold, with a wreath of wheat and poppies. Hades' attendants wear ghostly fluttering black or white, with white ghostly makeup on. Four of them wear headdresses that resemble the skulls of horses, complete with black bridles and reins.*

*Honored guests can be cast as as Helios, a man dressed in yellow or gold with a sun painted on his face; as Zeus, a middle-aged man dressed in regal robes the color of the sky; and as Hermes, a young man dressed in a short white tunic and cape, with winged sandals and a winged hat. Remaining attendants can be drummers.*

chorus: Welcome, all, to this sacred place. We stand between the collision of two whirling worlds, and yet we celebrate the coming moment with hope and joy. The daughter of Demeter, sweet Persephone, has spent all her days dancing in the light of the sun and moon, wrapped in the glory of the spring's fields. She is Spring's child, and flowers bloom in her footsteps. Yet this world is a world of dark as well as light, and darkness too can be beautiful . . . and necessary.

persephone: I am the daughter of my mother,

And little know I of passion and pain,

Light and darkness, laughter born of tears.

These things are strange to me,

Sheltered as I am in the bosom of love

And I long to know of the deeper world

Beneath the bright one.

chorus: As Persephone walked through the fields, she could put her ear to the ground and hear faint whisperings. It seemed to her that terrible cries came from under the earth, though she could barely perceive them. And this caused her great wonder.

persephone: Mother, what are the cries and whisperings I hear from deep under the earth?

demeter: My darling, those are the dead souls who abide in the realm of sad Hades. They weep because no one comforts them. Pay them no heed; enjoy the sun and the wind and the bright flowers. Go play with your friends.

*Persephone dances in a simple circle dance with her attendants.*

chorus: But the whisperings of the dead began to haunt Persephone in her sleep, and she became weary of the everyday joys of sun and flowers and dancing, and spent many hours laying in the fields with her ear to the ground. Then one day, she came upon a great flower springing up from the earth. *(Attendant comes forward with a potted plant, from which sprouts a large flower. If the plant is not real, a silk flower should be wired on in such as way that it is easily pluckable.)* In spite of herself, she reached toward the flower and plucked it. *(Persephone does so)* Immediately the ground rumbled like thunder and a great crack opened in the earth.

*Drummers begin a loud, driving beat. Hades steps forward, holding the reins to the four dead horsemen who trot in front of him. He circles the area and comes to a stop in front of Persephone.*

persephone: Who are you? I do not know you, and yet you stir memories in me that I have not yet known.

hades: I am your destiny, and you are mine. For whosoever plucks this flower from the earth offers themselves to this path. Will you take my hand? *(he carefully removes his glove and holds out his hand)*

persephone: I am afraid. You are all that is unknown, and you smell of the dark places under the earth and in the soul.

hades: I, too, am afraid. You are a ray of light that will penetrate my dark kingdom and change it forever.

*Persephone timidly takes his hand, and the second she does, he seizes her and gallops off with her. Demeter comes forward.*

demeter: Persephone? Where are you? *(she searches throughout the crowd, calling Persephone by name)*

chorus: Demeter searched everywhere for her child, but Persephone was nowhere to be found. Finally she begged aid of Helios, the Sun.

helios: Demeter, Lady of the Corn, I have seen your daughter. She was carried off to the Underworld by that King of the Shades, Hades, he with his hands black from the soot of a thousand cremations, he who dines with ghosts.

demeter: Aaaiiiee! *(she weeps and mourns for a moment, then whirls about and lifts her arms to the sky)* Zeus, father of my child! Come and hear what has happened to our daughter! Quickly, I need your aid!

*Zeus appears.*

zeus: What is it, Lady of the Corn?

demeter: Our daughter, Persephone, has been stolen away by Hades, Lord of Shades, the Gate Fastener who lives with ghosts! He has taken her away to his shadowy realm! You must order him to return her!

zeus: Do not fret, Demeter. Our child is of age to be married anyway, and Hades is no mean suitor. He is wealthy, with all the jewels of the world, and important as well, for little is as inevitable as death. Could you not find it in your heart to accept him as a son-in-law?

demeter: Never! My child? With that dark monster? Never! If you will not help me, then curse you forever! *(storms off, and throws a ragged grey cloak over herself; wailing and mourning, she wanders about the circle)*

chorus: And in her mourning Demeter made this the most terrible year ever on this earth that feeds so many. The earth did not take seed that year, for Demeter in her beautiful crown concealed it. And the cattle many times pulled their bent plows in vain over the land, and many times the white barley fell uselessly upon the earth. And in fact, she would have wiped out the whole race of talking men with a painful famine and deprived those who live on Olympus of the glorious honor of offerings and sacrifices, if Zeus hadn't noticed it.

*Zeus comes forward with Hermes.*

zeus: That woman! She's starving all of them! Will nothing move her?

hermes: I have pleaded with her, great Zeus, as you asked. She will not make the land grow unless her daughter is returned to her.

zeus: Very well. I shall have to do something about it. Go down to Hades and tell him to return the girl, assuming of course that she has eaten nothing while she is among the spirits.

*Hermes salutes and runs off. Zeus withdraws in the opposite direction from Hermes, and does not step forward again until Hermes returns with Persephone. Hades and Persephone come forward.*

hades: You have made my kingdom brighter by your presence, my love. You lend a kind ear to all my mourning shades. All the dead have come to love you, even those tortured souls in Tartarus. Will you marry me and live here forever?

persephone: Dark One, Sad One, I have come to love you as well, and to love the work I have found here. But I do miss my mother, and I wish to return to the upper world and spend time with her before our wedding.

hades: Then go, my love. But before you go, let us plight our troth, so that none may keep us apart. *(he holds forth a pomegranate, and peels it, and they feed each other six seeds apiece)* One for secrets, that we share only with each other . . .

persephone: And one for patience while we are apart.

hades: One for memory, that we shall always remember and never take each other for granted . . .

persephone: And one for forgetfulness, that we shall be able to forgive each other all wrongs.

hades: One that we may not fear the dark places in and between us, for we delve them together . . .

persephone: And one that we shall shine the light of our love into all those places.

hades: One for loyalty . . .

persephone: And one for trust in that loyalty.

hades: One that anger shall come and pass quickly . . .

persephone: And one that laughter shall visit often and stay long.

hades: One that our love shall bear us up under all burdens . . .

persephone: And one that our love shall be an inspiration to all who know us.

hades: With this, I bind myself to you. You are the queen of my heart, my hearth, and my realm.

persephone: With this, I bind myself to you. You are the king of my heart, my hearth, and my realm.

hermes: *(stepping forward)* Persephone, it is time to go. Your mother awaits in the upper world.

*She moves towards him, one hand still holding Hades', and takes Hermes' hand. For one moment she stands, poised, looking back and forth in indecision, and then goes forward with Hermes. When she comes to the other side of the circle, she rushes into Demeter's arms with glad cries.*

chorus: And the spring flowers and green grass grew up beneath her feet as she ran, and the earth sprouted with all good things, and the famine was over, and all rejoiced with the coming of the spring.

demeter: My beautiful daughter, I feared I would never see you again!

persephone: Mother, I have something to tell you. I have plighted my troth with Hades. I have eaten of the sacred pomegranate with him. Though I will spend this summer with you, when the autumn comes and the grasses wither, I will go down again to be married to him whom I love.

**demeter**: No! You are my child! I will not have you leave me! Not to be with him!

**zeus**: *(stepping forward)* Demeter, she has chosen. She is a woman now, and you must let her fulfill her word, and her destiny. Yet I will say this: For the months of the spring and summer, each year, she may come again to visit you, yet in the autumn she must rejoin her husband. This bargain must satisfy all, for it is the best you will get.

**demeter**: *(sighing)* I accept. Though it goes hard with me, I accept. I wish you all joy in your new life, my daughter. *(embraces her)*

**chorus**: And the spring and summer passed in a blaze of happiness. But as the days grew longer, Persephone's heart turned toward her beloved, until finally on the equinox, the time when night and day, darkness and light, are equal, she prepared to go forth to her wedding.

**hades**: *(stepping forward)* My bride! Are you still willing to keep the promise you made to me?

**persephone**: I am, beloved! *(runs to him and takes his hand)*

**hades**: You are the dawn at the end of every night. I promise to love and honor you above all others, never taking you for granted, and be there when you have need of me.

**persephone**: You are the jewel buried deep in the earth. I promise to love and honor you above all others, never taking you for granted, and be there when you have need of me.

**hades**: You are the flower that blooms in the heart. I promise to see the divine power in you, and through you worship Goddess herself.

**persephone**: You are the fire that springs up deep inside. I promise to see the divine power in you, and through you worship God himself.

**chorus**: We witness your oaths and pronounce you married!

*All repeat. The lovers kiss, and then all go forth to feast and make merry.*

*chapter 10*
# nontraditionalists

We get a lot of comments from non-Pagans who take a peek into our faith(s) that there seems to be a surprising number of Pagans with nonheterosexual and/or nonmonogamous sexual preferences. Although in my estimation the majority of Pagans are still heterosexual and monogamous, there does seem to be a higher percentage of queerfolk and polyamorous folk in neo-Paganism—and why not? It's nice not to be told that you're going to hell for whom you love. It does, however, increase the likelihood that Neopagan clergy will, sooner or later, have to deal with people who are not merely one male-identified biological male and one female-identified biological female.

Since marriages that don't look like the above situation are not at this time legal, the handfasting is even more important emotionally, as this may be the only ceremony these people will get. The illegitimacy of queer and polyamorous weddings is a source of frustration and resentment for many, and a clergyperson should be sensitive to this issue and take extra effort to treat these handfastings with the same weight as a legal heterosexual marriage. It might be good to be versed in the legal alternatives that provide most of the financial and political benefits of legal marriage. Any two people, armed with an attorney, can give each other medical and financial power of attorney, sound wills, child adoption, and other legal paperwork that will do nearly everything but convince their insurance company that they are spouses. Check with the Gay and Lesbian Alliance Against Defamation (GLAAD) for more information (www.glaad.org or 212-629-3322).

We have officiated at many nonheterosexual weddings, handfastings, and commitment ceremonies. Most people don't know that there are many, many different combinations of gender presentation and sexual preference in marrying couples. We've seen them all, and we try to present here examples of the best queer wedding rites we know. Hopefully, you'll be able to find something here that suits your needs, or at least something that inspires you to write your own.

All the rituals in this chapter are classed as Level 3. Frankly, if people know that they're coming to a queer wedding, it's unlikely that they'd be the intolerant sorts who'd object to the religious context anyway. During some of the rituals, the audience is exhorted to cry an affirmation to the question of whether they will support this union. We've found from experience that this is a powerful thing, and that once they've shouted out their promise, even if they didn't intend to do so, they feel much more protective of the couple in question and their love, and much more willing to defend them. It's useful to have some people present—perhaps the wedding party and a few friends—who have been briefed about this part of the ritual and will shout out the correct line at the correct time. Authorize one of them—preferably someone with a loud voice and a commanding presence—to turn around and get the crowd to repeat it if not enough of them followed your shills quickly enough and managed to respond.

# men's handfasting ritual
### *(level 3)*

*This ritual was designed for the commitment ceremony of two gay men. When we saw it done, the officiant wore animal skins and horns. Both men dressed in different white outfits—one loose trousers and an embroidered shirt, the other a long robe over gathered Sufi pants. Four people dressed in bright colors invoked the quarters and their spirits, and two others, one in light-colored clothing and one in dark clothing, invoked the deities. You could change the costumes as necessary.*

123

**east caller:** I sing the song of the Boy Child,

Rising with the dawn,

Eyes full of wonder,

Spirit like a kite riding the winds,

Spirit flying among the gulls and swallows,

Golden with the light of all beginnings,

Climber of the Eastern Mountain,

You breathe possibilities.

You remind us that long before these lovers met

This moment was destined to be.

By breath and scent, by bud and blossom,

By hands that play and feet that wander,

We call you into our presence!

**south caller:** I sing the song of the Youth,

Hot as high noon,

Eyes full of the sight of your beloved,

Passionate in your anger and your pride,

Spirit like a flame that leaps and scorches,

Scarlet with strength and joy,

Runner of the Southern Mountain,

Your focus burns like sunlight through a crystal prism.

You speak to us of electric nerves

And remind us that all lovers are also warriors.

As all warriors should also be lovers.

By eye and will and muscular intent,

By hands that caress and phallus that rises,

We call you into our presence!

**west caller:** I sing the song of the Protector,

He who stands guard late into the evening,

Heart full of love for those he calls his own,

He who has much to lose and the strength not to lose it,

He who finds oceans of care to give to others,

Blue as the colors of sea and twilight,

Dancer of the Western Mountain,

Your love runs like a river through all of us.

You are the Maker and Builder of all safe spaces,

And you join hands into circles, tribes, communities, homes.

By lips and tongue and beating heart,

By hands that shape and legs that carry us,

We call you into our presence!

**north caller:** I sing the song of the Sage,

Drummer of starry midnight,

Wise and bent with years,

For whom the veils between worlds are thin and open,

For whom anger has evolved into compassion,

Green and brown as the leaves and bark of trees,

Walker of the Northern Mountain,

You are rooted to this earth like a strong oak.

You speak of permanence and commitment,

Of things meant to last more than a mortal life.

By skin and bones and sinew that hold on,

By hands that heal and the memory of a hundred years,

We call you into our presence!

*Two men step forward to call the deities.*

**first caller:** I call upon the Bright God, the Lord of Laughter and Joy. Lugh, Bright Sun Face, Horus Hawk's Eye, Green Man who stretches your arms toward the sun, bless this couple with a thousand moments of humor to lighten their burdens and a thousand smiles to cheer them in the face of adversity.

**second caller:** I call upon the Dark God, the Guardian of the Gate. Hades of the Dark Places, Dionysus of the Shaman-Madness, Herne the Hunter, bless this couple with knowledge of each other's depths, and keep them from fear in the face of difficulty and tears.

**officiant:** Do you come here today of your own free will to be joined as one?

**couple:** We do.

**officiant:** Your love is sacred, as is all love. Yet there will be hardships ahead. Many will not understand, and their words and actions will be cruel. Will you join together in spite of all who may speak against you, in living testimony to the power of love?

**couple:** We will.

**officiant:** Go then to the four quarters of the universe, and proclaim your love with pride.

*The couple walk to the east, then face each other, holding hands.*

**partner a:** We stand in the east, the place of the dawn. You, my dear one, make me feel young again in your presence. I swear that I will always think of you as my friend as well as my lover and that I will work to uphold our friendship.

**partner b:** I swear this as well. We stand in the east, the place of the spring. You, my dear one, help me to think clearly and speak my feelings. I swear that you will always be brother to me as well as lover, and that I will share my thoughts and conversation with you.

**partner a:** I swear this as well.

*The couple walk to the south.*

> **partner a:** We stand in the south, the point of energy. You, my lover, are the one that I desire. I swear that I will not let the spark die out between us, but will always look for new ways to stoke that fire.

> **partner b:** I swear this as well. We stand in the south, the place of heat. You, my lover, teach me more about myself every day that passes. I swear that I will always be fair to you, even when I am angry or hurt.

**partner a:** I swear this as well.

*The couple walk to the west.*

> **partner a:** We stand in the west, the place of harvest. You, my beloved man, make me feel truly loved and safe. I swear that I will make you the centerpoint of what I call family and defend you with my body and heart.

> **partner b:** I swear this as well. We stand in the west, the place of twilight. You, my beloved man, make me feel secure enough to speak my feelings to you. I swear that I will not close you out or distance you from even my most terrible pain and dissatisfaction, but will always bring honesty to our relationship.

**partner a:** I swear this as well.

*The couple walk to the north.*

> **partner a:** We stand in the north, the place of winter. You, my partner, have earned my greatest respect as a wonderful human being. I swear that I will always be proud to stand with you and that my actions shall show that respect and pride, in public and in private.

> **partner b:** I swear this as well. We stand in the north, the place of bedrock. You, my partner, are the one that I wish to grow old with. I swear to you that I make this commitment with no reservation in my heart and that I wish to be bound to you until our bones return to the Mother.

**partner a:** I swear this as well.

*The couple walk back to the altar.*

**officiant:** You have heard this declaration of love. Do you support this couple, your friends and family and tribe, in this, their commitment to one another?

**all present:** We do!

**officiant:** Do you all swear to stand up for their vows today, to defend them as they have defended you and to speak out in their favor against those who would thrust them apart?

**all present:** We do!

**officiant:** I now bind you with this cord, man to man, heart to heart, lover to lover. By Eros who brings love, by Ganymede who offers the cup, by Hermes who opens the lips, by Pan of the animals, and by all the spirits of earth and sea and sky: behold! You are two men, but there is one life before you. Walk together in glory.

*The couple kisses. All cheer.*

**east caller:** By the powers of Hermes, rider of the winds, messenger to the gods, he who moves in and out of darkness unharmed, I thank you, gentle breezes, and send you home.

**south caller:** By the powers of Eros, whose sharp arrows inflame the heart, he who inspires all to embrace, I thank you, fires of imagination, and send you home.

**west caller:** By the powers of Ganymede, whose cup is always full, youth of promise and beauty, I thank you, oceans without and within, and send you home.

**north caller:** By the powers of Pan, who is all that is male in Nature, he of the mountains rising high and the wild places, I thank you, earth beneath our feet, and may we always come home to you.

*The rite is ended.*

# women's four corners wedding rite
## (level 3)

*For this ritual, four women act as officiants and marry the couple. One should be a young girl, preferably a teenager, dressed in white. One should be an adult woman who has not born children, dressed in red. One should be a mother with children dressed in green, and one should be an elder dressed in black.*

128

*The altar should be in the center of the space rather than at the end. It can be laid with flowers, wreaths, trinkets, a bell, two taper candles and a large pillar candle, and a large goblet of some sweet substance—wine, mead, juice, etc. Four cords, each about a yard long and colored in white, red, green, and black, lay across the altar. The couple stands on either side of the altar, facing each other. The four officiants stand facing outward at the edge of the circle and call the quarters.*

**officiant in white:** Breathe!

Gate of the Winds,

Soaring birds in flight,

Fragrance of a rain-washed spring morning

Swallow, kestrel, and butterfly

Bring the rosy dawn,

Hail to all new beginnings,

Hail Aradia

Diana's silver daughter.

**officiant in red:** Behold!

Gate of Fire,

Sun-scorched desert,

Lioness prowling the savannah,

Fierce and ready to leap,

High noon of summer heat,

Lava of the volcano

Hail to all great passions,

Hail Ishtar

Lady of Love and Battle.

**officiant in green:** Drink!

Gate of the Waters,

Fishes in rippling schools,

Vast and endless ocean

Salty womb from which we sprang,

Rushing river and lakes like blue jewels

Dolphin leaping with joy,

Sharks guarding the mysterious depths,

Hail to all engulfing feelings,

Hail Aphrodite,

Foam-born, we taste your sweetness.

**officiant in black:** Touch!

Gate of the Earth,

Hunting wolf and great bear,

High mountain chain my spine,

Green hills my breasts,

My belly a midnight valley cloaked in snow,

My bones the solid rock beneath your feet

I am hard and old, the grandmother of all,

Hail to all firm commitments,

Hail Gaea

Who surrounds us.

*Officiants walk around the circle, going around one full turn on the edge, and then spiral inward until they are close to and face the couple and the altar in the center.*

**officiant in white:** *(smudging the couple with incense)* Breathe deeply, both of you. You stand at the center of the universe, and all powers are listening to you at this moment. I am the Maiden, one-in-myself, standing alone and seeing everything new for the first time. You once stood where I stand now, independent and centered in myself. I ask this of you: Do you swear to keep your own separate individual identities, no matter how strong the urge to merge together in love?

**couple:** We do.

**officiant in white:** Do you swear to renew your love together whenever it becomes stale?

**couple:** We do.

**officiant in red:** *(bringing out a lighter)* Welcome, lovers. You stand at the center of the universe, and all powers are listening to you at this moment. I understand love, as I am the Lover who knows all the fires of the body. I know how bodies sing to each other, their insistent pulse and shouted desire. I am Desire, and I am also the Warrior who fights honorably with honorable opponents. You stand now where I stand, wrapped in a love sweeter than ripe fruit, warmer than a summer day. I ask this of you: Do you swear to keep the fires of your love fed and burning, no matter what troubles may assault each of you in turn?

**couple:** We do.

**officiant in red:** Do you promise to fight fairly with each other and not destroy each other's trust in rash anger?

**couple:** We do. *(they light each of the taper candles in turn)* This is the light of my soul . . . *(they light the large candle together with their individual candles)* . . . which is my gift to you that I bring to our marriage, two flames burning as one.

**officiant in green:** *(taking the goblet from the altar)* Drink of me, of the life from my breasts, of the sweetness of my love. *(she hands them the goblet, and they each hold it for the other to drink out of)* You stand at the center of the universe, and all powers are listening to you at this moment. I am the Mother, the one who knows selfless love and sacrifice, the joy of nurturing, the pain of loss, and the tears of sorrow. My road is a hard one, yet it is what makes us human. You will soon stand where I stand, trying your best to support each other on hard roads. You will watch each other suffer and feel helpless to anything, but give more love, and you will suffer in turn. And this, too, is part of love. I ask this of you: Are you willing to sacrifice your convenience for the happiness of your beloved?

131

**couple:** We are.

**officiant in green:** Do you swear that you will aid and support each other willingly and with joy, and care for each other above all others?

**couple:** We do.

**officiant in black:** Take hands in this sacred space, children. *(couple joins hands across the altar)* You stand at the center of the universe, and all powers are listening to you at this moment. I am the Wisewoman, who has seen many years and lived many joys and hardships. And I say to you, you will also see those joys and hardships. You must learn patience and endurance, and learn also when to hold on and when to let go. I am the Elder who is the rule of tribal law, and I say that rules can be a good thing. I ask this of you: Are you willing to set strong boundaries between you and respect them as you respect your own life?

**couple:** We are.

**officiant in black:** Do you swear to love each other the same when you are old and grey, and nurse each other through illness and death?

**couple:** We do.

**officiant in black:** You have answered eight questions, and eight is the number of commitment. I ask you one more question, to make the sacred nine: Do you, of your own free will, wish to be bound together in the sight of the Goddess?

**couple:** We do.

**officiant in black**: We bind you now with four cords. These cords represent the phases of the moon—waxing crescent, full and bright, waning crescent, and dark moon becoming new again. They represent the woman's cycle, which you both know with your own bodies—the time of preparation, the time of the release of fertility, the time of sorrow and waning, and the time of the Moon Blood. They also represent the faces of the Goddess—white for the Maiden in her innocence, red for the Lover who knows passion, Green for the mother who nurtures, and black for the Crone who knows wisdom.

**officiant in white**: *(takes the white cord and tying it about the couple's clasped hands)* Do you, _____, promise to love and honor and trust _____ as your partner and spouse, to listen and to laugh, to need and to know, to depend and to defend, to stand shoulder to shoulder against any who would sever you from each other?

**partner a**: I do so swear.

**officiant in white**: You have my blessing. May you always find something new to love in each other.

**officiant in red**: *(takes the red cord and tying it about the couples' clasped hands)* Do you, _____, promise to love and honor and trust _____ as your partner and spouse, to listen and to laugh, to need and to know, to depend and to defend, to stand shoulder to shoulder against any who would sever you from each other?

**partner b**: I do so swear.

**officiant in red**: You have my blessing. May your bodies always sing to one another.

**officiant in green**: *(takes the green cord and tying it about the couple's clasped hands)* Do you swear this oath before the Goddess in all her forms, including that which you see in the face of each other?

**couple**: We do so swear.

**officiant in green:** You have my blessing. May you be each others' greatest gift.

**officiant in black:** *(takes the black cord and tying it about the couple's bound hands)* Do you swear this oath before all the ancestors, the brave women who have come before you, and those who will come after you, to whom you will be example and inspiration?

**couple:** We do so swear.

**officiant in black:** You have my blessing. May you grow old together in happiness. We now pronounce you handfasted in the sight of the Goddess. You may kiss.

*They do. All applaud.*

**officiant in white:** Breathe out! Gate of the winds, close with our thanks. Go forth on your new path.

**officiant in red:** For behold, you are one. Gate of Fire, close with our thanks. Go forth with a hunger for life.

**officiant in green:** We have drunk of you and your love. Gate of the Waters, close with our thanks. Go forth and cherish your days together.

**officiant in black:** Remember this day every time you touch. Gate of the Earth, close with our thanks. Go forth bound, yet newly free.

*The rite is ended.*

# women's chalice and wand wedding
### (level 3)

*This handfasting was created for two women who considered them-*
*selves to be a butch-femme couple. Although both identified as women,*
*one felt comfortable in a more traditionally feminine role, and the*
*other felt more authentic as a fairly masculine woman. Although they*
*felt that many of the male-female handfasting trappings suited their*
*social genders, they also felt strongly that their ritual needed to acknow-*
*ledge and respect the fact that they were two women, not a heterosex-*
*ual couple, and that this was a perfectly valid style of being two women*
*together in a love relationship. To express this fact, they used the tradi-*
*tional Great Rite, but changed it somewhat.*

*The couple we created the ceremony for dressed in a fairly tradi-*
*tional white wedding gown and man's tuxedo. This was important to*
*them, as it was a reclaiming of conventional wedding customs. Each*
*wore a wreath of flowers and ivy. The butch member of the couple had*
*a beautiful wrought-steel chalice made by a friend who was a black-*
*smith, set with stones and elaborately carved. She filled it with plum*
*wine just before the ritual. The femme member of the couple had*
*another friend make a wand carved out of an oak tree, decorated with*
*feathers, beads, and animal and bird claws, with a stone in the tip.*

*Cast the circle with a simple quarter calling. The caller should*
*walk around the whole circle with a lit candle to consecrate the*
*space. The femme member of the couple comes forward on the arm*
*of a friend or family member—in our case it was her butch ex-lover,*
*with whom she was still good friends. Wedding attendants of various*
*genders and in various outfits followed her in, bringing her up to the*
*altar, where the officiant waits.*

**officiant:** Friends, family, and community! We are gathered here tonight to bless the
union of _____ and _____, who have come here to seal their commitment
before all of us. Their love has been a testament of courage and faith in the
face of great odds, giving hope and encouragement to everyone who has

known and loved them. Tonight we celebrate that love, giving them our support and standing by them as they have done for all of us. Friends, family, community, and tribe will you stand by them in the future as well?

**all present:** We will!

**officiant:** By Lilith and Aphrodite Urania, by Artemis and Athena, by all the wild goddesses who run with the wind, I bless you both.

*The couple then faces each other.*

**femme partner:** *(brings out the wand and presents it to her partner)* This wand reminds me of you. It is strong, and yet its feathers are soft. It is beautiful and makes me long to stroke it. Its stones are hard and of great value. I love both your hardness and your softness, your strength and your gentleness. You are a work of sacred art in my eyes and my most precious treasure.

**butch partner:** *(brings out the chalice and presents it to her partner)* This chalice reminds me of you. It holds more than anyone could guess, and it is filled with sweetness. Its curves enchant and capture the eye; it makes me want to stroke it and drink from it. It looks delicate, but it is made of steel, and it is strong enough that it will never break. I love both your softness and your hardness, your gentleness and your strength. You are a work of sacred art in my eyes and my most precious treasure.

**butch partner:** *(lowers her wand into the femme partner's chalice)* As I give to you, so does the Lord give to his Lady . . .

**femme partner:** And as I receive from you, so does the Lady receive from her Lord.

*They place the wand and chalice on the altar and faced the officiant.*

**officiant:** *(to butch partner)* Do you, _____ take _____ as your handfasted spouse, to love and honor and respect, to tell your dreams and sorrows to, to hold in your arms and defend to the death, to enjoy as the greatest gift that the universe has to offer?

**butch partner:** I do.

**officiant:** *(to femme partner)* Do you, _____ take _____ as your handfasted spouse, to love and honor and respect, to tell your dreams and sorrows to, to hold in your arms and defend to the death, to enjoy as the greatest gift that the universe has to offer?

**femme partner:** I do.

**officiant:** These rings are made of gold, and I know that you bought them together in the store, excited at picking out the symbols that so many would deny you. Some will see them on your hands and misinterpret or disapprove. But I think that more folk than you might expect will smile fondly or perhaps even be envious of your obvious happiness and joy in each other.

*The partners then exchange rings. They can say the traditional words,* "With this ring I thee wed, and with my body I thee worship, and with all my worldly goods I thee endow," *or they can pick other sentences.*

**officiant:** I now pronounce you married. Go in peace and harmony, and be protected by all the gods from all the world's ills.

# shapeshifter's handfasting
## *(level 3)*

*This handfasting was created by a rather unusual couple consisting of one gay man and one gay drag-queen-feminine-two-spirited-shape-shifting man. He felt that his identity was not strictly male, but nor was it female. As someone who frequently "shifted shape" back and forth from male-appearing to female-appearing, he wanted acknowledgment that his lover was marrying all of him, and not just part. This wedding was built around that premise.*

*The officiant was a transgendered person. Four friends of theirs, each dressed as some sort of totem animal, cast the quarters by making animal noises and doing a sort of power dance in the direction indicated, and then speaking out.*

**east caller:** By eagle and hawk, by sparrow and kestrel, by all that flies on the wind, I call Spirit into this circle.

**south caller:** By panther and lion, by wolf and jackal, by all that runs hot on four feet and tastes the warm blood of life, I call Spirit into this circle.

**west caller:** By dolphin and whale, by salmon and piranha, by all that swims in river and sea, I call Spirit into this circle.

**north caller:** By serpent and lizard, by beetle and worm, by all that crawls upon the breast of the Mother, I call Spirit into this circle.

**officiant:** We come here today to celebrate love, the love of _____ and _____ for each other. Love takes on many shapes that appear to us throughout our lives. First it appears as the love of parent for child, then, as we grow older, that of child for parent and for brother and sister. Then we learn the love of one friend for another. Then, as we come of age, we learn the love of romance that binds two people together, the fireworks and bells, the golden moment. Then as we grow older, we learn the love that comes when this love burns away— the long, stable love, a warmth as eternal as the sun, as enduring as the Earth.

We learn also the love of children again, this time from the other side, and so the circle renews itself, over and over. What shape has your love taken?

**partner a:** My love for you first took the form of fire, burning in me. I had to be with you or I felt that I would perish. You were my warmth and my light, the flame that I circled like a moth, half adoring, half afraid that I might be burned. Then, as we walked down the path of years together, my love for you burned down to coals that kept a steady glow, like that of a hearth. My love for you is now something that I can work with and find useful. It is the lamp in the window after the long journey, and the warmth that is always there in the cold winter. And I know that if I stir the coals, sparks will fly up!

**partner b:** My love for you first took the form of water, a trickle pouring in. I did not take it seriously at first, like a mere leak in the roof. Then the leak grew greater and greater until it was a river pouring in to sweep me away. At first I was frightened, and then, as I learned to swim in the flow of my love for you, I began to crave it as the water of life, the source of all things. Then, as we walked the path of years together, my love for you became like wind that blew about me, a force that tried its hardest to caress and wrap you in its embrace. It has become the air that I breathe, my atmosphere.

**officiant:** Do you promise to love each other, no matter what shape each of you may take in the future? For nothing is certain save change itself.

**partner a:** When I first met you, I saw you as one person. Then I met your other side, and I was confused at first! But I soon grew to love her too, and to see her both as separate and as the same, one and many. I love you for your manhood and for your womanhood also, and for the fluid balance that you dance. No matter which way I turn, you complement me. I promise always to love, honor, and cherish every part of you.

**partner b:** I love you for your singleness, your trueness, your constant and sane knowledge of who you are and where you stand. You are my anchor, as stable as the earth beneath my feet, and yet like the earth you too have your seasons, and you surprise me day to day with your own small changes. I promise always to love, honor, and cherish every part of you.

officiant: Will you now take out the rings and make many into one?

partner a: These rings are two rings that link together into one. By these rings, I vow that I will always love every face you wear and the oneness that is behind them, and may Spirit bless our path together.

partner b: By these rings, I vow that I will always love you in all your many complexities and the oneness of your bright soul, and may Spirit bless our path together.

officiant: *(binds their hands together with a cord)* By this binding, I declare you handfast. So mote it be!

all: So mote it be!

*The rite is ended.*

# the rite of aphrodite urania
### (level 3)

*A transgender wedding is a difficult thing to delineate because the self-images of people who could be classed as transgender vary wildly. Many primary transsexuals consider themselves to be simply men or women, albeit raised in the wrong gender with a difficult and unusual medical history. They consider their conditions to be mistakes that were corrected and that they are now past, and they do not wish to class themselves in a wedding as anything other than a man or a woman. They would probably prefer to choose one of the many traditionally gendered rites in this book.*

*On the other hand, there are a lot of folk out there who do not consider themselves to be wholly male or female, and they may want this represented in a ritual. Some are intersexuals, who have a clear and present physical and medical reality of being dually gendered to deal with. Some are crossdressers or "genderqueers" living as their birth gender but in very nontraditional ways. Some are transsexuals who may have changed their bodies but still consider themselves androgynes of some sort.*

*When we wrote the rite of Aphrodite Urania, we wanted a ritual that would be expandable for a single-gendered person marrying a transgendered person, or two transgendered people marrying each other, or for two single-gendered bisexuals marrying who do not wish to be classed as straight or gay. It's also good for more than two people. It has become the bi/trans/poly ritual of choice in our Pagan church.*

*The quarters are called—not in the four traditional directions, but in the cross-quarters. Although technically anyone can call them, we are always careful to choose the quarter callers by their gender energy, as specified below. Sometimes the individual performing the ceremony is the northwest caller, who invokes Aphrodite Urania; sometimes the officiant is separate from the callers. If possible, an altar should be set up in the northwest. It can have whatever ritual implements you choose on it, but for this rite we always use a large conch shell, modified so that it can be blown like a horn.*

*The northeast caller should be one or more of the following: a masculine woman, a warrior woman, an intersexual living as female, a pre-transition FTM transsexual, or a woman (biological or otherwise) with facial hair and preferably lots of body hair. S/he should wear light brown or tan.*

*The southeast caller should be one or more of the following: a neuter androgyne, a feminine or genderqueer man, an intersexual living as a male, a pre-transition MTF transsexual, or a man (biological or otherwise) who wears long hair down on one side and tied up in a bun on the other. S/he should wear orange.*

*The southwest caller should be one or more of the following: a feminine or genderqueer man (biological or not), a drag queen, a MTF transsexual, or a transgendered person who has had much experience with altered states. S/he should wear purple.*

*The northwest caller can be any person who considers themselves to be transgendered and/or two-souled. S/he should wear a beard (which does not have to be real) and a long gown of aqua. Choose them carefully, for they will be the official personification of Aphrodite Urania for the couple in question, the union of male and female into one body and soul.*

**northeast caller:** Spirits of the northeast, who span the length from earth to air,

Who bridge the gap between body and mind,

Be with us on this day

And bless us with clarity in our physical feelings,

Joy in the body without dishonesty,

Lust without lies,

And tongues that speak each other's body language.

I call Lilith, Hairy Goddess, Barren One,

Asker of the hard questions,

Whirling scirocco, desert wind,

Bless this couple's passion

With the honest lash of your serpent tongue.

**southeast caller:** Spirits of the southeast, who span the length from air to fire,

Who bridge the gap between mind and will,

Be with us on this day

And bless us with discipline in our dealings,

Imagination in our words,

Minds that fly together light as ashes on the wind,

And the ability to rise from those ashes and start anew.

I call Shiva, the lord who is half woman,

Destroyer of the Universe of Illusion,

Lord of those who are outcast,

Bless this couple's promise

With your stern witnessing of truth.

**southwest caller:** Spirits of the southwest, who span the length from fire to water,

Who bridge the gap between heart and soul,

Be with us on this day

And bless us with ecstasy in all its forms,

Seeing God/dess in one another,

Knowing that our love is merely part

Of the greater love of the universe.

I call Dionysus, Womanly One,

Shaman-god of the vine, Lord of the Dance,

Opener of the Doors Between Worlds,

Bless this couple's joy

With the cup of your eternal bliss.

**northwest caller:** Spirits of the northwest, who span the length from water to earth,

Who bridge the gap between body and heart,

Be with us on this day

And bless us with love in all its forms,

Crossing all boundaries,

Sweeping us away with its beauty,

Drawing us like magnets to the ones

Who will reveal our inner selves.

I call Aphrodite Urania, the Bearded Love Goddess,

Joiner of hands and hearts,

Two in one and one out of many,

Bless this couple's love

As they stand on your shore

Where the tide of Ocean's feeling meets the flesh of the land.

*The northwest caller then steps forward into the center of the circle*

**northwest caller:** I am the builder of bridges,

The slender line of love across the deepest of abysses.

When you leap off that cliff,

Holding your breath,

Knowing nothing is certain but your feelings,

You find yourself not tumbling, terror-stricken,

As you had feared

But walking safely on the great span of my heart

Where you meet each other on the sacred middle ground

And cross to a more joyous land.

**partner a:** We stand before you today, taking pride in our love and our joy, and ask to be blessed and bound before all witnesses.

**partner b:** We stand before you today, ready to make a promise with all our hearts, ready to make solid as earth what has flowed like water.

*At this point, either the northwest caller becomes the officiant, or a separate officiant steps forward and beckons them to stand in front of the altar. If the latter is the case, the northwest caller should stand beside the officiant throughout the ceremony.*

**officiant:** Dear hearts, you come before us today to allow us the honor of looking with wonder upon the sacredness of your love. You truly remind us that love crosses all boundaries and brings all hearts together. We are proud to stand with you and honor your relationship and your promises. Yet each of you *(or "one of you," if only one person is transgendered)* has both a goddess and a god within. Let us hear them speak.

*Here each of the partners steps forward and says something of their own making. The idea is that each line begins with "The Goddess within me . . ." or "The God within me . . ." and that those who feel that they have both male and female qualities/selves/personae/energy/what-have-you may speak both lines, whereas a nontransgendered partner need speak only one. We give below a couple of examples created by real people, in order to help inspire original words.*

## example 1

**partner a:** The Goddess in me loves you for your integrity, your honesty, and your great conversation. She values your strong sense of spirituality and your strong sense of justice. The God in me loves you for your caring and nurturing, and the open way you show your love. He values your incredible courage and strength. Both parts of me love you beyond life itself and see you as my true and equal match.

**partner b:** The Goddess in me loves you for your insight and your wit. She honors you for your sacrifices and your concern for your fellow beings. She values your tenacity and your sense of hope for tomorrow. The God in me loves you for your sensuality and adaptability to new situations. He honors your sense of reason as well as your ability to compromise when needed and to remain steadfast before daunting odds. Both sides of my being would feel lost and empty without you, and your love gives me completion. I will be devoted to you throughout this existence and beyond.

*example 2*

**partner a:** The Goddess in me is drawn to your smile and your laugh and the way that you accept me. She loves sharing everyday things with you, like making breakfast or lying together just holding each other while the rain falls on the roof. The God within me is drawn to the way you defend our relationship like a tigress, the way your passion shows in how you fight for the causes you believe in. He loves working side by side with you in our shared passion. Both parts of me love you and want to spend the rest of this life with you.

**partner b:** The Goddess in me loves both parts of you. She loves your Goddess, for her softness and vulnerability, her soft skin and beautiful eyes, and her stubborn strength in not hiding herself in spite of all fear. She loves your God for his dedication and honesty, his dreams, and his soothing hands. You are my beloved, two-in-one, and I am fortunate to know and love you in this lifetime.

*The officiant at this time takes up the conch shell and pours water into its open lip, so that it holds it like a cup. S/he hands it to one of the partners.*

**officiant:** When you blow a strong blast through this horn, you celebrate the masculine. When you drink from this cup, you celebrate the feminine. Both are one, in you and between you and in your hands. So do as thou wilt!

*The first partner either blows a blast through the horn (we suggest practicing first) or drinks from it, or both in turn, in whatever order s/he desires. S/he then hands it to the other partner, who does the same.*

**couple:** *(to each other)* I celebrate all of you, and all of us.

*The couple then hands the conch shell to an onlooker, who makes the same choice of drinking or blowing, and passes it on. The shell makes the rounds of all the guests; any who choose to refrain may do so with no disrespect. Finally, it is handed back to the officiant, who drinks and/or blows, then pours the remainder out on the ground as a libation. Next, the couple takes what vows they will (see chapter on vows or create your own) and their hands are bound.*

**officiant:** Today we have seen the mystery and the miracle of the two become one. You who have been blessed this day in marriage, take this memory with you all the days of your life. You who have been blessed by witnessing, take this memory with you to teach you how love is a bridge across every abyss. So mote it be!

**all:** So mote it be!

**officiant:** Will you stand forth, *(gestures for audience to rise)* all of you who will defend this couple and their love to the ends of the earth, with words and deeds, letting no lie go by unchallenged?

*All who are so willing stand forth.*

**officiant:** Do you swear, as these two have sworn, to champion this marriage with the sword of truth and to stand by these your friends and loved ones, against whomever would tarnish the name of their love?

**all:** We do!

**northwest caller:** By Aphrodite Urania, I bless you both. May your love surmount all boundaries between you. Spirits of the northwest, wash out again on the tide!

**southwest caller:** By Dionysus, I bless you both. May your love bring ecstasy to every moment of your lives. Spirits of the southwest, quench your flame once again!

**southeast caller:** By Shiva Mahadeva, I bless you both. May there be no illusions between you. Spirits of the southeast, fly away like ash on the wind!

**northeast caller:** By Lilith, I bless you both. May you always be honest with each other, and may your passion never die. Spirits of the northeast, dance away on desert winds!

*The rite is ended.*

# many hands of love: a polyamorous handfasting rite
*(level 3)*

As the Neopagan movement grows, a small but constantly increasing number of Pagans are coming out as polyamorous, and wanting to join in loving groups of more than two people. Polyamory, as opposed to promiscuity or mere nonmonogamy, implies a high level of honesty, openness, communication, and agreement between partners over who may do what with whom. Each polyamorous relationship is very different from every other one, as only the individuals involved can determine which rules and boundaries are most effective for the security and happiness of everyone concerned. Some have one central person with two lovers, some have a triangle with all three people involved, or a square with four, or a long chain where each person has two partners. In some, there are primary, secondary, and tertiary levels of commitment; in others, everyone has an equal share of every other person's time, energy, and affection. Within these relationships there may be any number of sexual preferences, orientations, and combinations.

It is assumed that, since the legal definition of marriage still includes only two people of opposite sexes, this is a nonlegal ceremony. In order to make this ritual as flexible as possible, we have designed it in interchangeable parts. The opening and closing are used with all the variations, the middle section with the vows has two different versions, of which one may hopefully fit your group of lovers.

Everyone stands in the boundary of the circle, with the lovers next to the officiant. The callers of the four quarters should have either long scarves that they can wave about, ribbons tied to sticks, or something else that flows through the air. They recite their invocation facing the direction of their element, and then they walk (or run, or skip, or dance) around the entirety of the circle, waving their fabric to sweep away negative influences, returning to the direction in which *they began. Each caller waits until the last one has completed the circle before beginning their invocation.*

**east:** I call the Great Winds of Change

And the Words of Power!

May language spring forth

And never be thwarted!

May clarity spring forth

And never be muddied!

May honesty spring forth

And never be suppressed!

May all the hateful words of the past

Be blown clean away!

**south:** I call the Great Flame of Passion

And the Hearth of Power!

May heat rise between bodies

Like a volcano!

May love burn strong

And never die out!

May inspiration spark

And bloom into manifestation!

May all the smoldering anger of the past

Be burned clean away!

**west:** I call the Great Ocean of Feeling

And the River of Power!

May tenderness flow forth

And never be scorned!

May compassion flow forth

And never be slighted!

May joy flow like water

And never be dammed!

May all the old jealousies of the past

Be washed clean away!

**north:** I call upon the Great Stone of Enduring

And the Mountain of Power!

May patience grow

And never be stunted!

May caring grow

And be well tended!

May laughter be seeded

And joy grow from its sprouting!

May all the old assumptions be but fertilizer

To grow a new kind of love in a clean ground!

**officiant:** We call upon Aphrodite, goddess of love and beauty, on this day of celebrating love. We call especially on her aspect of Aphrodite Urania, builder of bridges, joiner of hands across incalculable abysses, she who brings together. Lady of Love Unexpected but always welcome. Your presence shows us that there can never be too much love in the world. We call also upon her son Eros, the will to love that cannot be overcome or underestimated. Lord of Love Irresistible, your presence shows us that no matter what anyone says, love cannot be denied. And you, _____ and _____ and _____ and _____ *(speak first names of lovers)*, do you all come here of your own free will to join in the bonds of love?

**lovers:** We do!

*For the next part, we have two alternate versions. This first version is for a primary couple relationship where one person is adding a new lover who will not necessarily be lovers with the other spouse. The officiant should have two cords, one golden and one silver.*

*version 1*

**officiant:** You, _____ and _____ *(primary partners)*, have been committed to each other for some time now. We here honor that bond by showing it to all. *(ties their hands together with the golden cord)* Many blessings be on your love, and may it be the solid ground from which each of you fly.

**partner a:** Our love is strong and solid, and nothing can change it. Any addition to our family will only add love, not subtract it.

**partner b:** Our love is stable and constant, and nothing can lessen it. Any addition to our family will simply add to our commitment.

**partner a:** I love you now and for always.

**partner b:** I love you now and for always.

**officiant:** Now you have come to a new voyage of discovery. _____ has found great love with _____ *(third partner)*, and wishes to be bound in marriage with her/him as well. Speak now your love with pride!

**partner b:** *(speaks about how s/he met the third partner, and what love has grown between them, and speaks of new beginnings, and then says:)* I would bring you into the circle of love that is my family, for there is no reason to break and part what can be shared with more joy.

**partner c:** *(speaks about how s/he loves the second partner, and how s/he sees this new family, and speaks of new beginnings, and then says:)* I will gladly come into the circle of love that is your family, and I wish to bring it still more love and joy.

*They take hands, and the officiant binds the silver cord around their hands, so that the second partner is bound on both sides.*

**partner b:** I love you now and for always.

**partner c:** I love you now and for always.

**partner a:** *(to partner c)* I swear to be a sister *(or brother)* to you, _____, and I swear always to believe in your love for me, _____, and I swear to never let fear and insecurity override the goodness that I know is here in this circle.

**partner c:** *(to partner a)* I swear to be a sister *(or brother)* to you, _____, and I swear always to believe in your love for me, _____, and I swear to never let fear and insecurity override the goodness that I know is here in this circle.

**partner b:** I will be your friend now, and for always.

**partner c:** I will be your friend now, and for always.

151

## version 2

*This next version can be used for a handfasting where three or more people are hand-fasted all together. We have used an example of four, but this ritual can be expanded or contracted to any number of people. The quarters are called and the officiant speaks as above.*

*Each lover stands forward and presents his or her cord. It should be twelve feet long, with knots tied at specific places that correspond to the following measurements: their height, the width from fingertip to fingertip when the arms are out-stretched, the diameter of the chest encircling the heart, and the diameter of the head around the forehead. Although they will be in different colors, chosen by each lover to symbolize themselves, they should all be about the same thickness. Each cord should be marked in some way with some bodily fluid of the person who has knotted it. This is the classic witch's measure.*

**officiant:** In elder days, when witches would meet in a coven at night, their lives depended upon secrecy. The coven elders would take their measure with a cord, and use this against them if need be. Today, however, we live in happier times, where we can practice openly both our faith and our different ways of loving, and each of these lovers has brought with them their measure, as a gift and not a hostage, to offer up to this marriage in the name of love. Come forth, you who love and would be bound in love, and show the gifts of your-selves that you bring.

*The following are examples of possible things to say, in order to inspire you to create your own lines.*

**partner a:** My cord is green, symbolizing growth. I bring to this marriage the ability to grow and change, and to help my lovers also to grow and change, and to always see the new green of spring in the frost of each passing winter.

**partner b:** My cord is red, symbolizing passion. I bring to this marriage my intensity. I will passionately love and defend this marriage and everyone in it, and I will never let things become dull and flat and boring.

**partner c:** My cord is silver, symbolizing communication. I bring to this marriage an almost unlimited ability to talk, and process, and keep the lines of communication open. I will never let there be unsaid words that create resentments or secret pain.

**partner d:** My cord is brown, symbolizing work and loyalty. I bring to this marriage the ability to keep going in spite of hard times, to remain faithful and be patient, and to work hard at whatever I can do to make things better for us.

**officiant:** Place your cords together, end to end, and each take a turn knotting them together at one end.

**partner a:** By this first knot, I honor our new beginnings.

**partner b:** By this second knot, I honor the path we walk together.

**partner c:** By this third knot, I honor the future we face together.

**partner d:** By this fourth knot, I honor the love we share.

**officiant:** Now I will hold the end of this cord, as the gods hold firmly the silver cord of your souls in place on this Earth. You will all do the work of braiding these separate cords into one.

*They begin to braid. This may take a while. During this, the circle of people may drum, or chant, or sing. At the end, they tie the final knot all together. The officiant takes the braided cord. Then each lover places their right hand into the center of the circle, and the officiant wraps the braided rope around their hands.*

**officiant:** You are now bound each to all, each with all, each by all. Each strand alone may be broken, but together they are truly unbreakable.

*At this point, the two alternate versions merge, and the officiant continues the same for both.*

**officiant:** Each lover that you have had in the past has enriched your life with the experience of their love. You bring that wealth to this handfasting. Use it wisely, taking the best as an example but not allowing the worst to stop you in your tracks. It takes many hands to carry a great love. Grasp this love with both hands, and do not hold back.

    This handfasting will not lie easy in the eyes of many people. Some will raise their voices against you and your choices. Do you swear to close your ears to their doubt, and hear only the love and support of your chosen family?

**lovers:** We do!

**officiant:** Do you swear to be considerate of one another, to be patient with one another, and to see as often as possible the divine spirit within each other?

**lovers:** We do!

**officiant:** Do you swear to hold strong to your love, to not be swayed by hard times, and yet always make every effort to ensure the happiness of every partner in this circle?

**lovers:** We do!

**officiant:** Do you swear to work through jealousy, insecurity, and fear and to do what is necessary to appease all inner demons, no matter how hard the path?

**lovers:** We do!

**officiant:** *(to all present)* I ask all present, all witnesses, to stand and answer this question: Do you all here swear to honor the love and the handfasting of these your friends, no matter what the voices of others say?

**all present:** We do!

153

**officiant:** I then declare you all handfast in the eyes of the Gods, in the name of Aphrodite Urania, and the archer Eros. May love and joy be your constant companions, and lie in your beds with you every night. Good fortune to a new-formed family! You may now embrace and kiss.

*Lovers kiss, and the rite is ended.*

*chapter 11*

# children and ritual

These days, many couples are going to have the added complication of children from prior relationships. It's not easy to be a kid and see your parent marry someone new. Even if you like the new person (which you might not), and the divorce wounds aren't fresh (which they might be), and you're old enough to understand why your parent needs a new partner (which you might not be), there are likely going to be complications. It's a tricky subject, and one which should be handled with a great deal of patience. As a parent, you can start by telling your children about the wedding as far in advance as possible, so they have a long time to get used to the idea.

Frankly, no one has more potential for being hurt by a wedding than a young child of the bride or groom. The couple's relatives and friends may have their own issues, but they are adults. They can choose to avoid the couple, and they have (or should have) the self-control and experience to say, "I don't like this, but you have to go your own way." A child does not have these privileges. It's likely that he or she will be living under the roof of the new marriage or at least seeing it on a regular basis. A child must put up with watching his or her parent go through the googly newlywed stage, which is particularly bad if it's been "just me and Mom/Dad" for some time.

In deciding a child's role in a wedding or handfasting ceremony, base the situation solely on each child's wishes. Obviously, you've decided to get hitched, whether your kids like it or not. They don't get to decide that, and this is probably galling enough to them. Don't rub salt in the wound by forcing them to be part of—or even attend—a wedding that they are unhappy about. Ask each child whether they would like to participate or just attend. It may be difficult for you, but if your child would really rather just stay home and play video games and pretend it isn't happening, it's best to let him or her. You're the parent and the adult, and you can live with that disappointment. Besides, nothing puts a wet blanket on a wedding like an angry, resentful kid.

If your kid does decide to sit it out, whether at home or in the audience, she may change her mind gradually as all the wedding plans flurry on apace. If you think this is happening, you might try asking again whether she'd like to be involved, and don't get down on them if the answer is still no. Conversely, she may back out at the last minute. Raven recalls, "My daughter had an attack of adolescent stage fright a week before our wedding and decided to jettison her speaking part. It was easier on all our nerves just to find someone else to say those lines; we felt that we were going to have enough performance anxiety on our own without forcing a reluctant kid through it as well. As it turned out, her godfather had been asked to do the musical accompaniment, and he arrived with his guitar and encouraged her to get hers and play with the musicians, so she was able to contribute something she felt more comfortable with."

Another thing that you can do to make your children more comfortable (which most parents, unfortunately, don't do) is to give them a lot of input into what clothes they are going to wear to the wedding. A child who is already feeling powerless in the situation may feel more so if he is forced to wear something that he feels doesn't show who he really is as a person. If he's only going to be in the audience, don't make a big deal out of wearing fancy clothes; although that favorite T-shirt and ripped jeans may be too far out of line, try to come to a compromise that you can both live with. Remember that people are going to be looking at you, not the kid in the audience.

If your child does want to be in the ceremony, stress that the outfit is a costume, as in a play or theatrical production of some sort. (After all, that's really what a wedding is—sacred theater.) Let your children help design what they are going to wear, if possible, or at least pick out the colors. It will make a big difference in whether they feel listened to. If they are going to be saying lines, make sure that they are given the parts far in advance, more so even than the adults in the party, and that they have cards to read off of anyway, in case of last-minute jitters. Make sure, also, that the lines are ones that your kids don't feel stupid saying, or they'll say them stupidly.

Also, make sure that what you are asking any given child to do is appropriate to his or her age and ability. Don't give the dyslexic kid with ADD lots of lines to memorize or have the klutzy kid carry things that could spill. Letting any child under the age of puberty walk around with lit candles is risking disaster. If the kid isn't yours, ask the parents for a clear assessment of what that child can handle, and stick to it.

## flowergirls and ringbearers

In former days, the purpose of the flower girls was actually to scatter flower petals before the bride, so that she would symbolically walk on happiness. These days, flower girls simply clutch artificial baskets and stand around, as most churches and halls would have a fit if you "littered" in this way. (If you actually have an outdoor wedding, though, it's a wonderful custom to bring back, and the girls of all ages love flinging petals around.) Ringbearers, too, have been reduced to a mere prop; as their ages got younger and younger, they were generally not allowed to carry the actual rings, as they would probably roll away under the feet of participants and be lost forever. The current situation usually involves them carrying a stuffed cushion with artificial rings sewn to it.

Rather than repeating these roles, which have become empty and superficial, you might want to think about creating entirely new roles for children in the wedding party (and that includes nieces, nephews, and other beloved young ones). For example, one couple costumed a dozen kids (offspring of the adults in the wedding party) as faeries, elves, sprites, and nature devas, complete with leafy half-masks and tunics, and wings of wired gossamer or feathers or leather bat-wings. They came in first and ran in a circle around the entire gathering, tossing glitter into the air and shouting,

"We bless this space with faery gold!" This was incorporated into the circle-casting, as the children had already delineated the sacred space, and symbolically invoked the blessing of the Good Folk. (The kids also were in charge of leaving food and drink from the reception out for the faeries afterwards.) This way they got to wear neat costumes and do something characteristic and easy (run giggling in circles and throw stuff), and the effect was charming to the onlookers as well.

One bride, in her thirties, decided that she disliked the idea of being "given away" by parents from whom she was estranged, and whom she had hardly seen since her teens. On the other hand, she had been a professional nanny for many years with several families, and her wedding was marking the end of this career, as she intended to bear and raise her own children instead. She decided to let the children she had taken care of, as a group, walk her to the circle and "give her away," as it was they who would suffer most from losing her.

## blended family vows

Some families have chosen not to make the children speak at all, but to speak to them as part of the ritual. It's a chance to reassure them that even at this moment, when the relationship between the two adults is paramount, they haven't forgotten their kids' presence. One of these vows goes as follows.

# couple addressing a child
*(level 3)*

*When our friends David and Jezanna got married, they incorporated David's daughter from his first marriage, nine-year-old Lydia, into their ceremony. First they called her forward to stand before them, and then they spoke the following words to her.*

**david:** Lydia, on this the day of my marriage to Jezanna, I want you to know these things: You have a place in our home, in our love, and in our lives. My marrying Jezanna does not diminish the love I have for you; it gives it a companion. I am blessed that you and Jezanna are so close. It brings me great happiness to see you laughing and talking together. I promise to always remember how special you are, to find time to hear your stories, to watch you skate and dance. As you grow, I will not try to hold you back but instead help you fly. I will ask you to find space for Jezanna and myself in your life; we will not force ourselves upon you. I promise to be an ear when you need one, a lap when you're tired, a shoulder when you cry. I promise to love and cherish you for all the days of my life.

**jezanna:** Lydia, you are not a daughter of my body, but you are a daughter of my heart. I promise to love and care for you, while always respecting your special relationship with each of your parents. I promise always to be your friend—to listen to your ideas and your feelings, to teach you when you ask me, to protect and comfort you if you should need it, and to help you to grow in any way that I can. You have been a joy to me since the day I met you, and I am honored to now be family with you.

**david and jezanna together:** We give you this pin to remind you of these promises. You are always in our hearts, and always part of our family.

# children addressing bride and groom
## *(level 3)*

*These vows were incorporated into the wedding of a family with three children, a mom, and a stepdad who had lived with them for some time and was finally tying the knot. Luckily, in this case, all three children got along well with their stepparent. First, the kids all walked their mother into the wedding circle, and the ceremony proceeded as planned. Just before it was time to do the actual hand-tying, the kids all came forward.*

160

**child a:** *(addressing the groom)* _____, you're going to marry our mother. Do you promise that you will never come between her and us?

**groom:** I swear that I will never interfere in her relationship with you. I would like to think that _____ and I will be married forever, but no matter what happens to us, she will always be your mother, and I respect that. I will remember that I am the adult and you are the children, and I will not compete with her for your attention.

**child b:** *(addressing the groom)* _____, do you promise to treat her well and not make her cry?

**groom:** I promise to love her and treat her as best that I can. I will never deliberately hurt her, and if I accidentally make her cry, I'll make it up to her immediately. You and I are all in on a secret that no one in the whole world knows like we do: what a special person she truly is.

**child c:** *(addressing the groom)* _____, will you be our friend and treat us like friends should be treated?

**groom:** Yes, I swear that I will be your friends for as long as you'll have me. I will do my best to make peace in the home and listen to you as closely as I can.

**child a:** Then you have our blessings. Get married and be happy.

*At this point, the kids took out a cord, and all three of them tied the couple's hands together. Then they took out long scarves, and each held the ends so that they made a circle around the couple while they kissed, and they ran in a circle three times around them for luck.*

# child addressing bride and groom
*(level 3)*

*This was written by a teenage son whose dad was getting married again. He stood up and spoke the words as part of the wedding.*

**son:** *(addressing the groom)* Dad, I'm here to see you get married to _____. At first, when you told that you were getting married, I wasn't too happy about it. I didn't think that I could take one more parent telling me what to do. But then I thought about how happy she makes you and how much easier you are to get along with now that she's in your life, and I figure she's the best thing for you. And I'm proud of you for going out and finding her in the first place. I know how down you were for a long time, and I know it wasn't easy to start thinking about dating. So I'm proud to be here today.

*(addressing the bride)* And _____, well, at first I wasn't sure about you. You're real different from my mom, and I was afraid that you'd want me to be someone I'm not. But you earned my trust the hard way, from the beginning. You put up with me when I was a pain, and you were always patient, and you didn't tell Dad how to deal with me. I think I trust you now, and I'm glad that you're here to make Dad happy.

So get married already, both of you!

# couple addressing children
### *(level 3)*

*These vows were written for a family with two adults and four children, two belonging to each parent. The parents turned to their children and invited them to come forward. As each spoke, they joined hands with the parents and each other and finally formed a circle.*

**bride:** We are all going to be a family now, even if we have to learn to grow into each other. We are each a valued part of that family, and we each bring something valuable to our home. I bring really good lasagna, and help with homework, and lots of love and support, and seeing the best in everyone.

**groom:** I bring patience, and a barbecue, and rollerblading with everyone, and common sense, and being a storyteller.

**child a:** I bring fun, because I like to play games and laugh.

**child b:** I bring imagination, to make stuff up.

**child c:** I bring honesty, because I tell it like it is, even when it hurts.

**child d:** I bring love, because I have lots of it.

**groom:** Welcome to the family. We are all made richer by every one of you. The more of us there are, living together in love, the stronger this family is. You are all unique, and I am honored to have you as family.

**bride:** Welcome to the family, and I am blessed three times over today.

*chapter 12*
# interfaith marriages

$\mathcal{I}$n this day and age of eclecticism, interfaith marriages are becoming increasingly common. Twenty years ago the question "In which faith shall we raise our children?" was the crux of many a couple's arguments; now, in the infant steps of our twenty-first century, couples are stuck on the question of which aspects of whose religioculture will be reflected in their wedding. As ministers, we have both witnessed and played a part in this process. Sometimes one partner is Pagan and the other practices another faith entirely. More commonly, both currently practice some brand of Paganism, but at least one person wishes to acknowledge the traditions of his or her childhood.

Usually there are one of two motivations for this, and you should understand which is your own. The first (and best in our opinion) is that you see emotional and cultural values in your former faith that have stayed consistent even after your adoption of Pagan ways. You wish to pay homage to your roots and acknowledge the seed that started the tree of your spiritual growth. This scenario contains quite a different set of factors than the second possible motivation, where you wish to please relatives and/or friends who practice the faith that you have drifted away from. In this case, the concern is usually over making your marriage (and coincidently your choice of life partner) more acceptable to family and peers. It is natural to desire to want our loved ones to feel comfortable during such a crucial and presumably joyous occasion. After all, if their witness and blessings were not important, the couple would have opted for a much more private ceremony, or even two separate ceremonies. That said, however, this second motivation can add additional stress.

In either case, it may be prudent to consider the following: The individual who wishes to incorporate some aspects of the faith of her birth should think about what aspects of that religious culture she would like to see incorporated into the ceremony and how it is going to reflect not only her values themselves but her partner's. A lovely example of this occurred during a summer wedding of friends of ours. The man came from a Jewish family. He and his partner wished to have their own home and to raise a family together, consisting both of children he had had in a previous relationship and ones to come in the future from this one. In traditional Jewish weddings, the couple is united under a canopy called a *chuppah* (see the section on Jewish wedding traditions, pages 191–193). Most significantly, the chuppah represents the couple's new home together, physically and spiritually. His Pagan bride-to be loved the symbolism but requested that instead of the typical pole frame and opaque cloth awning that the structure should be constructed of a wood framed trellis festooned with fresh flowers, fruits, and other vegetation. The resulting structure was splendid and resulted from a combination of hearts and common values.

On the other hand, the couple who wish to further the cause of positive relations with one of their families by including elements of this family's faith's wedding traditions may be treading on rather tricky ground. One of the most difficult issues is deciding how large a role the non-Pagan elements are going to play in the ceremony. Do you wish them to predominate in the wedding ceremony but be flavored with Pagan overtones? Perhaps you would like to give them only a nod—if not also a wink. Take into consideration at this point the feelings and possible reservations of your intended audience. While ecumenicalism is on the whole a noble thing, there is another "ism" that occasionally slithers in its shadow: tokenism (defined as "presence without meaningful participation"). Consider the awkwardness that resulted from the following situation.

*In a small town in New Jersey during the early winter of 1977, a school board attempted to address concerns that were raised by some parents the previous year concerning its decoration of the elementary school for its holiday concert. In the interest of being more reflective of its student body, board members decided that instead of just decorating for Christmas, Hanukkah decorations should also bedeck the halls and classrooms. This idea was met with much acclaim, and students and teachers were recruited to help. Along with the usual reindeer, Santas, and snowflakes, Stars of David and menorahs were constructed and posted on the walls along with banners that read "Joyeux Noel" and "Happy Hanukkah." A magnificent tree adorned with feathery angels, colorful glass baubles, and glittery blue and white six-sided stars was placed in the lobby. Within a week, the office was inundated with calls from upset Jewish parents. A local synagogue sent a polite but firm request that the Stars of David be immediately removed from the Christmas tree. The principal was at first mystified. He couldn't understand why the local Jewish community was so angry. After all, his staff took the Hanukkah decorations straight out of a book called* Christmas Celebrations Around the World. *A secretary finally explained to him that Hanukkah is not in fact the "Jewish equivalent of Christmas" but a completely separate holiday (see page 191 for Judaic/Pagan wedding suggestions) and that Jews didn't "do the Jesus thing."*

Part of religiocultural sensitivity is understanding that you need to pay attention not only to the content but to the context of the elements that you wish to include in your ritual. Doing your homework never hurts. Take time to visit a public library (some churches like Jewish synagogues, Krishna temples, and Catholic churches also have libraries that may be accessed by the public, though books are not usually subject to removal by nonmembers), or try consulting faith-based websites. In addition to book- and Internet-based research, it is also helpful to consult with a person who is deeply familiar with the tradition from which you are borrowing. Preferably, this person should at least be an acquaintance with whom you are comfortable enough to speak about your wedding plans. It also may be helpful to keep the following guidelines while consulting your various sources.

In the case of special items, ask: Where can you find one? (Sometimes the source is a simple as an ethnic gift shop, or it may have to be borrowed from a close friend or relative.) How is the item maintained? (When not in use, is it kept in a particular carrying case? Does it need to be spiritually cleansed before or after each use?) Who normally is permitted to carry and utilize the item? (Clergy? Male? Female? Particular family member?)

In the case of a special ritual item (Navajo wedding jar, chuppah, athame and chalice) you may want not only to inquire about its meaning but also about the proper way to treat it. For instance, in Thai and Tibetan Buddhism, it is considered blasphemous for ritual items such as singing bowls and cymbals to come in contact with the floor or someone's feet. Accidental contact defiles the item. In some cases, many days of prayer, fasting, and mourning are required before reconsecration, while in others, the spiritual damage is considered irreparable.

## sacred eclecticism versus sacrilege

Probably the most difficult handfastings of all to arrange are the ones that involve one Neopagan and one member of a different faith, yet we seem to get them time and time again. Part of the reason for this is the growing number of interfaith marriages. Even clergypeople of mainstream faiths have, for the most part, accepted this, and many are creating structure and context for interfaith marriages as part of their normal rituals. It's unlikely that this trend will do anything but increase.

Neopagan clergy tends to be ahead of their mainstream cousins when it comes to tolerating interfaith unions between Neopagans and members of other faiths. If you go to a Catholic priest or Pentecostal minister or Islamic mullah and ask him to create and officiate in his own building a ceremony that is half Neopagan and half drawn from his own faith, the strong likelihood is that you'll get a shocked and fervent refusal. Some of the Pagan or heathen clergy that you approach with such a ceremony may also have strong reservations about performing any kind of a non-Pagan ceremony, but most Neopagan clergy will sigh and agree to try. We've also had good luck with some Unitarian Universalist clergypeople who were quite willing to do a ceremony in conjunction with a Pagan clergyperson, and if that clergyperson was not legally licensed by the state to perform the marriage, the Unitarian minister was willing to sign the certificate.

Whether Pagan or non-Pagan, however, any clergyperson may or may not know much about the other faith in question if it is not one that they were raised in. Don't count on your Pagan clergyperson to be able to find a clergy member of another faith to co-officiate and help with the writing of the ritual and vice versa. An interfaith union of this sort will call for some extra effort to assemble all the necessary elements. The couple should have in-depth discussions over each line, and whether the ceremony makes each of them feel heard, honored, and respected.

The following rituals were written for all the different sorts of unions that we've listed. We do not suggest that you bring them to your local church or temple or mosque. They are not likely to be well received there. However, many Neopagan clergy may be willing to attempt them. If you do actually know a flexible member of the non-Pagan's religion who would be willing to participate in rituals like these, that's terrific. We're all for ecumenicalism. But don't go in to an unknown clergyperson carrying these rituals and expect him or her to be thrilled. The policy of many mainstream faiths is that to invoke any deity in a building dedicated to a certain god other than that god is sacrilegious and unacceptable. Clergypeople who are willing to perform interfaith ceremonies in tandem with a Neopagan clergy person will usually tend to prefer a neutral place to perform it. If you cannot find a clergyperson of the other faith, you might try someone who is a non-clergy scholar or practitioner of that faith—perhaps a friend or family member—assuming that, if the wedding is to be a legal one, the Pagan officiant is properly licensed.

Interfaith weddings can be acts of incredible hope and courage, where two people of (possibly radically) different faiths, worldviews, values, opinions on fidelity, sex, childrearing, etc. promise to spend the rest of their lives negotiating around these differences, trusting in their mutual love and individual integrity to bridge the rifts that will come up. An interfaith wedding can also be a terrible mess, depending on the willingness of each partner to inconvenience themselves for the other's needs and, of course, the willingness of each family to put aside prejudices and throw their support behind the happiness of the couple.

# pagan - catholic interfaith handfasting

*This is designed to be a two-officiant ceremony. As it is unlikely that you will be able to find a Catholic priest to do half of it (although don't throw out the idea completely), you may want it done by a friend in the faith. If you do get two clergypeople involved, make sure that it is worked out beforehand who will be signing the marriage certificate, if it is to be a legal wedding. For a nonlegal handfasting, just pick two people that you love and trust to do the honors.*

*Four chosen wedding attendants face in the proper direction and call the quarters thusly:*

**east:** Hail Saint Raphael, Archangel of the Eastern Light, protector of travelers! Bless this couple as they begin their long journey together.

**south:** Hail Saint Michael, Archangel of the Fiery Sword, protector of those who guard! Bless and protect this couple from all that would thrust them apart.

**west:** Hail Saint Gabriel, Archangel of the Western Sea, messenger of heaven! Bring us hope for the future and the music of the spheres!

**north:** Hail Saint Uriel, Archangel of the Northern Star, who comes forth in hope! Light their way as they take their first steps on this path.

*The couple walk in from opposite sides and stand before the officiants.*

**catholic officiant:** Friends, families, and communities of both _____ and _____, we gather here today to celebrate the union of this couple. We ask that you surround them in a circle of love as unconditional as that of God's love.

**pagan officiant:** We celebrate not only their love and their commitment, but the bridge that their marriage will create between two families, two tribes, two communities, two ways of being in the world. We celebrate also their courage, to build that bridge between two far places, and to cross it together and find home and family where none was expected.

**catholic officiant:** Lord, look with love upon this woman, who wishes to be joined in marriage. May she put her trust in you, and see you as her equal, heir with you to a life of grace. Lord, look with love upon this man, who wishes to be joined in marriage. May he put his trust in you, and see you as his equal, heir with you to a life of grace.

**pagan officiant:** Lady of Light and Darkness, in the dust of whose feet are the hosts of heaven, whose body encircles the universe, grant your blessing to this couple who stand here before you to be joined as one. Lord of Darkness and Light, seed sower, Horned One, dancer in the heart, grant your blessing to this couple who stand here before you to be joined as one.

**catholic officiant:** "'Who is she who looks forth as the morning fair as the
   moon, clear as the sun, awesome as an army with banners?' . . .
Make haste, my beloved, and be like a gazelle or a young stag on the mountains
   of spices." *(Song of Solomon 6:7, 8:14)*

**pagan officiant:** My love is like the sun that shines down upon my life.
   My love is like the moon that lights the way in the darkness.
   My love is like the earth that supports and nourishes me.
   My love is like the sea, ever-changing and yet ever-constant.
   My love is like the fire that warms me when I am cold.
   My love is like my breath which gives me life.
   My love is like the Great Spirit, which dwells within us all
   And gives us the strength to face each new day together.

**catholic officiant:** Saint Nicholas was the bishop of Myra, and he was a good and just and generous man. It is said that when the daughters of a poor miller wept because they could not afford dowries to get married, he stole up to their house at night and threw in three bags of gold, enabling them to afford to start out on new lives and marry. From this parable, we learn that it is godly to be generous, and this is especially true for couples starting on this path. There will be many times in your lives ahead when you will feel the need to disagree, sometimes strenuously. Rather than attacking each other and causing unnecessary wounds of the heart, try to remember the example of Saint Nicholas' generosity, which is a reflection of God's own generosity to all of us. Remember that it is better to give than to demand, and that it is better to give unacknowledged than to receive resentfully. May the blessing of Saint Nicholas be on you, and also that of the Blessed Virgin Mary, and her earthly husband Joseph, and the Father, Son, and Holy Spirit keep you as well.

**pagan officiant:** The word "bride" is related to Brigid, the Irish goddess of old for whom Saint Brigid was named. It is said that Saint Brigid was an abbess who desperately wished for more land for her nuns. She went to the local lord, who was a cruel and heartless man, and begged him for land to support themselves and build an abbey. He laughed at her and told her that tomorrow he would give her as much land as she could surround with the edges of her cloak.

There are two ways that the story here ends. One tale says that during the night, her cloak magically grew to many times its size, covering many acres, and the lord was struck with amazement at her divine grace and humbly agreed to grant her the land. But yet another tale tells a different story. It tells how Saint Brigid spent the dark night unraveling her cloak, thread by thread, tying each thread together into one long string, knot by knot, and walking about the edges of the land laying it down, step by step, until she had surrounded many acres with her one thin thread. In the morning, the lord realized her wisdom, her ingenuity, and the strength of her commitment, and he agreed to hold to his bargain.

As a union between people from two different faiths and families and cultures, not everything will come easy for you. There will be many days spent unraveling your assumptions, thread by thread, and many nights spent finding ways to join together in agreement and compromise, knot by knot, and many miles of road walked together, step by step. In time, you may learn to balance each other's needs and faith so well that it may look, to those who stand outside and do not know, like a miracle, a thing of amazement, a cloak of love that has grown to encompass everything. And indeed, they will not be wrong, for this is what miracles are truly made of.

May Lady Brigid bless you with patience and persistence, tolerance and trust, enlightenment and endurance, laughter and love, all the days of your life on this Earth.

**catholic officiant:** *(to bride)* _____, do you take _____ to be your husband? Will you love him, comfort him, honor and keep him in sickness and in health, and be faithful to his love?

**pagan officiant:** *(to bride)* Do you give yourself to him and accept the gift of himself and his love that he gives to you? Do you pledge to endure all pains and hardships that life may bring you, and share all joys together as well?

**bride:** I do.

**catholic officiant:** *(to groom)* _____, do you take _____ to be your wife? Will you love her, comfort her, honor and keep her in sickness and in health, and be faithful to her love?

**pagan officiant:** *(to groom)* Do you give yourself to her and accept the gift of herself and her love that she gives to you? Do you pledge to endure all pains and hardships which life may bring you, and share all joys together as well?

**groom:** I do.

*The rings are brought forth.*

**catholic officiant:** Lord, bless these rings which we bless in your name.

Grant that those who wear them

May always have a deep faith in each other.

May they always live together

In peace, good will, and love.

We ask this through Christ our Lord.

**pagan officiant:** Mother of all things, Lady of the heavens,

Blessed be these rings, and the hands upon which they will reside,

May they always reach for each other

And always find there support and love.

May they move with grace through the cycle of life

And be to each other an anchor in the world.

*Couple places rings on each other's hands.*

**bride:** With this ring I thee wed.

**groom:** With this ring I thee wed.

**catholic officiant:** For as much as _____ and _____ have consented together in this sacred covenant, and have declared the same before this company, I pronounce you husband and wife, in the name of the Father, and the Son, and the Holy Spirit.

**pagan officiant:** As you have come together here of your own free will and declared your commitment to each other, I bless you with all the power of the Lord and Lady in all their forms, and especially with the blessing of Hera, goddess of marriage, and Aphrodite, Lady of Love, and I pronounce you married. You may kiss!

*Some couples may choose to end the ceremony here and process out. In other cases, it may be important to the Catholic officiant to do the final blessing afterwards; in which case keep going to the end of this ceremony. Discuss with your officiants as to what their strong preferences are.*

**catholic officiant:** Most gracious God, we thank you for blessing the union of this man and woman. By the power of your Holy Spirit, pour out the abundance of your blessing upon them. Defend them from every enemy. Lead them into peace. Let their love for each other be a seal upon their hearts and mantle about their shoulders and a crown upon their foreheads. Bless them in their work and companionship, in their sleeping and in their waking, in their joys and in their sorrows, in their life and in their death.

Grant them wisdom and devotion in the ordering of their common life, that each may be to the other a strength in need, a counselor in perplexity, a comfort in sorrow, and a companion in joy. Give them grace, when they hurt each other, to recognize and acknowledge their fault and to seek each other's forgiveness and yours. Give them such fulfillment of their mutual affection that they may reach out in love and concern for others. Grant that all married persons who have witnessed these vows may find their lives strengthened and their loyalties confirmed. Let your Spirit so direct all of us that we may each look to the good of others in word and deed, and grow in grace as we advance in years.

**pagan officiant:** Mother of All Things, whose love is poured out upon the Earth, Lord who is Guardian and Guide, Great Spirit of the Universe who is one with all things, Fates and Fortune who stand with us on this turning point in two lives, bless this couple with all the good and bountiful things in life. May they never hunger for food or family or friendship; may they never thirst for water or wonder or words of love. May their love be the foundation from which they go forth and to which they return, even as all things proceed from the Earth and return to her again. May this foundation also be the sturdy ground in which they can place their trust, giving them the courage to face their fears, separately and together. And may that foundation be a safe space where they can grow and change with no derision, scorn, or denial.

May everyone who stands here today, from every community and tribe, remember this day as a true coming together, a meeting of minds and hearts, a bridge built where there was only an abyss, which may be traversed by others now that it has been bound into the flesh and blood and bones of these two courageous adventurers. May the broad sea of love be garlanded by islands of understanding, and may we all stand on one today. Inspire us with this knowledge, that we may all go forth in greater understanding ourselves and thus change the world for the better. So mote it be.

*While the Catholic officiant speaks these words, the Pagan officiant quietly walks the circle, silently dismissing the elements.*

**catholic officiant:** The peace of the Father, the Son, and the Holy Spirit, which passes all understanding, keep your hearts and minds in the knowledge and love of God, in light and truth and love now and forever. Amen.

**pagan officiant:** The circle is open though unbroken. May the peace of the Spirit of the Universe go with you every day of your lives. Merry meet, and merry part, and merry meet again. Blessed be.

# pagan–protestant interfaith handfasting

*This is a fairly neutral ceremony, with little mention of deity on either side. However, we have provided the clergypeople with two sets of invocations and final prayers, one set we consider to be level 1 and one set we consider level 2, so that the couple may choose their level of religious neutrality. Couples are also free to substitute other Christian Scripture readings that are meaningful to them. The quarters are cast using the "Call to the Beloved" Quarter Casting (page 34) read by the bride and groom themselves. If you are using two clergypeople, note that the Protestant officiant reads the Christian lines and the Pagan officiant reads the Pagan lines. Alternately, one clergyperson can read both sets of lines.*

**protestant officiant:** Friends, we are gathered here today to witness and bless the joining together of this man and this woman in holy matrimony. The union of husband and wife in heart, body, and mind is intended by God for their mutual joy, for the help and comfort given one another in prosperity and adversity, and that society may stand on firm foundations. Into this holy union _____ and _____ now come to be joined. If any of you can show just cause why they may be lawfully married, speak now, or forever hold your peace.

**pagan officiant:** We come as a family, as a clan, as a tribe of friends and caring well-wishers, to see two individuals join into one life. The love of one person for another is the central hub of every wheel of human existence, and every union is cause for joy.

**protestant officiant:** Divine Providence, we rejoice in your life in the midst of our lives. You are the light illuminating everyone; you show us the way and the life. You love us even when we are unfaithful. You sustain us with your Holy Spirit. We praise you for your presence with us and especially in the act of solemn covenant. Amen.

**pagan officiant:** Great Spirit of the Universe, we stand here in affirmation of one sacred point in the hallowed cycle of life that you have ordained for us. We praise this cycle of life and love, and affirm you as the living manifestation of the power inherent in all creation. May your blessing be on us all.

*invocations (level 1)*

**protestant officiant:** "Love is patient and kind; love is not jealous or boastful;

it is not arrogant or rude. Love does not insist on its own way;

it is not irritable or resentful;

it does not rejoice at wrong, but rejoices in the right.

Love bears all things, believes all things, hopes all things, and endures all things.

Love never ends." *(1 Corinthians 13:4–8a)*

**pagan officiant:** Love is the dance that takes years to learn,

And must always be relearned

With the changing tides of time.

Love is the diamond, brilliant as the star

The strongest stone there is,

With a cutting edge sharp and keen

That once was a tender green plant

Growing in the breast of the Earth.

Love is the mainspring of the Universe

And its guiding spirit.

**protestant officiant:** "My beloved spoke, and said to me, 'Rise up, my love,

my fair one, and come away.

For lo, the winter is past, the rain is over and gone,

The flowers appear on the earth, the time of singing has come, and the voice of

the turtledove is heard in our land.

The fig tree puts forth her green figs, and the vines with the tender grapes give a

good smell. Rise up, my love, my fair one, and come away!'"

*(Song of Solomon 2:10–2:13)*

**pagan officiant:** A marriage is like two trees rising from the sacred earth

That grow close together, but from different roots,

Different colors of leaf, different textures of bark,

Different flowers in the spring,

Yet the same bees that drink their nectar,

The same birds that nest in their branches

And sing the spring into their unfolding buds,

The same shower of leaves falling in autumn

The same flood of cold bringing winter sleep.

And sometimes, two trees may entwine so closely

That we who watch them see only one tree

With different leaves, and wonder at the miracle,

For miracle it is.

176

## invocations (level 2)

**protestant officiant:** "Put on then, as God's chosen ones, holy and beloved, compassion, kindness, lowliness, meekness, and patience,

forbearing one another, and if one has a complaint against another, forgiving each other; as the Lord has forgiven you, so you must also forgive.

And above all these put on love, which binds everything together in perfect harmony.

And let the peace of Christ rule in your hearts, to which indeed you were called in the one body. And be thankful.

Let the word of Christ dwell in you richly, as you teach and admonish one another in all wisdom." *(Colossians 3:12–3:17)*

**pagan officiant:** "I who am the beauty of the green earth, and the white moon among the stars, and the mystery of the waters, I call upon your soul to rise and come unto me. For I am the soul of nature that gives life unto the universe; from Me all things proceed and unto Me all things must return. Let My worship be in the heart that rejoices, for all acts of love and pleasure are My rituals." *(Charge of the Goddess by Doreen Valiente)* protestant officiant: "He answered, 'Have you not read that he who made them from the beginning made them male and female,

and said, "For this reason a man shall leave his father and mother and be joined to his wife, and the two shall become one flesh"?

So they are no longer two but one flesh. What therefore God has joined together, let no man put asunder.'" *(Matthew 19:4–19:6)*

pagan officiant: "So let there be beauty and strength, power and compassion, mirth and reverence within you." (paraphrased from the *Charge of the Goddess)* We witness here the Hieros Gamos *(hee´-ros gahm´-os)*, the sacred marriage wherein two become one, woman half of man and man half of woman. Go forth blessed by the gods, and the Spirits of the Earth, and all the Ancestors who came before you, and be thou an example to those who will come after you.

*For the vows, the couple can choose either to utilize the vows below or go with any Level 1 vow in the Vows chapter.*

protestant officiant: *(to bride)* _____ and _____, if it is your intention to share with each other the joys and sorrows and all that the years will bring, with your promises bind yourselves to each other as husband and wife. _____, do you take _____ to be your husband, to live together in holy marriage? Will you love him, comfort him, honor and keep him in sickness and in health, and be faithful to him for as long as you live?

pagan officiant: *(to bride)* Do you give yourself to him, and accept the gift of himself and his love which he gives to you? Do you pledge to endure all pains and hardships which life may bring you, and share all joys together as well?

bride: I do.

protestant officiant: *(to groom)* _____, do you take _____ to be your wife, to live together in holy marriage? Will you love her, comfort her, honor her and keep her in sickness and in health, and be faithful to her for as long as you live?

**pagan officiant:** *(to groom)* Do you give yourself to her, and accept the gift of herself and her love which she gives to you? Do you pledge to endure all pains and hardships which like may bring you, and share all joys together as well?

**groom:** I do.

**protestant officiant:** Who stands with this man *(or woman, depending on which one is the Christian)* to symbolize the traditions and family out of which he *(or she)* comes?

**family members or friends:** We do.

**pagan officiant:** Who stands with this woman *(or man, depending on which one is the Pagan)* to symbolize the traditions and family out of which she *(or he)* comes?

**family members or friends:** We do.

**protestant officiant:** The union of \_\_\_\_\_ and \_\_\_\_\_ brings into one marriage two different traditions, two backgrounds, and two sets of beliefs into one marriage, one family, and one trust in the overarching love of Divine Providence. This takes courage, both to make such a decision and to be willing to follow through in the labor of love that is in their future. Although this marriage is the choice and the responsibility of this couple, still, their life together will be enhanced by the support of their families and friends.

**pagan officiant:** It is always more glorious to try to build a bridge together across a great gap than merely to stand on either side and attempt to hold hands across it. Such endeavors should be met with praise and wishes for success. Will you *(addressing family members and friends)* encourage and support \_\_\_\_\_ and \_\_\_\_\_ in their union, for better or worse? Will you stand behind them and not between them? Please signify your support by saying, "We will."

**family members and/or friends:** We will!

**protestant officiant:** Bless, O Lord, the giving of these rings, that they who wear them may abide in peace and continue in thy favor. Amen.

**pagan officiant:** Blessed be these rings that symbolize the circle of life and the cycle of death and rebirth, and blessed be they who wear them. So mote it be.

**groom:** With this ring I thee wed, and with my body I thee worship, and with all my worldly goods I thee endow.

**bride:** With this ring I thee wed, and with my body I thee worship, and with all my worldly goods I thee endow.

**protestant officiant:** For as much as \_\_\_\_\_ and \_\_\_\_\_ have consented together in this sacred covenant, and have declared the same before this company, I pronounce you husband and wife, in the name of the Father, and the Son, and the Holy Spirit.

**pagan officiant:** As you have come together here of your own free will and declared your commitment to each other, I bless you with all the power of the Lord and Lady in all their forms, and especially with the blessing of Hera, Goddess of Marriage, and Aphrodite, Lady of Love, and I pronounce you married. You may kiss!

*Some couples may choose to end the ceremony here and process out. In other cases, it may be important to the Protestant officiant to do the final blessing afterwards; in which case keep going to the end of this ceremony. Discuss with your officiants as to what their strong preferences are.*

**protestant officiant:** Most gracious God, we thank you for blessing the union of this man and woman. By the power of your Holy Spirit, pour out the abundance of your blessing upon them. Defend them from every enemy. Lead them into peace. Let their love for each other be a seal upon their hearts, a mantle about their shoulders, and a crown upon their foreheads. Bless them in their work and companionship, in their sleeping and in their waking, in their joys and in their sorrows, in their life and in their death.

Grant them wisdom and devotion in the ordering of their common life, that each may be to the other a strength in need, a counselor in perplexity, a comfort in sorrow, and a companion in joy.

Give them grace, when they hurt each other, to recognize and acknowledge their fault, and to seek each other's forgiveness and yours. *(All say "Amen.")* Give them such fulfillment of their mutual affection that they may reach out in love and concern for others.

Grant that all married persons who have witnesses these vows may find their lives strengthened and their loyalties confirmed.

Let your Spirit so direct all of us that we may each look to the good of others in word and deed, and grow in grace as we advance in years. Amen.

**all:** Amen.

**pagan officiant:** Mother of All Things, whose love is poured out upon the Earth, Lord who is Guardian and Guide, Great Spirit of the Universe who is one with all things, Fates and Fortune who stand with us on this turning point in two lives, bless this couple with all the good and bountiful things in life. May they never hunger, for food or family or friendship; may they never thirst for water or wonder or words of love.

May their love be the foundation from which they go forth, and to which they return, even as all things proceed from the Earth and return to her again. May this foundation also be the sturdy ground in which they can place their trust, giving them the courage to face their fears, separately and together. And may that foundation be a safe space where they can grow and change with no derision, scorn, or denial.

May everyone who stands here today, from every community and tribe, remember this day as a true coming together, a meeting of minds and hearts, a bridge built where there was only an abyss, which may be traversed by others now that it has been bound into the flesh and blood and bones of these two courageous adventurers.

May the broad sea of love be garlanded by islands of understanding, and may we all stand on one today. Inspire us with this knowledge, that we may all go forth in greater understanding ourselves and thus change the world for the better. So mote it be.

**all:** So mote it be.

*While the Protestant officiant speaks the following words, the Pagan officiant quietly walks the circle, silently dismissing the elements.*

**protestant officiant:** The peace of Divine Providence, which passes all understanding, keep your hearts and minds in the knowledge and love of God, in light and truth and love now and forever. Amen.

**all:** Amen.

**pagan officiant:** The circle is open though unbroken. May the peace of the Spirit of the Universe go with you every day of your lives. Merry meet, and merry part, and merry meet again. Blessed be.

**all:** Blessed be.

# pagan – muslim wedding

*Traditionally in many countries, the night before a Muslim wedding is spent by the bride and her female relatives in the ritual of Mehndi. This is the application of henna to the bride's hands, and sometimes to the feet and other parts of the body, in designs and patterns symbolizing good luck and good fortune. A Pagan/Muslim couple may want to take part in this custom, although there is no reason why both individuals cannot be decorated, perhaps by their friends (or, as in traditional culture, by a henna professional) with various signs and symbols. (If you need inspiration, check the symbols appendix on page 293.) Each may prefer symbols of his or her faith, or both may want a sign that they hold in common or created together.*

*Muslim wedding ceremonies tend, for the most part, to be short, perfunctory, and somewhat sexist. As it is unlikely that any Pagan will stand for any of this, we have softened and equalized the tenor of the ceremony. Traditionally, the big part of a Muslim wedding is not the ceremony but the festivities afterwards, which should be lavish.*

*Finding a Muslim clergyperson to perform a wedding with a Pagan clergyperson will be extremely difficult. We suggest that you might check with Al-Fatiha (www.al-fatiha.net or 202-319-0898), the support organization for nonheterosexual Muslims. Even if the couple is heterosexual, Al-Fatiha members may be able to find you someone more willing to do an interfaith ceremony. If not, perhaps the ceremony could be co-officiated with a Muslim friend and a Neopagan minister.*

*When the wedding begins, it is traditional for at least the Muslim partner to wear yellow. However, it is not a hard and fast rule. One trusted friend or family member should hold a handfasting cord and stand nearby; the task may also be shared by the two official witnesses. The Muslim person who is the acting clergy should have a small copy of the Koran; the Pagan clergyperson should have a green branch of a tree. The bride and groom should carry small gifts for each other. The family and friends sit or stand in a circle, holding per-cussion instruments such as drums, rattles, and sticks. As the couple enters, one from each side, escorted by family members or close friends, the circled family and friends begin a drumming rhythm. The couple circle the room in opposite directions, coming together at the far end and moving together into the center next to the clergypeople.*

**muslim officiant:** Do you, _____, and you, _____, come here of your own free will to be bound in marriage?

**couple:** We do.

**pagan officiant:** Do you come here to show your faith in the endurance of your love?

**couple:** We do.

**muslim officiant:** And one of his signs is that he created mates for you from your-selves that you may find rest in them, and he put between you love and com-passion; most surely there are signs in this for a people who reflect. And what-ever alms you give or whatever vow you vow, surely Allah knows it. Be faithful to each other, and remember that he hears your promises.

**pagan officiant:** Your love will be a bridge over a wide river. At times, the waters will rise and be tumultuous, but you will survive and not drown. Your love will be an example of tolerance and compassion to everyone who knows you, and you must remember to be proud of that love in the face of all who would stand against you. Remember also that the Goddess smiles on diversity, for it is in this model that she created the Earth.

*The bride and groom now face each other.*

**bride:** I give you this gift as a token on my love. *(hands him the gift and explains why it is appropriate for him)*

**groom:** I give you this gift as a token of my love. *(hands her the gift and explains why it is appropriate for her)*

**muslim officiant:** Place your hands together. *(they join hands in front of him, and he gently rests the small Koran on top of them)* May the blessing and wisdom of Allah be always over you and your union.

**pagan officiant:** *(brings branch up beneath their clasped hands, so that they rest upon it)* May the blessing and wisdom of the Goddess be like the Earth beneath your feet. Now speak your vows!

**bride:** I, _____, offer you myself in marriage, as has been done throughout time. I pledge in honesty and with sincerity to be faithful and helpful to you, to strive to live in blessed peace.

**groom:** I, _____, offer you myself in marriage, as has been done throughout time. I pledge in honesty and with sincerity to be faithful and helpful to you, to strive to live in blessed peace.

*At this point, the two witnesses step forward with the cord and bind the bride and groom's hands together.*

**muslim officiant:** I now pronounce you married! Go and be happy, and be good for each other.

**pagan officiant:** May the road that you walk together be light beneath your feet. You may kiss!

*They do so, and there is a general cheer. All now retire for feasting and celebration, which should be alcohol-free in order to respect the Muslims present.*

# pagan - buddhist wedding

*Buddhism is not necessarily a polytheistic faith, nor, in some forms, even a deistic faith. However, it is remarkably tolerant of other faiths and can usually find some common ground with Paganism—or at least not clash terribly. Buddhist friends of ours have sometimes managed to find quite acceptable common ground by comparing the Pagan deities to Buddhist spirits, dakinis, or demigods. In most Buddhist traditions, the monk or lama does not perform the marriage so much as merely bless it; the couple and their families actually perform the ceremony. This suggests that the Buddhist clergyperson (and, for that matter, the Pagan one) may be a friend rather than a priest, but this is up to the couple. Buddhist marriage rites vary widely from country to country, as they tend to reflect the culture of that area more than the faith that they may all practice, and they all tend to be fairly brief. This ceremony draws from several Buddhist cultural sources.*

*The room is prepared either with several sets of large pillows on the floor or else a table with large pillows laid on it. On these pillows are various short, thin pieces of cord in many colors (which will be worn until they wear off), with one very long piece of a color that is especially suitable to the couple. If they wish, an altar can be set up, with a figure of the Buddha on one side, with the appropriate trappings, and a figure of the Goddess on the other side, with the appropriate trappings. A conch shell is traditionally set in a place of honor next to a bowl of water.*

*The couple comes into the space from two directions, each flanked by a band of family and friends. The Buddhist member of the couple may carry the traditional o-juju, a rosary of twenty-one beads symbolizing Buddha and his deeds. The Pagan member of the couple can carry the long cord, if it is not left on the altar, or a sheaf of greenery. They stand before the altar.*

**buddhist officiant:** In the future, happy occasions will come as surely

as the morning,

And difficult times will come as surely as the night.

When things go joyously, meditate.

When things go badly, meditate.

Meditation in the manner of the Compassionate Buddha

Will guide your life.

To say the words "love and compassion" is easy.

To accept that love and compassion

Are built upon patience and perseverance is not easy.

**pagan officiant:** Live joyfully in this world,

And take your happiness from each other,

For you are each other's gift from the gods,

And the beauty and intensity of your love

Will be the gift you give back to them.

Love as the earth loves the touch of your body,

As the sea loves the dance of the dolphin,

As the fire loves to leap free,

As the wind loves the song of the lark.

*The couple either sit on the large pillows and lay their forearms across other pillows in front of them, or they stand and lay their forearms across pillows on the table. Family members and friends come forward, two or three at a time, and either sit next to the couple (if they are seated) or stand next to them, and each takes a cord of their choice (not the long one) and ties it around the wrist of one partner or the other. As they tie it on, they voice a wish for the couple. This goes on until you run out of family, friends, or cord. The cords will stay tied on the couple's forearms until they wear off. Then the Buddhist officiant steps forward, dips the conch into the bowl to fill it with water, and then pours it over both their outstretched hands.*

**buddhist officiant:** "The treasure of the body is more valuable than material treasure stored in the treasure house, but the treasure of the heart is the most valuable, and is much more than the treasure of the body." So said the Buddha in his wisdom, and so you will find in your journeys. Comfort one another with your bodies, but give freely of your hearts.

**pagan officiant:** *(anoints couple's foreheads with scented oil and speaks a blessing)* And the Goddess saith: behold, all acts of love and pleasure are my rituals. Or do I demand of you any sacrifice, for behold, I am the Mother of all things, and my love for you is poured out upon the Earth. May you both be blessed in your union, as the stars wheel down the heavens and the roses bloom in summer.

187

*The officiants step forward and take up the long cord, one at each end. They each loop one end a few times around the forehead of the person whose faith they represent, tying it in place. A piece about three feet long should hang between them. They should speak their vows, which should be personal to each of them and said to each other.*

**buddhist officiant:** In the name of the Compassionate Buddha, you are one, as we are all one with the Universe.

**pagan officiant:** By the Lady and the Lord, by fire and water, by earth and sky, by sun and moon, by all that lives and loves, I declare you married.

# pagan - hindu wedding

*Hinduism and Neopaganism have a few things in common that makes an interfaith wedding ceremony a little less difficult to put together. Hinduism is naturally polytheistic, and Hindus are familiar with the concept of Goddess, so it is a little easier to meet in the middle than it would be for monotheistic faiths.*

*The bride should wear a long veil and the groom a long sash; these will be wound around the couple as part of the ceremony.*

*Ideally, the Hindu half of the couple will say the lines marked "a," and the Pagan half of the couple will say the lines marked "b." However, they can both be said in unison or in some other alternation.*

a: Let us take the first step, to make our household a nourishing and pure place, avoiding those things injurious to healthy living.

b: Our home will be a mirror of our respect for the Earth and all its children.

a: Let us take the second step, to develop our physical, mental, and spiritual powers together.

b: We will encourage each other in fertility of the mind and soul.

a: Let us take the third step, to increase our wealth by righteous means and proper use.

b: May all the gods smile on us with good fortune and many resources.

a: Let us take the fourth step, to acquire knowledge, happiness, and harmony by mutual love and trust.

b: May our spirits fly together on wings of perfect love and perfect trust.

a: Let us take the fifth step, that we be blessed with strong, virtuous, and heroic children.

b: May we be the doorway to bring new life into the Earth, and nurture its passage.

**a:** Let us take the sixth step, for self-restraint, longevity, and consideration of others.

**b:** May we know when to speak and when to remain silent, when to reach out a hand, and when to stand aside.

**a:** Let us take the seventh step, that we may always live as friends and remain true lifelong companions.

**b:** You are my beloved, and all the light of the heavens are in you.

*The couple clasps hands together. The officiant, or honored family members, wind the bride's long veil and the groom's long sash down their arms to their clasped hands, where they knot them together, wind them about each other's hands, and knot again, so that they are tied together with and by the cloth. This next part can be memorized by the couple, or it can be a call-and-response from a officiant.*

**bride:** We are word and meaning united.

**groom:** You are thought and I am sound.

**bride:** May the nights be honey-sweet for us.

**groom:** May the mornings be honey-sweet for us.

**bride:** May the heavens be honey-sweet for us.

**groom:** May all the plants of the earth be honey-sweet for us.

**bride:** May the sun be honey-sweet for us.

**groom:** May the cows yield us honey-sweet milk.

**bride:** As the heavens are strong and stable,

**groom:** As the Earth is strong and stable,

**bride:** As the mountains are strong and stable,

**groom:** As the whole universe is strong and stable,

**bride:** So may our union be strong and stable,

**groom:** So may we always share our joys.

*Then another person steps forward to bless them; it may be a Hindu or Pagan officiant, or honored friend or family member, or if there are two, each speaks one of the two blessings.*

**blessing one:** As Brahma and Sarasvati were brought together by love of harmony, may your days together be harmonious. As Vishnu and Lakshmi were brought together by love of beauty, may your days together be filled with beauty. As Shiva and Parvati were brought together by love of discipline, may your days together be committed to love. Om Shiva-Shakti.

**blessing two:** As Geb and Nuit were brought together by the will to create, may you create wonders together. As Isis and Osiris were brought together by mutual respect, may you always honor each other. As the Green Man is drawn to the Spring Maiden by the tides of the universe, may your destiny lie with joy in each other. Blessed be!

# judeo-pagan wedding

*Note from Tannin: This section of the book has been one of the most difficult writing challenges of my adult life. It is not for a lack of material; between the rich Judaic education of my youth and the wealth of material available at local libraries (and online), there has been no shortage of information of beliefs, customs, food, and holidays. So what's the problem, you may ask? Well, summing up Jewish life in a few short pages in a Neopagan context is like trying to describe the changes of the sky to someone who has no concept of the color blue. Judaism is among the most ancient of the monotheistic faiths practiced today, the parent religion to Christianity and elder brother to Islam. The current Jewish calendar year is 5762. How is one to express in a few short paragraphs the myriad of beliefs, triumphs, tragedies, and traditions that have evolved over the past six thousand years?*

*Imagine, if you will, an unusual ornamental marriage ring that is several hundred years old. It consists of a fairly wide band decorated with stylized leaves and flower buds. It is crowned by a tiny, exquisitely detailed onion-domed structure, complete with a door, beautiful windows, and even carved brick facing. This ring, according to legend, was commissioned by an entire community of a Jewish village in Poland. It was to be lent by the community for wedding ceremonies, and the fact that it has a little house on top is appropriate. In my studies, I discovered again and again that the central symbol of any Jewish wedding is the home, which the couple will be building together.*

*This ritual contains both Ashkenazi (European Jewish) and Sephardic (Middle-Eastern Jewish) traditions. In terms of timing, you might want to keep in mind that the Jewish month begins when the moon shows its first sliver, just after the new moon. While it is against Jewish law to worship the moon per se, the moon had strong significance to them, as it controls the tides and the menstrual cycles of women, who are especially likely to celebrate the significance of the moon. The moon is often shown as a symbol of the Jewish people, while the sun sometimes represents their enemies, so lunar rather than solar energies are preferred. The period of the waxing moon is considered to be more fortunate in both Pagan and Jewish tradition, so it might make a good time for an interfaith wedding that seeks to find common ground.*

*Well-meaning Pagans have often put forth the fiction that there were widespread secret alliances between Jews and Pagans during the Burning Times. Unfortunately, there is no evidence for such a situation except in the slanderous words of the witch hunters. However, there is a spiritual kinship in the lunar symbols that can be appreciated as a metaphoric connection.*

*On the morning of the wedding, the bride and groom should take separate ritual baths. Add to each bath the following: sea salt, milk, and honey. Sea salt is traditionally a symbol of purification and permanence; milk and honey symbolize nourishment for body and soul. Place lit candles of blue and white around the tub. Blue candles represent the balance of sky and sea, above and below; white candles represent all that is light and the moon and stars. They should then be dressed in simple clothing. As part of this ritual, participants will place wedding robes or cloaks on the couple, so their outfits should not be so elaborate that they will interfere.*

*This ceremony is best performed out of doors, since the open sky is important to the symbolism. It can be performed indoors, but it should be in a spacious room, preferably with a lot of windows to let in natural light. Guests and friends can donate their artificial winter-holiday pine trees to make a symbolic forest, as well as potted plants and flowers. These should be placed around the door that the couple will enter. If it is outside, they will enter from where the foliage is thickest.*

*In the center of the space is the* chuppah, *the square canopy on four poles that represents the couple's first home. It is often a delicate piece of work, as it deliberately connotes the fragility of the peace in a new home. The poles are traditionally made of pine (for longevity) and cypress (for grace and endurance), and they may be held by friends or family members (to represent community support) or set into stands or the ground. For a Pagan touch, they may be decorated with ribbons and flowers to represent the four directions. Next to the chuppah is a small altar with a chalice of wine, a bowl of green olives, a string of flowers or vine (real or artificial), and a wineglass resting on a sturdy canvas bag. The couple might also want to include small votive candles (called* yahrzeit *in the Hebrew tradition), one for each deceased relative that they would like to honor.*

193

*The guests stand around the chuppah, and behind them is the* sukkah. *The sukkah is a small house, big enough for a few people to sit in and eat. It needs to have at least three walls and a roof. The walls can be made out of any materials—cloth, wood, or metal—but the roof must be made out of plant material, such as tree branches or bundles of straw or hay. (It is acceptable to put down a piece of lattice to support them.) There should be spaces between the branches so that the sky is visible. Inside the sukkah, a tray should be placed with a loaf of bread, partially sliced, and a bread knife.*

*The sukkah is associated with the holiday of Sukkot, a harvest festival that commemorates the time when the Jewish people were wandering in the desert after fleeing Egypt, and living in makeshift homes. Jewish people traditionally build sukkot in their back yards during this holiday, which celebrates the fertility of the earth. Sukkot is generally sometime in the fall, depending on the vagaries of the lunar calendar, but the symbolism is relevant is any time, and the sukkah can be used ritually at any part of the year.*

*To begin the ceremony, the bride and groom are brought together to the edge of the ritual area. Their entrance is heralded by the blowing of horns or a* shofar *(a traditional Jewish ritual instrument made from a ram's horn). The couple begins to step forward, but their progress is halted by a participant dressed as a Guardian of the Forest.*

*The Forest Guardian should wear green, have a crown or mask of leaves, and carry a tree branch, which he or she uses to block their path.*

**forest guardian:** Halt! I stand between the world of the wild things and the world of humans. I guard the borderlands! Who are you, who come to the edge of worlds?

**bride:** I am _____.

**groom:** I am _____.

**forest guardian:** Why do you seek to leave the wilderness? Here you have your freedom, and you need not answer to anyone for your actions.

**bride:** We come here hand in hand to start a home together.

**groom:** We come here together to receive the blessings of our community.

*The Forest Guardian shakes his head and looks sad. He takes a bowl of ashes, which is a symbol of mourning and transformation, and marks the foreheads of the couple with the ashes.*

**forest guardian:** I wish you well in your new life. However, remember that no matter how much you love each other, the call of the wilderness will find you through the walls of your home. May your love and commitment be stronger than the howling of the winds.

*The couple step beyond the Forest Guardian and are met by two well-wishers. These should be a happily married couple, who treat the couple like newly arrived royalty, bowing to them. They dress the couple in their wedding robes and place crowns—of metal, leaves, or flowers—on their heads. As they do this, each speaks in turn and gives them advice for their married life ahead. This should be personal to the married couple in question, and the bride and groom should not know ahead of time what will be said. The couple can either respond and say, "I will" or merely bow. Afterwards, the well-wishers should applaud them and step back. The couple comes forward, and the officiant meets them just before the chuppah.*

officiant: Welcome, _____ and _____, in the name of the Creator of the Universe and by the grace of all humankind. *(the couple bows)* Why have you come forth out of the wilderness?

couple: We wish to start a new life and build a new home, together as one.

officiant: Are you here by your own free will, with only love in your hearts?

couple: We are.

officiant: Then enter your new home!

*The bride and groom circle the chuppah seven times before entering; the officiant can lead them in order to keep count if necessary. The circles represent unity, and the number seven is indicative of the seven archaic planets. They enter the chuppah and stand facing forward.*

officiant: You stand beneath the chuppah, which represents your new home. It is a delicate creation, because the peace in a new home is always fragile and requires great care to maintain. Know, however, that the foundations of your new home are supported by your community. Together, you will both share in the sweetness of life. *(clergy gives the couple the wine cup and they drink from it)* You will also share in its bitterness, and the hardships and rewards of family and responsibility.

*Clergy holds out the bowl of green olives, and the couple each eats one. Here the bride and groom will make personal vows to each other and exchange rings. For ideas, please see chapter 7, Vows.*

officiant: *(ties vine or string of flowers about the wrists of the couple)* Above you are the stars; below you are the stones. As you go through life, remember: like a star should your love be constant. Like a stone should your love be strong. By this cord between you, you are made as one, and there is one life now before you. You may kiss!

*Couple kisses. Officiant places the wineglass in the canvas bag and places it at the exit route of the couple; they deliberately step on it on the way out, and crush it. The officiant says "Mazel tov!" and everyone cheers. The bride and groom enter the sukkah, cut a symbolic slice of bread together and feed it to each other, and then emerge and carry the tray around to all the guests, offering it to them.*

officiant: Bread is the staff of life. It is what we make to nourish each other, symbolic of the bond between the Divine Creator and humanity in their partnership to sustain life. As your community feeds you, so you shall feed them in turn. So mote it be!

196

*All shout "So mote it be!" and everyone adjourns to the feast.*

*chapter 13*
# full rites

The chapter that follows contains a wide variety of complete wedding rites. Some are unique creations of couples we know; others are tried-and-true rites that a great many couples have adapted for their own ceremonies. You can use these rites as they are printed here, or you can add elements from other parts of the book or of your own design. Either way, we encourage you to make these rites your own.

Practically speaking, it is a very good idea to go over your ceremony—whether you customize it or not—with your officiants and other key participants. Make sure everyone understands and is comfortable with their roles.

# rose garden handfasting
## (level 1)

*Stacey and Shawn sent us this description of their wedding ceremony, which we would class as a level 1 ritual, subtle enough for easily-spooked friends and relatives.*

To begin the ceremony, the officiants take baskets of multicolored rose petals and colored ribbons and walk around the circle sprinkling rose petals and dropping ribbons—yellow in the east, red in the south, blue in the west, green in the north. They mark out a circle quietly, without being obvious, saying, "We call upon the sacred elements and invite them to witness this union."

The bride and groom enter with their wedding party and circled clockwise about the marked-out area. Both the bride and the maid of honor carry large bouquets of multicolored roses. At Stacy and Shawn's wedding, the bride wore an ivory gown, the groom wore a semiformal suit in black and white, the maid of honor wore hunter green, and the best man wore a similar suit with a green vest.

A clergyperson asks the couple their intent, and they speak it. Then they light a large unity candle together and share a goblet of wine. They recite personal vows of their own making. Then the officiants tie their hands together with two ribbons, a silver one (for the bride and the Goddess, its length the bride's height) and a gold one (for the groom and the God, its length the groom's height). A broom is brought out; and the officiant slips it up between their bound hands so that when they slid their hands out, the knotted ribbons remain wrapped around the broom's handle. The officiant then pronounces them husband and wife.

Then a list of gifts are presented to the couple, with the officiant explaining each one. The gifts can include: a broom, as a symbol of family and the hearth; a loaf of fresh-baked bread, that they might never hunger; a bottle of homemade wine, that they might never thirst; a pouch of coal, that they might always know the warmth of love.

Finally, the officiants walk back around the circle and pick up the ribbons in order to open the space (leaving the rose petals to be crushed during the dancing and thus release scent), and the ceremony is over.

# language of flowers handfasting
## (level 1)

This wedding ceremony has lots of parts in it for bridesmaids and flower girls and as such is fairly modern/traditional. Unless you have your own herb and flower garden and a full year to grow things, we suggest that you contact a florist a significant amount of time in advance and work out the floral decorations with him or her. It's a subtle level 1 ritual, easily enjoyed by people of many faiths. We also suggest a program, explaining the various flowers and their significances. (Many thanks to Allyson Chaple of Ritual Fantastique Wedding Coordination for researching and creating the floral arrangements; see also appendix C for specific flowers and their meanings.)

Set up the ceremony space with three large vases: one for the bride's family, one for the groom's, and a third vase, empty save for water, between them. Two wreaths of Oasis block (a floral foam designed to be soaked with water and stuck with flowers) sit to the side. Eight more arrangements will be used to mark the four quarters, the three faces of the Goddess, and the Green Man; they can be vases or wreaths that surround candles, so long as they are portable by the bridesmaids. You will need a large quantity of fresh flowers and herbs of many varieties (see the Magical Aesthetics chapter) in buckets of water.

Before the ceremony begins, the groomsmen let in and seat each person. They also determine who is family and who is friend and direct them to choose an appropriate flower or herb. Family members choose one flower each and are asked to place it in the labeled vase belonging to their family. The family vases should already contain one flower apiece, a long-stemmed red rose, symbolizing the bride and groom. Mothers and grandmothers of the couple should also be given roses—white, peach, pink, or blue/lavender, if possible. Friends choose a flower or sprig of herb from a separate labeled vase, and two other individuals (perhaps the maid of honor and best man, if they are friend and not family) help them to stick their flower into one of the two wreaths, one for friends of the bride, one for friends of the groom. For appropriate floral meanings, see the flowers for magical wreaths in the Magical Aesthetics chapter (pages 12–13). Bride and groom wear wreaths with rosemary bases and other love herbs and flowers; bridesmaids' wreaths and groomsmen's boutonnieres are based on the friendship flower list (page 12). See also appendix C.

The arrangements for elements, the Green Man, and the three faces of the Goddess should be as follows. The air arrangement consists of plants special to the air element such as lavender, meadowsweet, love-in-a-puff, yarrow, lily of the valley, iris, lilac, lupines, periwinkle, pansy, heartsease, or white lily. If you have a candle or incense stick in the center, it should be scented with lavender. The fire arrangement consists of plants such as ornamental alliums, clover, carnation, pinks, mustard, toadflax, basil, nasturtium, thistle, chili peppers, Chinese lanterns, snapdragons, bee balm, marigold, or sunflowers. Candles or incense should be scented with carnation or cinnamon. The water arrangement consists of plants such as seaholly, foxglove, delphinium, marshmallow, water lily, heather, mint, borage, lemon balm, columbine, sweet pea, gardenia, or poppy. The candle or incense should be violet or mint scented. The earth arrangement consists of plants such as ferns, honeysuckle, tulips, daylilies, wheat, oats, magnolia, thyme, horehound, valerian, crocus, snowdrop, cornflower, narcissus, or pine. Candles or incense should be scented with honeysuckle or pine. The arrangement of flowers devoted to the Maiden, the first face of the Goddess, consists of moonwort, honesty, eucalyptus, daisies, mugwort, willow, pink and white rosebuds, or the blossoms of any fruit tree—apple, peach, cherry, or orange. The arrangement of flowers devoted to Venus, the second face of the Goddess, consists of pink, red, or yellow roses in full bloom, myrtle, cupid's dart, bleeding hearts, love-lies-bleeding, love-in-a-mist, violets, primrose, or catnip. The arrangement of flowers devoted to the Crone, the third face of the Goddess, consists of wormwood, southernwood, black *hollyhock, black lily, sage, rue, asphodel, comfrey, datura, hellebore, Solomon's Seal, or white or blue roses in full bloom. The arrangement devoted to the Green Man consists of lots of ivy, grapevines, and any green leafy branch.*

*The actual ceremony opens with one or more flower girls scattering flower petals (if you're inside, tell the hall management that you'll vacuum afterwards). They move in a deosil (clockwise) spiral until they are in the center of the circle, having thrown out about half their petal supply. Then four members of the wedding party each take the arrangements for the quarters and carry them to the appropriate corners.*

*The air arrangement is carried to the east. The attendant sets it in place, lights candle or incense.*

> **air attendant:** By lavender and meadowsweet, by lily and lilac *(etc., add in what flowers you have)*, may the four winds blow sweet upon this day.

*The fire arrangement is carried to the south. The attendant sets it down and lights candle or incense.*

> **fire attendant:** By *(add in what flowers you have)*, may the warmth of all our hearts light up this day.

*The water arrangement is carried to the west. The attendant sets it down and lights candle or incense.*

> **water attendant:** By *(insert flowers of choice)*, may all the waters of the world lay their blessing on this day.

*The earth arrangement is carried to the north. The attendant sets it down and lights candles or incense.*

> **earth attendant:** By *(insert flowers of choice)*, may our beloved ones be welcomed by the earth beneath our feet.

*The bride and groom come forth from opposite directions and meet together in front of the altar.*

**officiant:** *(gives any introductory lines that he or she wishes and then says:)* We bring flowers to weddings not only because they are beautiful, and fill us with joy but because they are the organs of love of the kingdom of plants. They remind us of love every time we see them.

*Then four more attendants come forward, one at a time. Their lines can be read by them or by the officiant. A young girl, not yet in any relationship, comes forward and places the arrangement of flowers sacred to the Maiden on the altar.*

**young girl:** Do you promise to be as honest and loving as two children, to share each other's joys and sorrows and never lose hope?

**couple:** We do.

*An adult female attendant comes forward and places the arrangement of flowers sacred to Venus on the altar.*

**venus:** Do you promise to think of each other first, and to give freely of your love to each other, without asking a price?

**couple:** We do.

*A female elder comes forward (perhaps the mother of the bride or groom) and places the arrangement of flowers sacred to the Crone on the altar.*

**crone:** Do you promise to stay together through thick and thin, promising love for the long road and not simply the easy path?

**couple:** We do.

*An adult male attendant comes forward and places the arrangement of plants sacred to the Green Man on the altar.*

**green man:** The ivy cannot stand without the tree, yet it takes nothing from the tree. It is neither parasite nor stranger, but enwraps the tree in its living embrace. Do you promise to embrace each other like the ivy, yet each have your own roots and sustenance, supporting each other like the trees?

**couple:** We do.

**bride:** By leaf and bud I pledge myself to you. *(places the ring on groom's finger)*

**groom:** By blossom and root I pledge myself to you. *(places the ring on bride's finger)*

**officiant:** *(asks selected members of each family to step forward)* Today your families will be joined forever, in a bond between these two lovers' hands. Do you support this joining and their love?

**family:** We do.

*Family members bring forward the two vases of flowers. They hold the vases as the bride and groom both pull white roses out and places them together in a third vase, held by the officiant. Then two representatives of the friends of the bride and groom come forward, bearing the herb wreaths.*

**officiant:** You have stood by these two for a long time, valuing their presence in your lives. Will you now accept and value both of them together, as a couple?

**friends:** We will.

*The bride and groom select their prechosen herbs from the wreaths and place them in the vase with the roses.*

**officiant:** So you join many with one act. May your lives blossom with hope and joy and never cease to grow.

*Attendants come forward and wrap the bride and groom's hands in a cord twined with a flowering vine.*

**officiant:** I now pronounce you married.

# heathen runic handfasting
### (level 1)

*This handfasting ritual is useful when there will be a large group of people who want to participate in the ceremony, but there is no time for briefing or rehearsal. It is also nice because it creates a rune set as a group wedding gift for the bride and groom. The rune set should be made beforehand, preferably by close friends of the couple, out of wood or fired clay or engraved stone.*

*The first time we saw this performed, each stone was taped to an index card with the accompanying line on it; these were passed out beforehand to anyone who wanted to participate. Each person in turn stepped forward, read their card, detached the rune, and placed it in the bowl on the altar. Because there was no time for rehearsal, the clergyperson in charge chose to let them go in any order, rather than the traditional order. A special bag had been made for the wedding runes, and it was given to the couple afterwards to keep them in.*

*This ritual lists both the Old Norse Futhark runes and the Saxon/Frisian/Northumbrian Futhorc runes. You may use either. You may also use this ritual in conjunction with parts of the other Heathen Marriage Rite (page 242) in this book. As it is, this ritual is level 1 because it does not mention deities or religious doctrine; it is good for heathen couples wishing to have a low-key, subtle ceremony but one that still honors their faith. Combining it with parts of the other heathen handfasting will raise its level.*

*Set the altar with an evergreen branch in a bowl of water, a honey cake, a horn of mead, and a wooden bowl to collect the runes in.*

*The runes and invocations are as follows:*

ᚠ Fehu (or Feoh) is the rune of wealth. May you gain riches and comfort, like the farmer with many herds of cattle.

ᚢ Uruz (or Ur) is the rune of strength. May you be strong for each other, like the wild aurochs and his mate.

þ Thurisaz (or Thorn) is the rune of the thorn. May you be a comfort to each other in times of pain and trial.

ᚠ Ansuz (or Aesc) is the rune of the divine message. May you learn to listen to one another, which is more important even than speaking.

ᚱ Raido (or Rade) is the rune of travel. Although you have walked two separate paths, may you now walk one road hand in hand.

< Kaunaz (or Ken) is the rune of fire and truth. May you speak only truth to each other, and never resort to deception.

✕ Gebu (or Gyfu) is the rune of the gift, of partnership, of the crossroads where you now stand. May you always give of yourselves generously.

ᚹ Wunjo (or Wyn) is the rune of light. May your path be bright; may your times in the darkness be few.

ᚺ Hagalaz (or Haegl) is the rune of hail. Misfortune will come, for it always does; may you hold together against the forces of chaos that rain down upon you.

ᚾ Nauthiz (or Nyth) is the rune of need. May you find ways to fill each other's needs, yet not depend on each other so much that you cannot look elsewhere for aid.

| Isa (or Is) is the rune of ice. May your hearts never freeze and turn cold to each other; instead, let your love melt all ice between you.

ᛋ Jera (or Jer) is the rune of the harvest. May all your hard work come to fruition, and may you reap the rewards you deserve.

Eihwaz (or Eoh) is the rune of the yew stave. May you protect and defend each other from all harm.

Perth (or Peorth) is the rune of the dice cup, the cave, the womb, the mystery. No matter how well you know each other, let there still be some small mystery left for the discovering.

Algiz (or Eolx) is the rune of the elk. May you meet all challenges with courage and exuberance.

Sowelu (or Sigil) is the rune of the sun. May you each be the Sun that brings life to each other's lives.

Teiwaz (or Tyr) is the rune of the warrior. May you stand together as shield-mates and not rend each other in mutual battle.

Berkana (or Beorc) is the rune of the birch tree, of growth. May you each encourage your mate to make new growth in all areas of life.

Ehwaz (or Eh) is the rune of the horse, of movement. May you always find fair footing along your path, and ever have good progress.

Mannaz (or Mann) is the rune of humanity. May you never forget that we are all human, and we make mistakes, and must be forgiven for them.

Laguz (or Lagu) is the rune of water. May you learn to flow together in harmony with each other.

Inguz (or Ing) is the rune of the sacrificial god. May you learn when it is the right time to make sacrifices for your relationship and when you should stand firm.

ᛞ     Dagaz (or Daeg) is the Rune of Dawn. May you wake up every morning in love with the one who lies next to you.

ᛟ     Othila (or Oethel) is the Rune of Heritage. May you have peace between your families, clans, and friends.

*(Next, we list the futhorc runes; use them or eliminate them as you choose.)*

ᚩ     Os is the rune of the bard. May the words that are spoken between you be magic, that you may always understand each other.

ᚪ     Ac is the rune of endurance. May you stand straight as an oaken stave together and never be ashamed.

ᛠ     Ear is the rune of the grave. May you be together even unto death.

ᛁ     Ior is the rune of the Midgard Serpent that surrounds the Earth. May you be willing to go to the ends of the Earth for each other.

ᚣ     Yr is the rune of the bow. May your sight be keen and sharp, and may you learn to aim in the same direction.

ᚸ     Qwert is the rune of the funeral pyre. May you be able to let go of what is necessary without ever losing hold of each other.

ᛥ     Stan is the rune of the stone, the keystone and the touchstone. May this marriage form a strong center for both your lives.

ᛣ     Chalc is the rune of the chalice, the Holy Grail. Whatever quests may take you away from home, may you always remember that your thirst for love can only truly be slaked at home.

✕ Gar is the rune of the spear, wrought from the World Tree. May you never forget your place in the universe, amid the branches of the World Tree, where all things are part of the same cycle and circle.

*After each rune has been placed in the wooden bowl on the altar, the officiant lifts the evergreen branch from the bowl of water and holds it high.*

**officiant:** *(shakes the branch over the couple as he says:)* With this I wish your love forever green and whole. *(to audience)* You who have gathered here to watch these two become one! Who will speak for this man, this groom?

*Some members of the groom's family or friends speak up and say, "I will speak for him." They proceed to say good things about him, telling of his excellent qualities and why he will make a good husband.*

**officiant:** Who will speak for this woman, this bride?

*Some members of the bride's family or friends speak up and say, "I will speak for her." They proceed likewise to extol her virtues and praise her as a good wife.*

**officiant:** The union of these two will bring together two clans of kin. Will you honor their marriage, and the bridge they make between you?

**family members:** We will!

**officiant:** Many of you have good wishes for this man and this woman. Stand forth now and give them the gifts that you would wish upon them.

*Each person with a card and a rune stands forth, one at a time, and reads the card, depositing the rune into the bowl. The couple then take what vows they will (see Vows chapter), exchange rings, are declared man and wife by the officiant, kiss, and share a honeycake and the horn of mead.*

# tarot handfasting ritual
## (level 2)

*The altar is laid with a chalice, a pentacle cookie, a sword, a wand, and a deck of tarot cards. If possible, large representations of the trumps should adorn the outside of the circle. This ritual can be done two ways. Either people dressed as each trump card, or at least symbolizing them, can say each part to the couple, or the couple and the clergyperson can do the stations themselves. If you have attendants standing as trumps, they stand in a circle. The bride and groom stand in the center, bearing a large bag or basket between them, and turn, facing each trump in turn. If only the couple and the officiant are participating, they stand in a circle laid with the items listed below, and the couple and the clergyperson walk around it picking up the items and saying the lines in parentheses below.*

*The trumps are dressed as follows: The Fool dresses in fool's motley. The Magician should be a man dressed in long robes. The High Priestess is a woman dressed in long robes with a crescent moon on her brow. The Empress is a woman in a long green robe and crown, carrying a sheaf of grain. The Emperor is a man in a cloak or red or purple and a crown and scepter. The Hierophant is a man dressed in long robes with a staff. The Charioteer is a man dressed in a red tunic. Strength is a woman dressed in brown and carrying either a live cat or a stuffed lion figure. The Hermit is a man in a long dark hooded robe carrying a lantern. Fortuna is a woman dressed as a gypsy. Justice is a person in blue robe with scales and a sword. Temperance is a person wearing a robe of lavender and carrying two small bottles filled with different massage oils. The Hanged Man is a man with a noose around his neck. Death is a person in a black robe with skull makeup and a scythe. The tower is a man or woman wearing torn clothing and is blackened with ashes. The Devil is a man or woman in a beautiful but sinister harlequin-like mask, and he or she dangles several human-shaped puppets his or her hands. The Star is a woman in a white chiton carrying an eight-*

*pointed star. The Moon is a woman dressed in silver with a crescent on her forehead. The Sun is a man or woman dressed in gold with a solar crown. Judgement is a person in a white robe. The World is a person dressed in dancer's clothes.*

**the fool:** You stand now at the beginning of a great and beautiful and ridiculous journey! If we were not fools at heart, we would never love. May only good luck follow you as you set out on your new path. *(drops an acorn into the basket)* *(alternately, the officiant says this line)*

**the magician:** You will need many new skills in order to make a life together. May they come to you with ease and mastery. *(places a handful of glitter in their basket)* *(Groom:* We promise to master those skills that we need to communicate and negotiate and make our life together.*)*

**the high priestess:** You have much to learn on this new path. May you have insight into each other's souls. *(adds a glass ball to the basket)* *(Bride:* We promise never to stop learning the mysterious depths of each other's souls.*)*

**the empress:** You will need to nurture each other. You are each other's support system now, and do not take that task lightly. *(places a sprig of grain in the basket)* *(Bride:* We promise to nurture and support each other.*)*

**the emperor:** You must respect each other's intelligence and talents. Always see each other as an honored consort. *(drops a glass gem [or a real one] into the basket)* *(Groom:* We promise to respect and honor each other's intelligence and talents.*)*

**the hierophant:** As you go through life, there are many traditions and structures that you can call upon to guide you. Do not cast aside the words of the elders. *(adds a small book to their basket, filled with marital advice written by their older friends)* *(the officiant says this line)*

**the charioteer:** You must aim at your goal together and never let anything stop you from achieving it. Learn to pull together. *(places a set of leather reins into the basket)* *(Groom:* We promise to aim at our goal together, and never let anything stop us from achieving it.*)*

**strength:** You must have patience and perseverance and never break beneath each other's needs. Be strong for each other. *(places a small lion figure in the basket)* (*Bride:* We promise to have patience and perseverance, and be strong for each other.)

**the hermit:** Be willing to grow old together, for the further you walk down the path of life, the more you will learn about each other. *(places a votive candle in their basket)* (*Groom:* We promise to grow old with each other in caring and devotion.)

**fortuna:** You must weather bad luck with good luck, endure the blows of fate together, and always take circumstances into consideration. *(places a small wheel in the basket)* (*Bride:* We promise to weather bad luck with good luck, endure the blows of fate together, and always take circumstances into consideration.)

**justice:** You must be fair to each other. Learn not to jump to conclusions before explanations are given. *(places a large silver coin in the basket)* (*Groom:* We promise to be fair to each other and not to jump to conclusions before explanations are given.)

**temperance:** You must learn to balance your individual needs with that of the needs of the couple. Do not lean too far in one direction or the other. *(places the bottles in the basket)* (*Bride:* We promise to always try to balance our individual needs against those of the relationship.)

**the hanged man:** Sometimes you will need make sacrifices for each other and for your marriage. Learn to do so joyfully. *(places a knotted piece of string into the basket)* *(the officiant says this line)*

**death:** You will both change and become new people in time and you must learn to love the new person that your lover is and not just mourn the old one that is gone. *(places a small skull in the basket)* *(the officiant says this line)*

**the tower:** Sometimes terrible disasters may come upon you. You may be separated by circumstance, pain, illness, or war. Learn to ride out the fearful times. *(places a bag of ashes into the basket)* *(the officiant says this line)* the devil: You will be plagued by fears, and mistrust, and insecurity, as we all are. You must work to defeat the small voice in your head that questions each others' true love, and not give in to those fears. *(gives them a small rubber monster)* *(the officiant says this line)*

the star: No matter what happens, you must never give up hope. *(places the star in the basket)* *(Bride:* No matter what happens, we promise never to give up hope.)

the moon: You must share the deep emotions that only surface in the middle of the night. Do not hold them back to spare each other the burden; take it willingly. *(places a small crescent moon in the basket)* *(Bride:* We promise to share each others' deepest emotions, and not hold back in order to spare each other.)

the sun: You must share your joys as well as your sorrows, and never completely lose sight of childlike wonder. *(places a small gold sun into the basket)* *(Groom:* We promise to share joys as well as sorrows, and we will never completely lose sight of childlike wonder.)

judgement: You must forgive each other, for we are none of us perfect, and we all make mistakes, and forgiveness is the gift that proves the worth of humanity. *(gives them a white rose)* *(Groom:* We promise to forgive each other, for we are not perfect, and we will make mistakes.)

the world: *(dancing up to the couple)* You must be willing to see things through to the end, which will only be a new beginning. *(she drapes a scarf over all the other offerings)* *(the officiant says this line)*

*The couple comes back to the altar where the officiant stands.*

officiant: The only card that we have not spoken of is the Lovers' card, and you two stand here before me and create the image of that card. The Lovers is a card both of love and of choice. Do you choose each other as life partners?

bride: *(to the groom)* I choose you.

groom: *(to the bride)* I choose you.

**officiant:** Do you choose to be married to each other today?

**couple:** We have so chosen.

**officiant:** You truly embody the Lovers today, and you have faced the whole round of Spirit that is the road of the cards. *(picks up the wand and waves it around them)* May you be blessed by the Spirit of Action, as you begin a divine action today. *(waves the sword between them)* May you be blessed by the Spirit of Boundaries, and always remember both that you are two and that you are one. *(hands them the pentacle cookie)* May you be blessed by the Spirit of Manifestation; nourish each other!

*They break the cookie and feed bits of it to each other.*

**officiant:** *(hands them the chalice)* May you be blessed with the Spirit of the Heart. Drink deeply of your love!

*They drink from the chalice, holding it for each other.*

*Then the clergyperson holds out a deck of tarot cards, preshuffled. Both the bride and the groom cut the deck and choose a card, and then they cut it together and choose a third card. These are not shown to anyone; they are a message from the universe especially for the couple.*

*At this point it is appropriate to recite what vows the couple may choose (see Vows chapter), have an exchange of rings, and be pronounced married. The rite is then ended.*

# astrological challenge handfasting rite
## (level 2)

*This requires a whole lot of people to put on properly. It's the sort of ritual that's great if you have dozens of friends whom you don't want to offend by leaving out of the wedding party. You will need twenty-two people, plus the bride, groom, and the officiant. You can start with the astrological circle casting in the quarter casting chapter (page 40). Then the twelve people representing the signs of the zodiac form a wide circle with several feet between each one, and the ten people representing the planets stand in a tight circle in the center, facing out. The couple begins to walk around the circle, in the aisle formed by these two groups. One by one, the participants representing zodiacal signs step out and challenge them. The couple should respond in the affirmative to each challenge.*

*The signs should be costumed as follows. Aries wears red and carries a flaming torch. Taurus one wears green and carries a large stone (a crystal, or just a big rock, as you choose). Gemini wears light blue and carries two knives or swords. Cancer wears silver and/or grey and carries a large seashell. Leo one wears yellow and/or gold and carries a Fourth of July sparkler. Virgo wears brown and carries a basket of grain. Libra wears pink and/or lavender and carries burning incense or smudge. Scorpio wears dark red and carries a goblet of wine. Sagittarius wears orange and carries a large candle or lantern. Capricorn wears black and carries a wooden bowl of salt. Aquarius wears purple and carries a great fan, fanning the couple with wind. Pisces wears deep blue and carries a chalice of water.*

*The planets should be costumed as follows. Venus is female, or at least feminine, and wears pink, rose, gold, or pale green and wears and carries flowers. Mercury can be male, female, or androgynous, and wears light shades of blue, grey, yellow, or white with wings fastened to hat and shoes. Neptune can be male, female, or androgynous and should wear flowing pastels and blow bubbles from a bubble wand in bubble soap. Mars should be male, or at least masculine, and wear armor of some kind and carry a sword or spear. Uranus can be male, female, or androgynous and should dress oddly or futuristically. Pluto can be male, female, or androgynous and should wear mostly black and dark red and carry a black veil. Moon should be female, or at least feminine; she should wear white and silver, with a crescent upon her brow. Moon carries a silver bowl of milk. Jupiter should wear regal robes of purple and a crown and carry a scepter. The Sun should be male, or at least masculine. He wears gold, yellow, orange, etc. and a solar crown on his head; he carries a golden staff topped with a many-rayed sun. Saturn should wear sober, dark clothes with little ornament and carry a scythe.*

### part 1

**aries:** By the power of all beginnings, I challenge thee! Will you defend each other from attack, abuse, scorn, and mistreatment, even if it endangers your own body and spirit? *(they agree)* Aries blesses you; go forth in innocence.

**taurus:** By the power of all that is valued, I challenge thee! Will you be constant and enduring in your commitment, never allowing time to wear away your vows? *(they agree)* Taurus blesses you; go forth in riches.

**gemini:** By the power of all that is spoken, I challenge thee! Do you each consider the other your intellectual equal, whose mind should never be underestimated? *(they agree)* Gemini blesses you; go forth in clarity.

**cancer:** By the power of kin and tribe, I challenge thee! Will you aid each other in building a safe home and help each other to work through the scars and heartaches of your childhoods? *(they agree)* Cancer blesses you; go forth in sanctuary.

**leo:** By the power of all that rules, I challenge thee! Will you each help the other to gain yet more confidence, and never belittle the other's spirit? *(they agree)* Leo blesses you; go forth in assurance.

**virgo**: By the power of all that labors, I challenge thee! Will you work hard and long at the continual maintenance of your relationship and never flinch from the most difficult of struggles? *(they agree)* Virgo blesses you; go forth in purity.

**libra**: By the power of all that bonds together, I challenge thee! Do you promise to be fair to each other, listening as much as you speak, and dancing always back and forth in mutual balance? *(they agree)* Libra blesses you; go forth in equality.

**scorpio**: By the power of all that desires, I challenge thee! Do you swear to forever stoke the flames of passion between you, never letting them burn out no matter how long and dull the days? *(they agree)* Scorpio blesses you; go forth in lust for life.

**sagittarius**: By the power of all insight, I challenge thee! Do you swear to trust each other forever, never faltering in that trust, nor letting false suspicions and insecurity overwhelm it? *(they agree)* Sagittarius blesses you; go forth in great adventure.

**capricorn**: By the power of all aspiration, I challenge thee! Do you swear to help each other achieve your goals, both singly and together, neither sacrificing your individual destinies for the relationship nor putting aside the mutual goal for personal ambition? *(they agree)* Capricorn blesses you; go forth in loyalty.

**aquarius**: By the power of all inspiration, I challenge thee! Will you always remember to be open to new things and not stagnate in the doldrums of repetition? *(they agree)* Aquarius blesses you; go forth in wonder.

**pisces**: By the power of all believing, I challenge thee! Will you remember always that you are part of a destiny much greater than yourselves and not lose sight of the many in the one and the one in the many? *(they agree)* Pisces blesses you; go forth in hope for the future.

*part II*

*The zodiacal signs step into the center of the circle, standing back to back and facing outward, and the ten representatives of the planets step out to take their places, spaced around the edge. The couple then makes a second turn around the circle to be challenged by the planets in turn. Here, the order is up to couple. The planets may challenge in linear order (Sun through Pluto) or, for the more esoterically minded, they may fall into the order of the planets in the composite chart of the handfasting couple. (This requires that a composite chart be drawn up for the couple well beforehand; the order would start with the ascendant of that chart and continue around through all the houses.) The order shown is the composite chart of the couple who wrote the ritual.*

venus: Hail, you who have come together in love! By the power of love itself, I challenge thee! Promise me, now, that you will never cease to touch each other with the greatest affection, that no sorrow can drive you apart! *(they agree)* Venus blesses you, go forth in adoration!

mercury: Hail, travelers on a new path! By the power of all that moves, I challenge thee! Do you promise always to communicate with each other, and never fall for long into oceans of silence? *(they agree)* Mercury blesses you; go forth in swiftness!

neptune: Hail, travelers with starry eyes! By the power of all that dreams, I challenge thee! Do you promise never to lose the story that brought you together, and to find yourselves in still other stories? *(they agree)* Neptune blesses you; go forth in beauty!

mars: Hail, companions in arms! By the power of all warriors, I challenge thee! Do you swear to fight fairly and honorably with each other, treating each other at all times as the most honorable opponent one could have the privilege of sparring with? *(they agree)* Mars blesses you; go forth under a shield of protection.

uranus: Hail, you who venture into the unknown! By the power of all that changes, I challenge thee! Will you learn to be open to the impossible and never dismiss possibilities out of hand? *(they agree)* Uranus blesses you; go forth in laughter.

**pluto**: Hail, you who stand at the crossroads! By the power of all that transforms, I challenge thee! Will you swear that no matter how your partner shifts shape, you will follow them still and learn to love them again? *(they agree)* Pluto blesses you; go forth in regeneration!

**moon**: Hail, you who move through a rite of passage! By the power of your flesh and blood and hearts, I challenge thee! Do you swear to care for any children that might come of this union forever, and put them first until they come of age, no matter what happens between you? *(If the couple does not wish to or cannot bear children, and this is not going to be an issue, an alternate challenge is:* Do you swear to care for each other in old age, until you are too feeble or death takes you? *Either way, the couple agrees.)* The Moon blesses you; go forth in compassion.

**jupiter**: Hail, you who are lucky to be here! By the power of all good fortune, I challenge thee! Do you swear always to be generous to all those around you, and always share in whatever Fortune has given you? *(they agree)* Jupiter blesses you; go forth in opportunity.

**sun**: Hail, lovers on this joyous day! By the power of every new day, I challenge thee! Do you promise to strive always to see each other, not as you would have each other be, but as you truly are, and love whatever you see? *(they agree)* The Sun blesses you; go forth in happiness.

**saturn**: Hail to you, who are about to make such a great commitment. By the power of all endings, I challenge thee! Mine is perhaps the hardest demand of all, but you may not turn it aside. Do you swear that if your love shall end and the two of you go separate ways, you shall treat each other only with the greatest respect and kindness, no matter what pain lies in your heart? *(the couple had better agree, or Saturn will take them off at the knees)* Saturn blesses you; go forth in eternity.

*Mars and Venus step forward and offer the couple rings, and they make their vows, with the help of a clergyperson or alone (see Vows chapter to fill some in). After the kiss, the signs and planets all join hands and make an arch, which the couple passes under on their way out of the circle.*

# faery wedding
*(level 2)*

*This handfasting was created by two people who are deeply drawn to the concepts of the realm of Faery, and wanted to reflect that in their ceremony. Many of the guests were "Otherkin"—people who believe that their souls are linked somehow to those of mythical creatures.*

*Decorate the hall and tables with bare branches sprayed silver and gold with glitter paints; some glittery silk leaves can be wired onto them. The centerpieces can be silk autumn leaves and artificial harvest vegetables, also glittering silver and gold. Sheer curtains of glittering cloth should hang everywhere, and the tablecloths can be of material woven with metallic thread. It's a lot of decoration, but in candlelight, the effect is a frosted twilight world where everything has a magic layer of faery dust on it.*

*When we saw this ritual, the bride and groom wore semi-medieval outfits in subtly glittering fabrics. The groom wore a robe with wide, ragged sleeves, a jeweled velvet cape, and he carried a sword. His head was adorned with a wreath of frosted flowers. The bride wore a long trailing gown of muted heathery colors and a great headpiece made of two frosted branches coming out from her circlet like antlers. The headpiece was hung with glittering flowers and a long iridescent veil over the entire thing. The wedding party was similarly costumed, except that they were all masked, as were most of the guests. Masks were of strange animal faces, feathers, or leaves—mostly only half-masks for comfort. Faery and goblin costumes abounded. Whatever costumes you choose, they should combine nature, the Faery world, and the glittering, frosted effect of the décor.*

*Drape the altar in silver and set it with two crystal goblets and three silver-grey candles in silver holders. The original ritual used two officiants; the priest wore a mask with great curving horns and trailing grey robes, and the priestess wore silver robes and a wreath of icicles.*

*Four members of the bridal party or other honored guest should cast the quarters. The east caller wears grey and pale violet, with long flowing layers of sheer fabric blowing in every direction. The south caller wears glittering clothes of gold, orange, and red and has a staff with a butane lighter built into the top of it. The west caller wears a flowing blue and aqua robe, with glinting silver jewelry and long strings of pearls, and carries a bubbling faux-stone fountain in her hands. The north caller wears a tunic and mask entirely of leaves and carries a carved staff and a great crystal. Cast the quarters as follows.*

**the east caller:** *(spinning around several times with a sword)* Sylphs of the air, gossamer-winged sprites who fly over the land, riders of the four winds, bear us tonight into a magical world where the wheel of time stands still.

**the south caller:** *(raising the staff)* Salamanders of the blazing fire, phoenix that dies and is reborn, devas of the dancing flames, enchant our eyes with glory and delight us with inspiration.

**the west caller:** *(placing the fountain on the head table, which is situated to the west of the circle)* Mermaids of the ocean, tritons who cavort with dolphins, sirens of the storm, nereids of the seven seas and naiads of the winding rivers and streams, bring harmony to flow between us like sweet water and sweeter wine.

**the north caller:** *(thumping his staff on the ground three times and lifting his crystal high)* Gnomes and kobolds under the earth, faery folk of the woods and fields and flowers, trolls born of stone, dryads living under bark and leaf, silver thorn and golden tree, red rose and lily of white, bring us the miracle of the turning seasons.

*Officiant A steps forward.*

**officiant a:** Herne, Horned One, Lord of the Forests, Leader of the Wild Hunt, who is king of all those who meet in shadow and dance in the dawn, be with us on this night, and bless us your followers, especially _____ and _____ who stand before us tonight as an embodiment of love.

*Officiant B steps forward.*

**officiant b**: Lady of the Animals, Queen of the Trees, Silver Moon, She Who Sings the Stars, Diana who is queen of all witches and faeries and magical creatures, be with us on this night, and bless us your followers, especially _____ and _____ who ask tonight to be joined as one.

*Bride and groom turn and face each other.*

**couple**: We are the moon and the sun,

The water and the fire,

The wind and the rain,

The light and the shadow.

We are all things between us,

And we complete each other.

**groom**: My beloved, you shine like the moon in my life, casting light into my darkness. You are the white doe who drinks at the crystal pool, and you are the stars reflected in that pool and the silver fish who gleams deep within it. You are the willow tree who bends its head over the stream and the birch who strides proudly into the burned fields. You are the rose on the tree, whose scent is sweet and whose thorns are many. You are the nightingale in the garden and the wild gull on the wind. You are all these things to me, and I am in awe before you.

**bride**: My beloved, you are the light of dawn that glories across the horizon. You are the stag of seven tines who runs the hills and the hare who is fleet of foot and the wolf who pursues them both. You are the great oak in all its strength and the thorned holly with its berries like drops of blood. You are the hawk of keen sight and the kestrel who rides the storm and the lightning when it strikes the earth in triumph. You are all these things to me, and I am in awe before you.

**groom**: *(kneels and places the bride's foot upon his palm)* You are my love, and I see the Goddess through you and through you, touch and worship her. I swear upon my life to love and reverence you forever and to defend you with all my

221

strength and to always be the roots that anchor you to earth. This I swear upon all the breath in my body, and may my breath leave me before I break this oath. *(releases bride's foot)*

bride: *(kneels and places the groom's foot upon her palm)* You are my love, and I see the God through you and through you, touch and worship him. I swear upon my life to love and reverence you forever and to defend you with all my strength and to always be the roots that anchor you to earth. This I swear upon all the breath in my body, and may my breath leave me before I break this oath. *(releases groom's foot)*

*Two members of the wedding party come forward, and pour white wine into the two goblets, and, bowing, hand them to the couple, who give each other a sip.*

bride: Drink of sweetness, and I promise you years more of it to come.

groom: Drink of sweetness, and I promise you years more of it to come.

*The rings are brought out; they should be engraved with either leaves or flowering vines.*

officiant b: Long ago, our forefathers and foremothers exchanged rings of twisted grass, pulled from the body of the Earth Mother, and thus she witnessed the oaths taken by those standing on her bosom. Today these rings are metal, pulled from her veins, but they still bear the mark of her sacred leaves. Take them, and make your promises true.

bride: *(placing a ring on groom's finger)* This is a token of my love, that you may never forget it and may always take comfort from its presence.

groom: *(placing a ring on bride's finger)* This is a token of my love, that you may never forget it and may always take comfort from its presence.

officiant a: Place your hands in the symbol of eternity. *(the couple clasp hands, right to right and left to left, and he binds them with a silver cord)* Thou art bound, and art bound well; thou hast found thy magic spell, the gods thy love will ever tell.

**officiant b:** I pronounce thee wedded, and may the blessing of Herne and Diana be on thee forever, no matter where thy paths do lead. May it follow thee down hill and dale, through forest and waste land, over mountain and into valley, pursuing ever like the faithful hound, and never lose sight of thee. Be thou joyful in thy choice.

*The couple kiss. Officiants begin quoting from Shakespeare's* A Midsummer Night's Dream (*V, ii, 24–36 and 47–52*).

**officiant a:** "Through this house give glimmering light,

By the dead and drowsy fire;

Every elf and every faery sprite

Hop as light as bird from brier;

And this ditty, after me

Sing and dance it trippingly.

**officiant b:** "First, rehearse your song by rote,

To each word a warbling note,

Hand in hand, with faery grace,

Will we sing and bless this place.

**officiant a:** "Now until the break of day

Through this house each faery stray,

To the best bride-bed will we,

Which by us shall blessed be.

**officiant b:** "With the field-dew consecrate,

Every faery take his gate,

And each several chambers bless,

Through this place, create sweet peace

Ever shall in safety rest,

And the owner of it blessed."

Each member of the wedding party, and each guest if they so choose, shall take water, salt, a candle, a feather, a stick of incense, a stone, wine, or other such thing and walk through the area and especially through the couple's home if it is held there, blessing each room and banishing all poison of any kind. The bedchamber especially should be blessed, and flower petals scattered across it, and afterwards the couple solemnly led in and put to bed so that they might consummate the marriage. Ideally the wedding party will be waiting outside, singing and playing instruments, serenading them until the deed is done, and then all go feasting.

# peasant tradition handfasting
### (level 2)

The Peasant Tradition is a Neopagan tradition specifically for Pagans who live rurally, on farms and homesteads, produce at least some of their own food, and whose spirituality revolves around working their land with the seasons. The details of the individual worship vary with area, climate, crops, and situation, but this handfasting is adaptable to any area. It is designed to be performed on land belonging to and worked by the marrying couple. No officiant is involved with this ceremony; if it is to be a legal wedding, you will need someone authorized to perform weddings who is willing to sign the license without taking part in the ceremony. Alternately, some of the lines may be adapted to be said by an officiant.

The bride and groom should fashion a doll out of leaves and grasses picked on the property. The groom fashions the bride doll and vice versa. Scraps of hair and clothing are appropriate, although not necessary. If it is the right time of year, a twining vine of some sort should be cut to bind them together; if there isn't one available, use a cord.

The bride's bouquet should be built around a sheaf of grain, traditionally tied with ivy. You may add flowers around the grain, but grain should form the core. The groom wears a wreath of leaves *gathered on the property, symbolizing the Green Man; the bride may wear leaves, flowers, or grain as she chooses.*

*Lay the altar with the largest iron pot or cauldron that the couple has, filled with grain that they can afford to sacrifice to the fire (popcorn is good for this) Also place on the altar a jug of water, a large stone painted with mystical symbols, their largest kitchen knife, and many flowers and leaves, if in season. A hole should be dug nearby, and a bonfire lit within easy distance. The quarters are called by trusted friends.*

**first quarter**: High mountain of trees

Deep valley of flowers

Bedrock strong on which we stand,

Green fields of Earth

Giving forth bounty,

Bless us as we care for this land.


**second quarter**: Stream dance and river run

Lake sparkles in the sun

Ocean brings forth life from deep below

Blood running in our veins,

Sweat we give with work and pain,

Water us with joy that we may grow.


**third quarter**: Spark of flame

Forge and form

Give us light and keep us warm

Heat and sun

Lightning strike

Bring us shelter from the storm.

**fourth quarter**: Wind that whirls

Wind that cools and blows

Bring the rain

To make our fields grow

Carry wings

That beat from long ago.

*The witnesses stand in a circle around the altar. The bride and groom stand in the center, facing each other and holding their right and left hands together so their arms are crossed, making the sign of infinity.*

**bride**: The springtime of love is the time of new growth, first stories, the blush of sunrise and cherry blossom and laughter, the breeze that brings each long-awaited letter.

**groom**: The springtime of love is beginnings, and we have made a beginning here. I want to wake up with you every morning and know renewal.

**bride**: You are my Green Man of the spring, awakening me like the earth.

**groom**: You are my Earth Maiden of the spring, leading me forward with laughter.

**couple**: May we weather all storms that may come.

**bride**: The summer of love is the time of heat and power, where we learn to love and to fight, and learn the electric points between us that crackle with inspiration.

**groom**: The summer of love is when we blossom into fullness, when we try our strength against each other and are surprised and dismayed and overjoyed and proud.

**bride**: You are my Sun God of the summer, sending sparks along my body and soul.

**groom**: You are my Hearth Goddess of the summer, warming and protecting our home.

**couple:** May we always keep each other from the cold.

**bride:** The autumn of love is the time of harvesting, when we gather and reap, and breathe the scent of woodsmoke and fresh-baked bread.

**groom:** The autumn of love is the time of accounting, when we secure our resources in the storehouse, when we plan for our future together, on a bed of many-colored leaves.

**bride:** You are my Grain God of the autumn, sacrificing for our love in so many ways.

**groom:** You are my Earth Mother of the autumn, giving of yourself selflessly to feed what is growing between us.

**couple:** May we always have enough and more.

**bride:** The winter of love is the time of cold winds that send us inside, to be alone together and wait out with patience the cold time of enduring.

**groom:** The winter of love is the time of the clean white cold that helps us to see each other clearly and brings us closer together.

**bride:** You are my Hunter of the winter, doing what is necessary for our survival.

**groom:** You are my Snow Queen of the winter, covering me with a blanket of beauty.

**couple:** May hard times never drive us apart.

*Then they bind the dolls together with ivy and place them in the hole together, throwing the flowers in after them, and shoveling dirt back into the hole until it is filled.*

**couple:** Now we are joined forever in the bosom of Earth, planted like a seed to grow.

*Rings are brought out.*

**groom:** I place this ring on your finger to symbolize that we are bound to each other in the circle of life.

**bride:** I place this ring on your finger to symbolize that we are bound in the circle of family and hearth and home that we have built.

**groom:** May our love, like a tree, shoot upwards toward the sky.

**bride:** May our love, like the earth, give forth in bounty.

*They kiss. Then they pour the bucket of grain into the fire as an offering.*

**couple:** From fiery Sun to Earth and back to fire. *(they pour out the jug of water onto the earth)* From earthly well to water and back to earth again.

*The quarters are uncast silently, and the rite is over.*

# romany-inspired handfasting
### (level 2)

*This wedding ceremony is based loosely on various observed Romany weddings of some centuries ago. It looks very little like anything practiced by the modern-day Roma, so we've chosen to refer to it as Romany-inspired, to be accurate.*

*This ceremony should ideally be outside and at night, although it can be adapted to daytime in a building if necessary. If possible, you should get permission to dig a hole about three feet deep and a foot in diameter, reassuring the landowners that it will be refilled afterwards. Set up an altar with the following items on it:*

- *A large wooden bowl, preferably at least mixing bowl size. It needs to be disposable, as it will be burned after the ritual (much in the same way that one crushes a wineglass at a Jewish wedding). You won't want to keep it after this ritual anyway.*

- *A cup of water from a running stream.*

- *A small bowl of freshly dug earth.*

- *A small nip bottle of brandy.*

- *Three stones, for the* urme *or Fates.*

- *A spoon carved out of horn.*

- *A large empty glass jug with a label on it bearing the names of the couple.*

- *A funnel, put into the neck of the jug.*

- *An apple and a sharp knife.*

- *If possible, a ram's horn that is blowable, like a shofar.*

*The individual who performs the ceremony was traditionally the Rom Baro, leader of the* kumpania *(tribe or clan). We are assuming that this will probably not be a legal ceremony, so the couple should ideally pick someone who is in a leadership position over them and whom they respect.*

**rom baro:** Do you, _____, come here to take this woman to wife?

**groom:** Uva. (*Yes.*)

**rom baro:** Do you, _____, come here to take this man for a husband?

**bride:** Uva.

**rom baro:** *(hands the wooden bowl to them)* You must mingle your fluids together as one.

*The bride takes the bowl first, and her closest female friend kneels and holds it between her legs, under her skirts, and the bride urinates into the bowl. (For purposes of making this part go smoothly, we suggest that both the bride and the groom forgo underwear and drink enough water before the ceremony so as to have decently full bladders. Obviously this is not a rite for the overly shy.) Then the groom's best male friend kneels before him with the bowl, and he urinates into it. Then the bowl is carefully given back to the Rom Baro, who sets it on the altar.*

**rom baro:** *(sprinkles into the bowl the contents of the cup of earth)* To your mingled fluids we add earth from the forest trees so that your union will be blessed by the *kesali*, the spirits of the trees. *(pours the cup of water into the bowl)* We now add water from a running stream so that you will be blessed by the *nivasi*, the spirits of the water. *(pours in the brandy)* We add a libation to beseech the *urme*, the Fates, to bless you with good fortune and keep you from the grasp of Martiya, the Angel of Death, until it is your time.

*Then the bride and groom take the apple and cut it in half, vertically, to show the star of seeds inside. Rom Baro takes up the horn spoon and stirs the mixture.*

**bride:** *(to groom)* As the stars of the sky appear in the fruit of the tree, so I will be the fruit that feeds you and you will be the star that guides me.

*They feed each other the apple pieces.*

**groom:** *(to bride)* As the stars of the sky appear in the fruit of the tree, so I will be the fruit that feeds you and you will be the star that guides me.

*They feed each other the apple pieces.*

**rom baro:** You are joined together in earth and water and spirit forever; I now declare you husband and wife.

*The bride and groom exchange rings.*

**bride:** (*to groom*) You are my *artha* (*wealth*).

*They kiss. The Rom Baro blows a blast on the ram's horn. Then the mixture from the bowl is carefully poured into the jug with the funnel by wedding helpers, and carried ceremoniously to the hole in the ground. It should be set in the hole, still open, with the neck pointing upwards, and then everyone at the wedding takes turns placing a shovelfuls of dirt into the hole. The Rom Baro should go first. The next two scoops should be dumped by the bride and groom, then their parents, then other relatives, and then other guests. When the hole is filled, the rite is over and all should go and have a grand party, preferably with lots of alcohol.*

# druidic handfasting rite
## *(Level 3)*

*This rite is inspired by the Celtic lore of standing stones, and is an amalgam of Druidic tradition, although it is not derived strictly from any one of them. It was created for a couple who were both of Celtic ancestry and wanted a rite that would reflect their genetic backgrounds.*

*This ritual opens with a classic circle casting by the officiant or by four chosen friends. If possible, four large upright stones should be set at the four quarters of the circle. The altar should have a wooden bowl of grain, a jug of wine, a sword, a branch of oak, a twine of ivy, and a sprig of mistletoe. The rings are strung on the branch of oak.*

**north:** All hail the Standing Stone of the North,

Guardian of the Earth!

Whose name is the Great Bear,

Whose name is Midnight Star,

Whose name is Sleep of Winter

Whose name is Constancy.

**west:** All hail the Standing Stone of the West,

Guardian of the Waters!

Whose name is the Salmon of Knowledge,

Whose name is Edge of Twilight

Whose name is Autumn Rain

Whose name is Yielding.

**south:** All hail the Standing Stone of the South,

Guardian of the Fire!

Whose name is the Coiled Dragon,

Whose name is High Noon

Whose name is Summer Solstice,

Whose name is Fervor.

**east**: All hail the Standing Stone of the East,

Guardian of the Air!

Whose name is Hawk in Flight,

Whose name is Light of Dawn,

Whose name is Equinox,

Whose name is Wanderer.

**druid**: We come together here in this place between earth and heaven

To join these two in holy union.

In the name of Brigid, Bride of Fire;

In the name of Aengus Mac Og, Lord of Love,

In the name of Olwen[1], Lady of Flowers, *ol*-wen

In the name of Lugh[1], Sun Face *loog* or *loo*

In the name of all the ancestors whose voices speak through us,

In the name of all our people united

May we be open to the bright waves of love this day.

*The Druid pours out about a third of the grain on the ground.*

**druid**: For the ancestors that came before, for those who gave us birth, and for those who are yet to be. May they all bless this union. *(Hands the bowl to the bride, who pours out another third, repeats this line, and hands it to the groom, who does the same. Then the Druid pours out a third of the jug of water onto the ground.)* For all the spirits of this good earth that we walk upon. May they bless this union. *(Hands the jug to the bride, who repeats the line and the action, and then to the groom, who does the same.)* You who have come before us today: Do ye walk the paths of the moon and sun.

*The groom walks about the circle deosil, and the bride walks about the circle widder-shins. They come together again at the altar.*

**groom:** I walk the paths of the sun, around the wheel of the year as he rises and fades and is reborn, and his path leads me again and again to my beloved.

**bride:** I walk the paths of the moon, around the turn of each of thirteen months as she waxes and wanes and becomes new again, and her path leads me again and again to my beloved.

**druid:** All life is a circle, and it revolves between the circle of the stars above and the circle of the stones below. You are at an important part in the circles of your lives; from here on you will spiral together below those same stars and around those same stones. *(takes the oak branch)* The oak is strong, the king of trees. It provides a backbone for all that live on it. Will you take its strength into you?

**couple:** We will be strong in our faith, our wills, and our love.

**druid:** *(waves oak branch over them)* May the Dagda, Eochaid Ollathair (ay-oh-kha-eed *ohl*-la-thair), bless you both! *(takes the ivy)* The ivy twines up the oak like a lover's embrace; it does not feed from it, as its roots are in the ground, but relies on it for support. Will you be support for each other?

**couple:** We will hold each other up in time of trial.

**druid:** *(waves ivy over them)* May Danu's (*dah*-noos) blessing be on you both. *(takes the mistletoe)* The mistletoe, sacred plant, cannot survive on its own, but is fed and succored by the great oak tree. It is like your love, which cannot exist without your effort and care. Will you care for your marriage as you would a child, nurture and guard it, feed it on affection and trust and hope?

**couple:** We will nourish each other's souls.

**druid:** Take now, each of you, the gift that you would give the other, the symbol of this cycle of life. *(they take the rings off the oak branch)* Speak now your vows to each other. Repeat after me *(to bride)*:

Your freedom is my freedom.

Your chains are my chains. *(she repeats)*

Your heart is my heart. *(r)*

Your tribe is my tribe. *(r)*

Your kin is my kin. *(r)*

Your joy is my joy. *(r)*

Your sorrow is my sorrow. *(r)*

Your hopes are my hopes. *(r)*

Your hand is bound to mine. *(r)*

I hereby pledge myself to you as wife, and through you I honor all men and all gods. *(r)*

*Bride places ring on groom's finger.*

**druid:** *(to groom)* Your freedom is my freedom. *(he repeats)*

Your chains are my chains. *(r)*

Your heart is my heart. *(r)*

Your tribe is my tribe. *(r)*

Your kin is my kin. *(r)*

Your joy is my joy. *(r)*

Your sorrow is my sorrow. *(r)*

Your hopes are my hopes. *(r)*

Your hand is bound to mine. *(r)*

I hereby pledge myself to you as husband, and through you I honor all women and all goddesses. *(r)*

*Bridegroom places ring on bride's finger.*

**bride:** By Brigid's flame and the light of Arianrhod (air-ee-*an*-rod), I swear this oath.

**groom:** By Aengus Mac Og and Lugh Sun Face, I swear this oath.

**friend:** *(takes a cord and binds their hands together)* You are so promised and so bound.

*They kiss as the Druid holds mistletoe over them.*

**druid:** By the power of all the gods, and the spirits, and the ancestors who came before us, I pronounce you handfast. Blessings to you and yours!

*Quarters are closed.*

**east:** We thank you, Standing Stone of the East! Hail Bealtaine[1]! *bel*-tane

**south:** We thank you, Standing Stone of the South! Hail Lughnasadh[1]! *loo*-nah-sah

**west:** We thank you, Standing Stone of the West! Hail Samhain[1]! *sow*-en

**north:** We thank you, Standing Stone of the North! Hail Imbolg[1]! *im*-bolg

*The rite is ended.*

# celtic sacred grove handfasting
## *(level 3)*

*This is another Celtic-inspired rite, built around the symbolism of the sacred grove of trees. Each specific tree in this tradition has a symbolic meaning, a letter of the Celtic Ogham alphabet, and a lunar month or calendar day associated with it. We've also given the blessings of Celtic deities to the tree that they chose.*

    *The bride and groom stand before the altar, which is laid with many leaves and flowers, a cup of wine or mead, and the rings, which should be marked with knotwork that has no end. Also on the altar should be a large bowl of water with a leafy branch in it for sprinkling. They bring forward a staff, carved with their names and made of whatever wood is special to them, and they stand before the officiant (perhaps a Druid, but perhaps not) holding the staff between them with their hands intertwined around it. A trusted friend stands by with ribbons of many colors, and ties them around the staff one at a time.*

**officiant:** Do you come here, _____to be made one with _____?

**groom:** I do, for she is the beloved of my heart.

**officiant:** Do you come here, _____, to be made one with _____?

**bride:** I do, for he is the beloved of my heart.

**officiant:** A marriage is not something that comes into being all at once; it grows slowly, and sometimes must be built and tended with care. A marriage is very like unto a sacred grove, with every tree in a different stage of growth and with a different purpose. We call now upon the powers of the sacred grove to bless you in your union. First we call upon Danu (*dah*-noo), mother of many! The first tree of the grove is the birch, pure as snow.

**bride:** Danu, bless us in this new beginning. *(an ivory ribbon is tied to the staff)*

**officiant:** We call upon Brigid, Lady of the Flame! The second tree of the grove is the rowan, tree of protection for the hearth and home.

**bride:** Brigid, bless our hearth with eternal warmth. *(an orange-red ribbon is tied to the staff)*

**officiant:** We call upon Lyr *(leer)*, Lord of the Sea! The third tree of the grove is the ash, which understands the ebb and flow of all the waters of the world.

**groom:** Lyr, aid us in flowing easily with each other. *(a translucent, iridescent ribbon is tied to the staff)*

**officiant:** We call upon Bran *(brahn)*, Singing Head of Wisdom. The fourth tree of the grove is the alder, which knows the secrets of fire and heat.

**groom:** Bran, give us the wisdom of truth, which burns like fire. *(a crimson ribbon is tied to the staff)*

**officiant:** We call upon Olwen *(ohl-wen)*, Lady of Flowers! The fifth tree of the grove is the hawthorn, the tree of love and the heart, with all its thorns and glories.

**bride:** Olwen, let our love be deep enough to survive every thorn. *(a deep purple ribbon is tied to the staff)*

**officiant:** We call upon Arianrhod *(ar-ee-an-rod)*, Lady of the Moon! The sixth tree of the grove is the willow, tree of enchantment and intuition.

**bride:** Arianrhod, teach us to sense what is in each other's hearts at every moment. *(a yellow ribbon is tied to the staff)*

**officiant:** We call upon the Dagda *(dahg-da)*, great king of ultimate strength! The seventh tree of the grove is the oak, tall and enduring against the bitterest winds.

**groom:** Dagda, give us strength to stand together against the world. *(a black ribbon is tied to the staff)*

**officiant:** We call upon Cuchulain (koo-*khull*-lin), greatest of warriors! The eighth tree of the grove is the holly, with leaves that stab and berries like drops of blood.

**groom:** Cuchulain, arm us with vigor and let no one come between us. *(an iron-grey ribbon is tied to the staff)*

**officiant:** We call upon Taliesin (tal-ee-*es*-sin), bard of the magical speech! The ninth tree is the hazel, whose nuts grant wisdom of the tongue.

**bride:** Taliesin, help us remember to speak our love often. *(a dark brown ribbon is tied to the staff)*

**officiant:** We call upon Lugh (*loo* or *loog*) Sun-Face, brightest of the gods. The tenth tree of the grove is the grapevine that loosens tongues and brings joy.

**groom:** Lugh, bring us laughter in the midst of grey skies. *(a blue-violet ribbon is tied to the staff)*

**officiant:** We call upon Goibniu (go-*eeb*-nee-oo), brewer of the ale of immortality! The eleventh tree of the grove is the ivy, which twines upward in the sacred spiral.

**groom:** Goibniu, let us dance together in the spiral of life. *(a sky-blue ribbon is tied to the staff)*

**officiant:** We call upon the Morrigan (*morr*-ig-gan), dread crow of the battlefield. The twelfth tree of the grove is the reed, which sings a haunting song in the wind.

**bride:** Morrigan, aid us in overcoming our fears. *(a blue-green ribbon is tied to the staff)*

**officiant:** We call upon Cerridwen (*kair*-id-wen), keeper of the magical cauldron! The thirteenth tree of the grove is the elder, tree of fate and destiny.

**bride:** Cerridwen, guide our feet on the path that is destined for us. *(a russet ribbon is tied to the staff)*

**officiant:** We call upon Boann (bo-*ahn)*, gentle white cow! The fourteenth tree of the grove is the silver fir, who shelters the shepherd under its boughs.

**bride:** Boann, help us to be gentle with each other. *(a black-and-white patterned ribbon is tied to the staff)*

**officiant:** We call upon Nemetona (neh-meh-*to*-nah), goddess of the sacred grove! The fifteenth tree of the grove is the aspen, which knows the promise of rebirth.

**bride:** Nemetona, give us always hope for the future. *(a scarlet ribbon is tied to the staff)*

**officiant.** We call upon Arawn (ah-*rawn*), Lord of the Underworld! The sixteenth tree of the grove is the yew, the tree of death and sorrow.

**groom:** Arawn, let our love continue even unto death. *(a pure white ribbon is tied to the staff)*

**officiant:** We call upon Mabon (*may*-bon), god of youth and beauty! The seventeenth tree of the grove is the Furze, which gives honey for the buzzing bees.

**groom:** Mabon, may we always see the beauty in each other. *(a tan ribbon is tied to the staff)*

**officiant:** We call upon Nuada (noo-*wah*-dah) of the Silver Hand! The eighteenth tree of the grove is the heather, which gives perfume to the summer air.

**groom:** Nuada, teach us when to step back and step down. *(a golden ribbon is tied to the staff)*

**officiant:** We call upon Rhiannon (ree-*ahn*-on), goddess of horses! The nineteenth tree of the grove is the apple, which nourishes us and bears the secret star at its heart.

**bride:** Rhiannon, let us move ever forward on a joyous path. *(a yellow-green ribbon is tied to the staff)*

**officiant:** We call upon Scatha (*skah*-tha), teacher of battle! The twentieth tree of the grove is the blackthorn, in the hedges that separate one man's land from another.

**bride:** Scatha, teach us to fight fairly with each other. *(a dark blue ribbon is tied to the staff)*

**officiant:** We call upon Aedh (*ayth, with a hard "th"*), sacred bonfire of the darkest day! The twenty-first tree of the grove is the honeysuckle, which brings the butterflies to feed on its nectar.

**groom:** Aedh, give us sweetness in everyday life. *(a pale yellow ribbon is tied to the staff)*

**officiant:** We call upon Diancecht (dee-on-*kekht*), healer of the gods. The twenty-second tree of the grove is the Guelder rose, which heals the unhappy womb.

**bride:** Diancecht, help us to heal each other's wounds. *(a pink ribbon is tied to the staff)*

**officiant:** You are now bound together by the powers of all the gods. May your lives flourish like the grove, and all the living things of the Earth.

*The officiant then sprinkles them with the sprig dipped in water. They drink from the cup together, exchange their rings, and are proclaimed married in the name of the gods. The rite is over.*

# heathen marriage rite
### (level 3)

*We created this ritual for a couple whose spiritual practices spanned heathen (Norse reconstructionist) and Norse Pagan practices. The heathen faith is strongly oriented toward family, hearth, and tribe; and this handfasting reflects those values.*

*This rite is arranged around the blessings of Frigga, Norse/Germanic goddess of marriage, and her handmaidens. Boughs from a tree that is still green should be placed across the threshold; if it is not winter, they can be deciduous; if winter, use evergreen boughs. For luck, everyone should step over the boughs in order to enter.*

*Set the altar with a horn of mead and lots of room around it for all the items that will be presented. The groom and bride enter from opposite sides, accompanied by family and friends. Both should wear wreaths and have belts on which can be bound later items. They both carry swords or long knives at their belts. These must be easily removed later in the rite.*

*The rite also calls for a happily married woman carrying a drop spindle on which is hand-spun a quantity of yarn or thread, a happily married man, an unmarried man, an unmarried woman with many lovers (she must wear a fine necklace to symbolize Freya), a strong and powerful man, and eleven people to invoke Frigga's handmaidens. Frigga's maidens are traditionally women, but need not be; anyone can call upon a goddess.*

**officiant:** Gods and goddesses all I hail,

Aesir[1], Vanir[2], Rokkr[3], all,  ·  ay-seer / vahn-eer / row-ker

Alfs and Idises[1] and Wights observe,  ·  eed-is-es

Salute the honored ancestors;

Bless what work is wrought this day.

Clans and tribes and families all,

Be with us in frith together.

We come here on this joyful day to honor the union of _____ and _____, who wish to be married. This will be a union of souls and of heart, and of households, and also of clans. *(turns to the groom)* Do you, _____, wish to take this woman unto your heart and your hearth?

**groom:** I do.

**officiant:** Do you, _____, wish to take this man unto you heart and your hearth?

**bride:** I do.

**officiant:** Then first lay aside all that might hinder your joy.

*The groom removes his sword or knife and lays it before the bride.*

**groom:** Thus I dedicate this to you, to serve you always with honor.

*The bride removes her sword or knife and lays it before the groom.*

**bride:** Thus I too dedicate this to you, to serve you always with honor.

*They take up each other's blades and lay them before the altar.*

**happily married woman:** We call upon Frigga, Lady of Marriage, spinner and weaver of relationships, peacemaker and welcomer, Mistress of Asgard. Bind these two together as one with your magical threads of contentment. *(places the spindle on the altar)*

*Next, the eleven people come forward to invoke Frigga's eleven handmaidens.*

**fulla:** We call upon Fulla *(fool*-ah), Lady of Abundance, you who make the grain bountiful upon the Earth. Bring wealth and riches to they who stand before us today. *(places a sheaf of grain on the altar)*

**lofn:** We call upon Lofn *(loaf*-en), Lady of Reconciliation, you who intercede between warring lovers. May battles in this new household be fair and quick to be resolved. *(places a knife on the altar)*

243

**gna:** We call upon Gna (g'*nah*), bright messenger who rides to bring good news. Spread the word of this great love to the four winds, that all may know of its glory. *(places a feather on the altar)*

**gefjon:** We call upon Gefjon (*geff*-yon), who aids the unmarried. Bless this couple as they leave your tutelage to start a new life together. *(places a white stone on the altar)*

**eir:** We call upon Eir (*air*), healer and physician, minister to the many wounds. Aid these two in healing each other of whatever ills have gone before. *(places a pot of healing salve on the altar)*

**snotra:** We call upon Snotra (*snow*-tra), you who study discipline and understand that virtue comes from labor. Teach us what labor is required to build the finest marriage. *(places a short-handled hoe on the altar)*

**huldra:** We call upon Huldra (*hool*-dra), lady of the herds, whose cattle meant wealth and security. Bless they who stand before you with eternal security of storehouse and pantry. *(places a cow's horn on the altar)*

**vor:** We call upon Vor (*vor*), prophetess who can see the future. May the future be bright and joyful for these most beloved, and may they live long in years. *(places a silver ribbon on the altar)*

**hlin:** We call upon Hlin (ha-*leen*), lady of consolation who mourns all that is lost, that these two may be so for each other, and may bear up with strength should one be lost. *(places a black cloth on the altar)*

**syn:** We call upon Syn (*sin*), who is all-fair and all-just, upon whose name contracts are sworn. May these two be honest and worthy in their dealings with each other. *(places a coin upon the altar)*

**vara:** We call upon Vara (*var*-ah), taker of oaths and promises, who sees every vow. May these two keep the oaths that are spoken today and not forsake them. *(places the two wedding rings upon the altar)*

**happily married man:** We call upon Odin, husband of Frigga, All-Father of Asgard. To be a good husband is as important as to be a good wife. No matter how urgent and important are your other duties, you should never take for granted this marriage nor forget the toil and support of your beloved. Duties may come and go, but if well tended, love will last forever.

**unmarried woman:** We call upon Freya (*fray*-ah), Lady of Love. May you never run short of desire and adoration, no matter how long and weary the years. May your life be fertile in beauty and harmony, and may the walls of marriage be a safe haven and not a smothering cell. (*she lays a bouquet of flowers on the altar*)

**unmarried man:** We call upon Frey (*fray*), Lord of the Fields. May this union be fertile in love, riches, and children. (*this last can be left out if the couple cannot or do not wish to have children*)

**strong man:** We call upon Thunor (*thoo*-nor), Lord of Thunder. May you both protect each other from the cruel words of the ignorant with strength and vigor!

**officiant:** The two of you have given up your weapons; shall you now take on the loving duties that shall replace them?

**happily married woman:** (*removes a ring of keys from her belt, and holds them out to the groom*) This keeps the house in order and unlocks all secrets. Do you wish for this woman to administer to your heart, your holdings, and your hopes?

**groom:** I do. (*he takes the ring of keys and gives it to the bride*) I trust you and you alone with all that I have and own. (*she fastens the keys to her belt*)

**happily married woman:** (*to groom*) This day you gain a treasure greater than any you have ever had. Guard her well and care for her always, for she is your good fortune.

**happily married man:** *(takes a small utility knife from his belt, and holds it out to the bride)* Not a weapon but a tool, to remedy and repair. Do you wish for this man to administer to your heart, your holdings, and your hopes?

**bride:** I do. *(she takes the utility knife and gives it to the groom)* I trust you and you alone with all that I have and own. *(he fastens the knife to his belt)*

**happily married man:** This day you gain a treasure greater than any you have ever had. Protect him well and care for him always, for he is your safe haven.

**officiant:** *(takes the rings from the altar)* The vows spoken today will be heard and hallowed by Sjofn, Syn, and Vara and all the gods and mortals present. Speak them with all integrity and sincerity.

**groom:** *(takes the bride's ring and puts it on her finger)* I take thee for my wedded wife, in darkness and in light, in summer and in winter, in weakness and in strength, through all of our days in Midgard.

**bride:** *(takes the groom's ring and puts it on his finger)* I take thee for my wedded husband, in darkness and light, in summer and winter, in weakness and strength, through all of our days in Midgard.

**happily married woman:** *(retrieves her spindle from the altar and unwinds yarn or thread from it)* By the power of Frigga, Holy Spinner and Weaver, I bind thee both together as one. *(winds the yarn around their hands, breaks it, and ties it off, so that their hands are loosely bound)*

**officiant:** By all the gods and goddesses, by all alfs and idises and wights, by all the names of the ancestors, by the ever-growing World Tree, I pronounce thee husband and wife.

*They kiss.*

**officiant:** Drink to each other's health and the health of all!

*The officiant hands the horn of mead to the bride, who pours a small offering onto the ground (or, if it is inside, into a bowl to be ceremonially emptied later) and drinks. She then hands the horn to the groom, who does the same. Then the horn is passed deosil around the circle, and all drink to the couple.*

**officiant:** *(takes the final drink)* Hail to the bride and the groom!

**all repeat:** Hail to the bride and the groom!

*Ideally at this point, the couple should be escorted with all speed to their bedchamber, where they should be partially undressed and put to bed by the members of the wedding party. The bed should be sprinkled with flower petals or at least scented with oil, and the horn of mead should be left for them. The visitors should wish them well, leave the chamber and close the doors, and proceed to sing and make music outside until such time as the nuptials are well and truly celebrated, and the couple comes out of the bedroom bearing the horn and no longer bound together. Then all should retire to a great feast.*

# grecian wedding
## (level 3)

*This is an updated version of the traditional ancient Greek wedding. One of its unique parts is that it has no officiant per se. The couple is married by their family and friends and their own words. If they wish the wedding to be legal, they should find an officiant who is willing to sign the certificate but take no part in the ceremony.*

*The ceremony requires many, many candles. If it is being held in an enclosed space, we suggest that they be put in jars where people can't bump into them and knock them over. (Check the candle etiquette section of the Magical Aesthetics chapter, pages 16–18, for more pointers.) Traditionally, rows and rows of candles were used, surrounding the room. The wedding was performed in front of the hearth, in which a fire was laid. If you have a fireplace, this is the appropriate time to use it, perhaps with some incense sprinkled on the burning logs. If you aren't lucky enough to have one, an arrangement of candles or a wok with a fire laid in it may do. The hearth is unlit at the beginning of the ceremony.*

*Many small figures of perhaps a couple of inches high should stand on the altar, symbolizing the* Lares, *or household spirits.*

*Traditionally, the bride wears a chiton, which is a simple draped tunic-gown with any Greek design embroidered on it as trim, and a himation, which is a long wrap draped around her. This outfit was traditionally white (yes, the Greeks did the white wedding dress, which was quickly lost until the nineteenth century) and also traditionally worn with a veil of flaming scarlet, and saffron-yellow shoes. Her wreath can contain myrtle for Aphrodite, wheat, rye, or barley ears for Demeter, bay leaves for Apollo, sage for Zeus, rosemary for fidelity, marjoram for sweetness, red and/or white roses for passion, marigolds for longevity, mint for amorousness, and orange blossoms for Hera. If she has long hair, it should be braided into six braids, the number of love. Originally it would have been parted into six sections with a spearhead, to give her courage. The groom should wear a knee-length form of her tunic and a piece of cloth draped around* him and brooched at one shoulder, also white, and he should wear a matching wreath. Both wear belts of thick cord which can be easily untied.

This wedding ceremony starts with a procession, traditionally from the bride's home to the groom's home. The procession should be made up of the following sorts of people:

- First, a number of small children sprinkling grains for fertility.
- Second, a number of older children carrying sheaves of wheat bound in bright ribbons.
- Third, the bride's mother, escorting her daughter.
- Fourth the maid of honor, carrying a sliced quince on a plate. (According to tradition, she should not be a young maiden, but a happily married woman, so that her contentment might rub off. However, this is up to the bride in question.)
- Fifth, bridesmaids with trays of small cakes or cookies to be shared after the ceremony. Traditionally there were ten of them. The cakes are made of barley flour, sweetened with honey and sesame, and decorated with almond paste in shapes such as suns and moons.
- Sixth, several young men (or women, if you like) dressed in Greek-style armor and carrying spears as an honor guard.
- Finally, everyone else, carrying candles, which will be added to the ones already at the site, and/or sprinkling salt, so as to protect the bride from evil.

In this modern version, if the mother of the bride is not able to participate, another older female who is important to her can escort her. The same goes for the groom's mother, who is to meet them at the door bearing a torch in each hand. In ancient Greek times, it would be the door of their family home, where the groom and his parents had been waiting for some time, but now it can just as easily be the hall where they are to wed. Either way, the groom's mother would have ritually anointed the lintel of the door with fragrant oils before the procession arrives.

**groom's mother:** *(lifts her torches high)* Who comes to this hall, and dost thou bring sorrow or joy?

**bride's mother:** We bring only the greatest joy, our most beautiful jewel, to offer up in marriage to your son.

*Everyone enters, and gather in front of the hearth, placing their candles between the ones already lining the walls. (We suggest laying several shelves just for candles, high enough up that people are less likely to knock them over.)*

**groom's mother:** *(kneels before the altar and sprinkles wine on the Lares)* May you bless our children with merriment and good cheer.

**bride's mother:** *(kneels before the altar and touches them with honey)* May you bless our children with everlasting love.

**groom's father:** *(kneels before the altar and sprinkles salt on them)* May you bless our children with wealth enough to be comfortable.

**bride's father:** *(kneels before the altar and sprinkles vinegar on them)* May you bless our children with the ability to work hard and not give up.

**groom:** *(kneels before the altar)* Venerable Lares *(lahr-ays)*, bless our new household, built together out of our love, and may my beloved always remain by my side before you.

**bride:** *(kneels before the altar)* Venerable Lares, bless our new household, built together out of our love, and may my beloved always remain by my side before you.

**youngest girls:** *(come forward and sprinkle the last of their grains on the ground)* Fortuna, bless this place!

**older girls:** *(come forward and lay their wheat sheaves before the altar)* Kore *(kor-ay)*, spring maiden, bless this marriage with happiness.

**members of the procession carrying cookies:** *(come forward and lay their trays down before the altar)* Mother Demeter, bless this marriage. May you always have enough and more.

**honor guards:** *(come forward one at a time and lay down their spears)* Zeus thunderer, King of the Gods, Holy Bridegroom, bless this marriage with fame and respect.

**best man:** *(a happily married man who has waited with the groom all this time)* *(steps forward)* Do you two take each other as husband and wife, to live and love together until such time as the Fates shall part you?

*The bride and groom face each other.*

**bride:** Where you are the husband I shall be the wife; where you are the father I shall be the mother; where you hold the hall I shall hold the keys.

**groom:** Where you are the wife I shall be the husband; where you are the mother I shall be the father; you shall hold the keys to my hall.

*He takes one of the candles and the bride takes another, and they light the hearthfire together.*

**couple:** So with the fire of our hearts we light the fire of our hearth, to make our home together.

*They are then given a cup of water by an attendant, and each pours a little out on the floor.*

**couple:** So with the river of our love we quench our thirst. So we take common possession of fire and water, to care for our home together.

**maid of honor:** *(takes their hands, and places them together)* By Great Hera, queen of all the gods, Lady of Marriage, Sacred Bride, I declare you husband and wife. May Hera bless you both. *(holds out the bowl of sliced quince)* Taste the sweetness of love. *(the couple each feed each other a slice)*

**best man:** *(takes one of the cakes, holds it over the bride's head, and crumbles it so that the crumbs fall onto her)* May you harvest only goodness. Take great care of my dear friend, for so long as you are together.

**maid of honor:** *(takes one of the cakes, holds it over the groom's head, and crumbles it so that the crumbs fall onto her)* May you harvest only goodness. Take great care of my dear friend, for so long as you are together.

**bride:** *(removes her veil—her attendants may help her—and lays it before the altar)* Gracious Lady Hera, I offer this to you in token of my promise. For the veil which separates me from my beloved is torn away forever, and there is nothing that stands between us. *(lays one of the cakes on top of the veil)* I offer this fruit of the harvest to you, that you shall know that I honor and value your gift, the gift of this man that I love, who loves me also, and is the finest gift I have ever received. I am grateful, Lady Hera. Always shall I treat him with love and care.

**groom:** *(lays a cake next to hers)* I offer this fruit of the harvest to you, that you shall know that I honor and value your gift: the gift of this woman that I love, who loves me also, and is the finest gift I have ever received. I am grateful, Lady Hera. Always shall I treat her with love and care. *(unties the bride's belt)* Now I have loosened your girdle, and I will worship you with my body from now on.

**bride:** *(unties the groom's belt)* Now I have loosened your girdle, and I will worship you with my body from now on.

*They lay the belts on the veil as an offering. The couple kisses, and all cheer. All repair to the wedding feast, which should serve, among other things, a copious amount of wine.*

# raven's star's thelemic marriage rite
*(level 3)*

*This ritual was designed by Raven's Star, a Thelemic priestess. It is not so much a Pagan rite as a ceremonial magic ritual, but there is a good deal of crossover between the Neopagan and ceremonial magic groups and philosophies. For more information on the Thelemic tradition, you might contact representatives of the Ordo Templi Orientalis magical group.*

*This ritual starts with the Lesser Banishing Ritual of the Pentagram, easily found in many books on traditional ceremonial magic. The couple should be standing in the center of the circle, with the spectators standing around the perimeter. Lay the altar with a wand, a chalice, a dagger, a pentacle, and the Alchemy card from the Crowley tarot deck.*

**officiant:** This rite of marriage is to be taken seriously, and the vows you will make to each other should be made with honor and without reservation. Are you both entering this union of your own free will?

**couple:** We are.

**officiant:** *(makes a circle around the heads of the couple with the pentacle)* Blessings to thee from Lady Nuit (noo-*eet*). *(touches right shoulder of each person with the chalice)* Blessings to thee from Lady Babalon (*bab*-ah-lon). *(touches the left shoulder of each person with the dagger)* Blessings to thee from Lord Therion (*thair*-ee-on). *(touches groins with wand)* Blessings to thee from Lord Hadit (hah-*deet*).

*Next the officiant performs the Banishing Ritual of the Hexagram as rewritten by Aleister Crowley in chapter 36 of the* Book of Lies. *The exception to the standard ritual is that the bride holds the chalice in the center of the circle, and the groom holds the wand. At the point where the priest would place the wand into the chalice, the groom should do the act with the bride. They should stay in this position, holding the wand in the chalice, during the next section of the ritual.*

*The officiant should now do a reading. Suggested passages are chapters 11, 28, or 29 from Crowley's* Book of Lies *or selected passages from chapter 1 of Crowley's* Book of the Law.

**officiant:** The Alchemy card represents the alchemical marriage of fire and water, blending them together to make something new and different, bringing about the gold of the philosopher's stone in each of them. Your union, when properly attained, will be like creating a precious stone that combines the best of both of you. Alchemy is meant to transform the soul into something higher, and by choosing to marry, you are choosing to undergo a transformation that will link your souls and your bodies to join your higher purpose.

Repeat after me: I promise to love you with all the fiery force of Lord Hadit. *(bride and groom repeat in unison)* I promise to love you with all the passion of Lady Babalon *(r)*. I promise to love you with all the strength of our Lord Therion *(r)*, and surround you with my arms as Nuit surrounds us *(r)*. I promise to respect your will as we respect Lord Ra-Hoor-Khuit (rah-hoor-koo-eet) *(r)*.

*After vows are over, couple removes wand from cup and sets them down on the altar; the officiant bids them take each other's hand.*

**officiant:** The vows you have made now alchemically bind you together as one spirit and soul united of purpose and of will. In the sight of the gods and these witnesses, I declare you married.

*They kiss.*
*Close with the Lesser Banishing Ritual of the Pentagram.*

# Warrior's Wedding
## (level 3)

This ritual was designed by a couple who considered themselves warriors. Both were trained the martial arts and had once had military careers. The bride, especially, did not want to be forced into a "delicate flower" image. They wrote this ceremony to be able to celebrate their love while not denying their true selves. As it is basically a gender-neutral ritual (none of the spoken words specify gender), it can be used by couples of any gender combination. It was also designed to be held outside, as there are cannons, fireworks, arrows, etc. It must be revised to be held indoors.

The bride and groom both wear breastplate and backplate armor—in her case over a simple red silk gown, and in his case, over a simple white shirt and pants. Both wear metal shoulder armor, bracers of metal or studded leather, scarlet capes, and a sword attached to the belt on one side and a knife on the other. They carry beribboned spears in one hand and shields in the other. Wreaths of metallic leaves, like laurel wreaths for victory, adorn their heads. The shields can be painted with symbols of their lives and beliefs.

Encourage members of the wedding party to array themselves similarly, in varying colors, sorts of armor, and weapons, from spears to halberds to swords to bows and arrows to quarterstaves. The bridal couple who designed this ceremony decided to keep the armor and weapons archaic for the sake of artistic vision, forgoing firearms and camouflage, but this is an individual decision. In their case, all spears, halberds, polearms, and length weapons were decorated with colored ribbons. The officiant dressed as the high priest of a war god with red robes, bronze armor, and a great horned helmet.

Set the altar with candles, a polished stone knife, a glass dagger, incense, and a goblet of wine. Ideally, a small cannon should stand a distance away from the party, with helpers ready to set it off on command. Other helpers can be ready with small fireworks, waiting for the signal. If you intend to have these for the ritual, make absolutely sure *that the individuals tending them are skilled and competent at handling pyrotechnics and that all explosives are a safe distance from the onlookers. Children should be under supervision by their parents and unable to approach the unsafe area.*

*The ritual begins with a quarter casting, for which you will need four members of the wedding party. They should be arrayed as follows. Air is dressed in white and carries a bow and arrow. Fire is dressed in red and carries a spear or other polearm. Water is dressed in blue and carries a net and trident. Earth is dressed in green and carries a mace or club.*

256

*Two members of the wedding party enter, carrying flaming torches. Behind them come the bride and groom, and behind them the rest of the party. The two groups enter from opposite sides, and the torchbearers plant the torches just behind the altar and then step back with the rest.*

**air:** Powers of Air!

Be with us on this day of elation!

Give us clarity and focus, clear sight and clear mind!

Athena, Shieldmaiden and Strategist!

Horus, Feathered Avenger of the Desert!

Be with us now!

*(puts the arrow to the bow and shoots it, preferably at a target outside the circle and with no humans in the way)*

**fire:** Powers of Fire!

Be with us on this day of victory!

Give us the heat of life and the dance of passion!

Sekhmet[1], Lioness fierce with tooth and claw!                    *sek*-met

Mars, Fighter and Protector of Cities!

Be with us now!

*(thrusts the spear at the sky)*

**water:** Powers of Water!

Be with us on this day of happiness!

Let us be vast as the ocean, wild as the river in flood!

Ishtar, Queen of Love and Battle!

Poseidon, King of Earthquakes!

Be with us now!

*(swings the net around)*

**earth:** Powers of Earth!

Be with us on this day of dedication!

May you be solid beneath our feet, so that we shall never lose our balance!

Scatha, Teacher of the Martial Arts!

Cuchulain[1], Greatest Warrior of the King!                    koo-*khull*-in

Be with us now!

*(strikes ground with club)*

*The officiant now walks all the way around the circle with a sword, cutting the boundary. Then he or she comes back to the altar.*

**officiant:** We come here today to witness the union of these two brave souls. Do you come forth today to unite with each other?

**couple:** We do.

**officiant:** Why do you wish to do so?

**bride:** Beloved, when I first saw you, I knew that you were strong enough to be my mate, my match, my companion, a lover who would not break beneath my desires nor flinch from my intensity. I knew also that you were honorable and would respect me as I am. You are as awe-inspiring as a great city under siege. I value you as no other in the world.

**groom:** Beloved, when I first saw you, I knew that you were my mate and match in every way, a lover who would not cling but stand independently at my side. I knew also that you were stalwart and constant, able to be firm in your word.

You are as beautiful and terrible as an army poised for battle. I respect and desire you as no other in the world for the warrior that you are.

**bride**: *(removes swordbelt, lays sword at groom's feet)* My beloved, my sword and my sword arm, are at your service, to fight at your side.

**groom**: *(removes swordbelt, lays sword at bride's feet)* My beloved, my sword and my sword arm, are at your service, to fight in your honor.

**bride**: *(removes knife, lays it across sword)* My wit and cunning are at your disposal.

**groom**: *(removes knife, lays it across sword)* My cleverness and agility are laid here for your use.

**bride**: *(lays spear on the pile)* My strength will defend your back.

**groom**: *(lays spear on the pile)* My power will defend your name.

**bride**: *(lays shield over the pile)* I will be a shield for your hearth and hopes.

**groom**: *(lays shield over the pile)* I will be a shield for your heart and holdings.

*Two of the bride's attendants now aid her in quickly removing her armor, which they drop to the side. She stands now in her gown, simple belt, bodice, and cape.*

**bride**: With you, I need no armor. With you, I can be vulnerable and know I will not be betrayed. I trust you.

*Two of the groom's attendants now aid him in quickly removing his armor. He stands in his simple shirt, belt, and pants.*

**groom**: With you, I need no armor. With you, I can be vulnerable and know I will not be mocked. I trust you.

**bride**: I will be your strong right arm. *(holds out her hand)*

**groom**: I will be your strong left arm. *(takes her hand in his)*

*Another attendant comes forth and binds their hands, across the pile of weaponry, with a red cord.*

**officiant:** Repeat after me. I, _____, *(bride repeats)* take _____ to be my shield-mate and companion *(r)*, my life partner and comrade-in-arms *(r)*. I vow that we shall be separated only by our own choice or over our dead bodies *(r)*. I vow that when we fight *(r)*, I will see you as my honorable opponent and always strike fairly and with respect *(r)*. I will be your sparring partner and keep you keen and sharp *(r)*. I will never take you for granted nor belittle you *(r)*. I will shore you up in times of weakness and take pride in your strength *(r)*. I will love you will all the passion of a warrior and treat every night as if it were our last *(r)*. *(repeat vow for the groom of the couple)*

Bring forth the rings! *(an attendant brings them forth)*

**bride:** *(placing ring on groom's finger)* With this ring I claim you for my own.

**groom:** *(placing ring on bride's finger)* I accept your claim. With this ring I claim you as my own.

**bride:** I accept your claim.

**officiant:** I now pronounce you married in the eyes of all the gods and goddesses we serve.

*They kiss, and the moment that they kiss, the cannon and the first of the fireworks should go off. When all the fireworks are finished, all attendants make an arch of weapons and they exit under it. The rite is ended.*

# night's children wedding
### (level 3)

*Not everyone thinks of romance in terms of pretty flowers and bright colors. For some, a more dramatic and macabre style is preferred, and this is not necessarily incompatible with a Pagan handfasting. The gods of polytheism are many and diverse, and most have their dark sides. Darkness does not have to mean evil; it can mean that which is hidden, mysterious, awe-inspiring, perhaps a little frightening. There are none of us who don't have at least some of those feelings before getting married.*

*This wedding has a dark, gothic aesthetic; when we did this handfasting, the bride wore a gown of trailing black lace with glittering red jewels, and a black lace veil over her face. The groom wore an eighteenth-century coat of dark red brocade, a shirt the color of bleached bone with lace ruffles at wrists and chin, and a black cloak. Both had dramatic, theatrical black-and-white makeup and each wore a sword. The wedding attendants were also dressed in black and white and dark red, with various sorts of makeup, and the officiant wore a long black shroud and a chain with a skull on it. Whatever costumes you choose, they should reflect this macabre, dramatic sensibility.*

*Drape the altar and the room with black lace, and place on the altar two goblets—one of red glass filled with wine and one of silver carved with skull-faces and filled with absinthe. (A note on absinthe: Absinthe made in a nineteenth-century manner is easily procured through Internet liquor retailers, but it is both very expensive and very potent. Pernod, the original absinthe distiller, produces absinthe without the wormwood extract—the toxin that gives absinthe its legendary effects—and it is widely available and comparatively inexpensive.) Also place on the altar a red glass dish with a bunch of black grapes, white anise-flavored crescent-moon cookies, and, ideally, a coil of cord had been braided from the couple's own hair. A large knife takes pride of place, and to the side of the altar place a clean* tray with sterilized razor blades, antiseptic, and bandages, as this is a blood rite.

A side note about blood rites: Many people find the idea of sharing each other's blood to be very romantic. It harkens back to the age of the "blood bond" that let you into a tribe, and today, when blood can kill, it is a way of saying, "I trust you to be clean and safe." It can be a symbol of "body fluid monogamy," implying that the couple will now have unsafe sex only with each other. However, the actual blood-drawing isn't something that you just do casually during a public ceremony. First of all, not everyone wants to watch that sort of thing. If you are set on it, make sure that you explicitly warn everyone, preferably in the invitation, so that they can decide whether or not to come. If they want to come but don't want to watch a blood rite, have someone announce it beforehand so that they can choose to leave the room.

Second, don't do something like this in a public place. Tannin was once approached by a couple who wanted to do their handfasting in a public museum—with spectators walking by in the hall—and include a blood rite. Obviously, such a thing was totally inappropriate, and they had to be talked out of it. Leaving aside the part about the strangers goggling through the door (and perhaps fainting), you might drip some of your bodily fluid onto the floor. Do remember that these days, blood is considered hazardous waste. Blood rites should be performed only on the private property of someone who knows about it and is fine with the idea, and in a place that is easy to clean up afterwards.

Third, be extremely careful with issues of safety. Cuttings should be done by a third party, not the nervous bride and groom, and only by someone who has done such things before and is skilled and steady. There's no need to go deep. If the cutting is too shallow, it can be touched up later in a less hectic place. Sterile procedures should be observed; that big old dagger may look romantic, but a packaged pre-sterilized scalpel is safer if less exotic. Even if it's just a needle prick, get a sterile medical sticker. Have antiseptic ready to paint on *the area before and after the cutting. We poured some into a crystal dish to keep the aesthetic and used a boiled paintbrush to apply it. Bandages may look unromantic, but they're necessary. Have a few microwave-warmed towels handy to sop up excess red stuff and a discreet plastic bag to pop everything into.*

*You will need four members of the wedding party to represent the quarters. They are dressed as follows. The south caller wears a red cloak. The west caller wears a long, shimmering robe of deep blue and a circlet with blue sparkling fringe that hangs down and covers her face. The north caller wears ragged grey robes and has rolled in a pile of dried leaves just prior to the wedding so leaves are stuck all over him. He carried a carved staff and limps, leaning on the staff. The east caller wears flowing white robes. She carries a blade and a whip.*

*Guests enter into a very dimly lit room, and stand in a circle around the altar.*

**south:** *(lights nine red candles in a great candelabra one by one)* By the first flame, I kindle a light in darkness.

By the second flame, I beckon to the seeker.

By the third flame, I make the spark between two hearts.

By the fourth flame, I create the lure of fascination.

By the fifth flame, I bring love into the world.

By the sixth flame, I kindle the hearthfire of one home.

By the seventh flame, I light the way down the paths of the future.

By the eighth flame, I warm old bones in one bed.

By the ninth flame, I smile into Death's embrace together.

**west:** *(lifts the chalice of wine in one hand and the chalice of absinthe in the other)* You have come forward together in love, which is both bitter and sweet. Do you promise to take the bitter with the sweet, every year you are together?

**couple:** We do.

west: Then taste bitterness, and know that it will follow in your footsteps, even as you laugh. You will know rage and regret, and sometimes you will weep for each other. And one day, one of you will die and leave the other alone, and this too is a part of love. *(the couple drinks from the silver cup of absinthe)*

And now taste sweetness, and know that it too will follow in your footsteps, even as you weep. You will know joy in the body, heart, and soul, and this will be your solace, even when all else is bleak. Your love shall be like the ocean, ebbing and flowing with the tide, encompassing the earth and the source of all life. May you drown always in your own passion. *(the couple drinks from the wine cup)*

north: *(limping to the altar)* Hail, children who would become one! Kneel, and feel me beneath you. *(the couple kneels at his feet, with bowed heads)* When you abase yourselves, you are merely closer to me, the source of everything. I gave you the bodies that you worship each other with, and I will take them back someday and bring your love beneath the cold clay. But if your love is true, it will not die but will live on in each green shoot that springs forth from my flesh. Eat of my flesh, and taste mortality. *(takes grapes from the altar, places them into the couple's outstretched hands, and they feed them to each other)* Eat of my bones, and know the immortality of the cycle. *(gives them moon-cookies, and they feed these to each other, and then rise)*

east: *(whirls into the circle in a swirl of flowing white. First she cracks the whip, being careful not to hit anyone)* The wind hears your promises, children, and asks if your words are true. *(places her blade's point against the bride's heart and says:)* Better to fall now on my blade than to make this vow with deception in your heart.

bride: I swear that all I say here is true. I come with open hands, and nothing is hidden.

east: *(places her blade's point against the groom's heart)* Better to fall now on my blade than to make this vow with reservation in your mind.

groom: I swear that all I say here is true. I come with open hands, and nothing is hidden.

*The officiant steps forward, dressed in black. He or she holds out the altar knife over their heads and draws a pentacle in the air over each of them.*

officiant: May you have good fortune all your days. Are you ready to share your lives, your tears, your laughter, and the very blood in your veins?

couple: We are ready.

264

*The officiant has them each hold their hand out over the altar. With the large knife, she traces a pentacle in their palms but does not cut the skin. Then she puts on a latex glove, takes out a sterile razor blade, and nicks each of their hands, being careful only to cut skin and not any deeper. When there is a little blood oozing from each wound, she places their hands together so that the blood is smeared together and binds them with the cord.*

officiant: You are bound, hearts pumping the red salt ocean of your bodies together. You are sealed together in love. You will defy and embrace life and death together. You will taste joy on each other's lips and eat ecstasy from each other's bodies. You are blessed. Now repeat after me: *(couple each repeats line of vows together)*

You are my chosen mate,

And I am bound to your side as is your shadow.

You are the keeper of my heart,

And my blood runs with yours.

I will share my life and breath with you

So long as the stars roll down the heavens

So long as the wheel of time turns

So long as there is breath in my body

And even after I shall want nothing more

Than to lie in a single grave with you

And for your spirit to become one with mine.

*The bride and groom kiss. A drummer plays a long, slow heartbeat rhythm on a skin drum. While the drumming goes on, each of the four directional players step forward in turn. The east caller sings a high, clear note to dismiss the winds. The north caller thumps his staff on the ground. The west caller dumps out the wine and the absinthe as an offering. The south caller blows out the candles, one by one.*

**officiant:** The circle is open. Go forth and master the night together.

*Everyone cheers, and the rite is ended.*

# pagan handfasting vow renewal
### (level 1)

*Handfasting vows are often renewed more often than traditional wedding vows; for one thing, if one is dealing with a trial year-and-a-day marriage, there's a good chance that the couple will be doing it all over again, perhaps on an even bigger scale, a year later. However, long-term vow renewals are a different sort of situation. These are usually taken by a couple who have spent many years together, preferably more than a decade and ideally well into middle age. Vow renewals are occasionally done at the same time as the wedding of a couple's adult child. They are for the sure thing, the long haul, the tried-and-true, the proven relationship. They are a way of saying that there are no regrets, and that love still burns just as bright.*

*The couple faces each other, clasp hands in the figure-eight symbol of infinity—right hand to right hand, left to left—and speak the lines, which they may choose and swap as they see fit. If they like, their hands can be rebound again, possibly by their children, if there are any, or by close friends.*

**spouse a:** Long, long ago, I asked all the assembled gods in their glory for one precious gift.

**spouse b:** Long. Long ago, I asked all the gods in their eternity for one ultimate blessing.

**spouse a:** Something that would be as strong as the earth beneath our feet.

**spouse b:** Something that would be as gentle as a warm feather comforter on a snowy night.

**spouse a:** Something that would fit me so well that I would wear it every day.

**spouse b:** Something that would grow with me as I grew.

**spouse a:** Something that would challenge me and stretch my mind's horizons.

**spouse b:** Something that would make me a better person.

**spouse a:** Something that I could always be proud of.

**spouse b:** Something that would always believe in me.

**spouse a:** Something that would accept me the way I am.

**spouse b:** Something that would make me feel, for the first time, what it was to be truly loved.

**spouse a:** Something that would fly with me every spring,

**spouse b:** Dance with me every summer,

**spouse a:** Share my harvest every autumn,

**spouse b:** Walk with me every winter,

**spouse a:** Lie with me every night,

**spouse b:** Awake to me every morning,

**spouse a:** Share my hopes and dreams,

**spouse b:** Share my pains and sorrows,

**spouse a:** Share my youth and strength,

**spouse b:** Share my old age and wisdom,

**spouse a:** Hold my hand,

**spouse b:** And love me forever.

**spouse a:** And the gods gave me you.

**spouse b:** And the gods gave me you.

**spouse a:** You are the companion of my body and mind.

**spouse b:** You are the companion of my heart and soul.

**spouse a:** Your presence is a blessing,

**spouse b:** And is still my greatest gift.

**spouse a:** All that I have is yours,

**spouse b:** And all that I am I became with your aid.

**spouse a:** All that I promised you before, I swear again with all my heart.

**spouse b:** All that I promised you before, I swear again with all my heart.

**spouse a:** No regrets.

**spouse b:** No regrets.

*Couple kisses. The rite is over.*

*chapter 14*

# handpartings

*I*n the modern Western world, 50 percent of all marriages end in divorce. To some, this is a terrible thing, foretelling the end of civilization as we know it. To others, it's just something that happens, like plants die in the winter and hurricanes hit and earthquakes swallow houses and people die all the time of all sorts of things. It's an ending to a cycle, and sometimes a cycle ends early for some reason. If you're a Pagan clergyperson trying to help a divorcing couple who want a ritual to separate themselves, as they had a ritual to bind themselves together, it is not your job to lay on guilt, make them feel like failures, or discuss deeply the reasons for their impending split. It's not your business, and it detracts from the energy of the handparting ritual.

Handparting ceremonies, with few exceptions, are not big productions. The majority of them are done with only the couple and perhaps a clergyperson present. Unlike a wedding, it's rare to have a bunch of friends witnessing it, although it has been done. Usually, the best use for bunches of friends is to take the two individuals out separately afterwards and spend the evening together in support and indulgence, whether with videotapes of violent movies, bottles of good wine, bitch sessions, or gourmet almond-fudge ice cream.

The atmosphere of a handparting ritual should not be angry or adversarial. It can be sad, detached, distant, or regretful, but it should attempt to avoid antagonism. It's not appropriate for someone to list all the faults of their ex during a handparting. That sort of thing is more appropriate for a ritual to mourn the death of the relationship, which should be done later, after the handparting and separately.

Of course, we realize that in many cases, the overriding feeling that the parting individuals have toward one another is quite antagonistic. In this case, it is the job of the clergyperson to point out to each of them that the handparting is more than just a ritual for each other. It is also a declaration to the universe and the gods that this union is now officially dead, and to be nasty to each other during its span is as dishonorable as sniping at a funeral. Stress that the ceremony will have more impact and be more effective, both emotionally and cosmically, if both parties remain well behaved, at least until they can get it over with and get away from each other.

Sometimes the acrimony between two people is so intense that they will not both be able to be in each other's presence for a handparting. This is especially true in those cases where one individual has moved far away or there are restraining orders involved. Perhaps one individual feels a need for the ritual, and the other doesn't care. In light of this possibility, we have provided guidelines as well as complete handparting rituals for both two-party and one-party situations.

## guidelines for couple handpartings

The soon-to-be-handparted couple needs to make one final decision as a couple before they go their separate ways. Both parties should agree on a symbol of their marriage or union that they are willing to destroy. They might use something from their wedding ceremony, such as the bride's bouquet, the wedding veil, the wedding floral arrangement (if it was kept), or the headwreaths (if they were kept). For a while now, it has been fashionable for Pagans who handpart and live near the ocean to fling their wedding wreath into the sea, often without consideration of components like silk and plastic flowers, floral tape, or wire. This is pollution and unfriendly to the Sea Mother. Unless your wreath is 100 percent organic, biodegradable material, don't throw it into a natural body of water or bury it in the earth. Burning it isn't recommended either, as artificial materials can create fumes.

If it is partly organic and partly artificial materials, they can pick it apart, burning or burying the organic bits and disposing of the rest in the trash. Please remember that glues and shellacs on organic materials make them only fit for the trash can. It may seem odd to do this, but it can actually be a symbolic mirror of what is going on in the lives of the couple at the moment. Divorcing partners are likely to be in the process of sorting out their belongings, priorities, and feelings; the picking-apart and slow undoing of what took so long to create can actually be an appropriate pre-handparting activity for both individuals.

If the couple's chosen items are photos, the safest thing is to snip them into tiny pieces and trash them. They can burn them—we've helped friends do that for a handparting—but they should do it in an extremely well-ventilated area (in fact, preferably outside) in a non-flammable metal bowl, tray, or bucket, and stand back from the fumes while they are burning. Rather then destroying the photos utterly, they might just snip their images apart and throw or give away the halves. Love letters, of course, burn easily, as does bad romantic poetry.

The couple should also choose two cords apiece, four in all. They can be yarn, string, ribbon, silk cord, whatever they prefer. Each partner should choose cords separately. One should be in a color that symbolized the best thing in the relationship—for example, red for passion, green for growth, yellow for fun, pink for romance, or blue for an intellectual bond. The other cord should be in a color that symbolized the hardest thing in the marriage—for example, red for anger, green for jealousy or money troubles, purple for class issues, icy blue for coldness and distance. In the end, the color should be symbolic to the individual involved; it doesn't have to match up with any traditional color correspondences. One woman we know chose sickly green to symbolize "the queasy feeling in the pit of my stomach whenever I would think about his infidelities." Another man chose a muddy grey to symbolize "the dishonesty and lack of clear communication that clouded every exchange." Another chose a bright, multicolored, but badly frayed ribbon to represent his former partner's mental illness.

The officiant will also have two cords, one white to symbolize marriage, and one black for endings. The cords should be the same length, all six of them. It's better to make them longer than shorter, as the couple may not want to stand all that close to each other, and the officiant will want room to do the cutting. If the couple prefers to stand one on each side of a room, just make the cords long enough. The couple should give their cords to the officiant beforehand, and she will twist or braid them all together. It doesn't have to be fancy, as long as they are all laid in one bundle that won't fall apart.

If there is a handfasting cord from the actual wedding, the couple can use it instead (as long as they can still slip their hands into it without untying knots), or they can tie it around the middle of the handparting cord in such as way that the officiant will be able to cut through it as well as through the longer bundle. Although a few couples preferred to use their original wedding cord, many didn't have one or preferred to make a new one symbolizing both the positive and the negative qualities of the marriage. It is important for the officiant to encourage them to think of something positive. Although they may not be able to see it now, they did marry this person for a reason once. It is worth it to make a concrete symbol of that reason, as they will be mourning it during the ritual.

These cords will be severed in half as part of the following ritual. How each partner disposes of their half is up to them and should be done on their own time. Some choose to burn them, some toss them in the trash. Some people keep theirs around to remind them of lessons learned that they do not wish to repeat. One woman, whose young daughter had watched her endure an abusive relationship throughout much of her childhood, gave her half to the girl when she grew old enough to date, in order that she never repeat her mother's mistake.

# handparting, both individuals present

*The ritual can take place in almost any space where a simple altar can be set up. The altar should hold their twisted or braided cords, a cup of water, a candle, some burning incense (or a fan, if people are allergic to incense), and some salt. Laid across the altar should be something that cuts—scissors, a knife, a sickle, even an axe or sword. The cutting instrument will be dictated by the strength, skill, and comfort of the officiant, and also the space in which the ritual is performed. Some officiants may like to have a large wooden block on the (hopefully sturdy) altar. They then can lay the cords across it and sever them with a dramatic chop of a sword or axe. Others may simply prefer to snip them with scissors, or cut them in midair with a small knife.*

*The couple enters and stands with the altar between them. The officiant should tie each end of the cord to one of each partner's wrists. Then the circle is cast as follows:*

**officiant:** Spirits of the east, Powers of Air, bring the winds of change to this place. We ask for your clarity and force. *(takes the incense and walks in a circle about the couple and the altar, smudging them or fanning them as the instruments require)* The winds bring hurricanes and tornadoes to batter and torment us, but they also sweep things clean, and carry us far away onto new paths of life.

Spirits of the south, Powers of Fire, be a beacon of light to we who stand now in darkness. We ask for your power of purification, which burns to the ground only to make way for new growth. *(takes the candle and circles the couple and the altar)* Fire can be the most destructive of all the elements, burning and charring everything in its path, like the force of anger and hatred. It can also be the warm coals that you carry safely against your breast to a new home, where they will kindle a new hearth and bring life again into your heart.

Spirits of the west, Powers of Water, bless with the never-ending tides that course through our bodies. *(takes the cup and circles the couple and the altar, anointing them with a drop of water)* The waters of life can drown you, drag you away and suck you down into what feels like death. But do not forget that they also quench our thirst and wash us clean. Like our feelings, and like love, we cannot live without it for long.

Spirits of the north, Powers of Earth, bring us your quality of solidity. Let our words and actions here be as heavy as stone, a bedrock upon which to build new lives. *(takes the salt and circles the couple, and then sprinkles a dab of it on each of their tongues)* The salt of the earth can be bitter and taste like the tears of sorrow that you shed, but it can also add savor to life in the future.

You who were once bound together, do you ask all the gods and powers of the universe to sever that bond, to free you from your oaths and vows?

**partner a:** I do.

**partner b:** I do.

*It is important that they answer separately, not with "we," as they are beginning separate lives where they cannot speak for each other as a couple.*

**officiant:** You have brought before the gods two things: your bond and that which your bond has created. Take now the symbol of that which your bond has created, and together destroy what was together made.

*Couple should now undo or unmake whatever item they have brought, or snip photos, or whatever. Proper space should have been made for this beforehand. They will still be bound, which is another reason for a very long cord. The officiant should encourage them to work together rather than having one do all the work.*

**partner a:** It is undone.

**partner b:** It is undone.

**officiant:** Throughout life, there will always be deaths, as death is a part of life. In the name of the Goddess of Death and her dark consort, I ask you now to bow your head and mourn the marriage at whose funeral pyre we now stand.

No matter how it ended, it began with love and hope and trust, and that is always worth mourning. With this death of one marriage, we rebirth two free people. Goddess, teach us to praise loss, death, and the passing of all things, for from this flux we know your blessings flow.

*Couple should bow their heads and make some attempt to mourn for what has been lost. If they wish, they can list the things that they will miss or that they mourn the loss of, but the officiant must be careful not to let it turn into a bitching session.*

officiant: With this blade and in the name of all gods of deaths and endings, I set you free. *(cuts the cord)* Go in peace, and do not look back. So mote it be.

partner a: So mote it be.

partner b: So mote it be.

*The couple should turn away from each other, and exit without looking at each other or speaking, preferably in opposite directions. Ideally, they should not communicate for three days. If they absolutely must communicate something important during that time, intermediaries should be used. The officiant quietly opens the circle and dismisses the elements, and the rite is over.*

# guidelines for single handpartings

If at all possible, a handparting should be done with both members, even if it's uncomfortable for them to be there. However, as we've noted, sometimes there are good reasons why one person can't come. The officiant needs to discern whether the individual asking for a solo handparting actually has a partner who would like to be part of it or not. Even if the partner doesn't want to participate, they should be notified that it is going to happen. It should never be done behind the other partner's back. Two people got into this marriage; two need to participate in getting out of it, even if one only reads a postcard saying that it will happen in eight days or something to that effect.

If there is a clear and present danger that one partner will be violent toward the other during the ritual, even if it is in a public space with lots of witnesses and friends to keep things calm, the partner should still be notified. It is unnecessary to tell him or her where it will be happening, however. The officiant can offer to do a separate solo handparting for him or her as well. The presence of a restraining order will obviously prevent a two-party ritual. If the partner wishes to participate, and there is no danger of violence, mere discomfort on the part of the petitioning partner is not a good enough reason not to invite the other partner. The living, breathing presence of that partner is a powerful force that will make the handparting more effective.

There is another reason why a handparting might have to be done solo, and that is when one partner is dead. Some people who lose their spouses find that they cannot wholly commit themselves to another relationship while the ghost of the first marriage is hanging over them, and they want a symbolic severing in order to begin new lives. Alternate lines for this situation are given in the ritual below.

# handparting ritual for one person

*For a solo handparting, many of the same things apply as in couple handpartings. The positive/negative symbolic colored cords should still be cut. The officiant will provide the black and white cords, and the ritual will be done with four instead of six. The attending partner should also bring a symbol of the absent partner—a photo, a drawing, or an object that the absent partner owns. Small stuffed poppets are not inappropriate, but they should not ever be used (nor have ever been used) for negative magic against the absent partner. Afterwards, the doll should be mailed to the partner to dispose of, with an assurance from the officiant that nothing more has been done to it. If necessary, a friend of the absent partner or a neutral party may be present to take charge of it immediately afterwards.*

*One end of the cord is tied to the petitioner's wrist, while the other is tied to this partner-symbol. The officiant then goes through the quarter casting for Handparting with Both People Present, stopping after saying "The salt of the earth can be bitter and taste like the tears of sorrow that you shed, but it can also add savor to life in the future" (page 274), and continuing as follows:*

officiant: You who are bound in marriage to _____, do you ask of all the gods and all the powers of the universe to be set free of this bond and go your own way?

petitioner: I do.

officiant: You have brought before the gods two things: the bond between you and _____ that was made by oaths and vows and what that bond has created. As you once took responsibility for making those oaths and vows, you must now take responsibility for destroying what they generated.

*Petitioner destroys the marriage-object in whatever way has been planned beforehand.*

petitioner: It is undone.

**officiant:** Throughout life, there will always be deaths, as death is a part of life. In the name of the Goddess of Death and her dark consort, I ask you now to bow your head and mourn the marriage at whose funeral pyre we now stand. No matter how it ended, it began with love and hope and trust, and that is always worth mourning. With this death of one marriage, we rebirth two free people. (*or, in the case of a handparting with a deceased partner, change this line to:* "Out of the darkness of endings comes new life; out of the night comes the dawn of new beginnings.") Goddess, teach us to praise loss, death, and the passing of all things, for from this flux we know your blessings flow. Speak, and say what you will mourn, and miss, and what it sorrows you to lose!

*The petitioner should now speak and list the things that he or she loved about the partner or the marriage and that he or she will now miss.*

**officiant:** Speak, and say what lessons you have learned from this loss!

*The petitioner should list the things he or she has learned from the relationship that is now ending and how those lessons will help him or her in the future.*

*alternate section for those whose spouse is deceased*

*After* "for from this flux we know your blessings flow" *above, continue as follows:*

**officiant:** Speak now to your beloved-that-was, and know that he (*or she*) hears you. Know that he (*or she*) knows your love and your sorrow, and understand. Know that he (*or she*) wants only your happiness.

*The petitioner then speaks directly to his or her dead partner, telling the partner that his or her love once shone brightly, but now he or she must move on and return to love in the land of the living—or something to that effect.*

*ending for either version*

officiant: With this blade and in the name of all gods of death and endings, I set you free. *(cuts cord)* Go in peace, but do not let one dimming of love's light dim your eyes to its radiant glory. There will be other loves in the future, if you do not close your eyes to it. May the earth support you; may the waters cleanse you, may the flames warm you; may the winds push you along to your new destination. So mote it be. *(dismisses the elements and uncasts the circle)*

petitioner: So mote it be.

*The rite is over.*

# guidelines for handparting with children

Parents who divorce have a much harder time than non-parents because they can't just pack up and walk away, never to speak again. When there are minor children involved, the demands of co-parenting force the couple to keep communicating, hopefully in courteous ways, until the children are of legal age and their responsibilities are over. Even after the children are adults, it is in the best interests of divorced parents to be civil at occasions such as the graduations, special honors, and weddings of their own children.

# handparting ritual for couples with children

*This ceremony is meant to be done with both parents present, or not at all. This is because it is as much for the children as for the parents, and to have one parent absent will not serve the purpose of reassuring them that both parents will still love them equally, even if they have ceased to love each other. If one parent refuses, or is in prison, or is under a restraining order, or cannot participate for some reason, the other parent should do a solo handparting without the children involved.*

*Bring cords and a marriage object as in Handparting Ritual for when both individuals are present (page 273). The officiant should also bring a length of red cord; each end of this cord should be knotted around the center of the long multistrand marriage cord, with the knots about six inches apart. When the cord is cut, it will be cut between these two knots so that the ends are still joined by the red cord.*

*Partners are bound by the ends of the marriage cord, and children are asked to stand holding the loop of red cord. The officiant does the quarter casting and the challenge, and the partners reply, as in handparting with both people present, stopping after both partners have said "I do" (page 274) and continuing as follows.*

officiant: You have brought before the gods these things: Your bond, which was formed by oaths and vows; your marriage, which was formed by your bond; and your children, born of your love and welcomed into the world within that bond you created. You will never be able to forget each other, for whenever you look into their eyes, you will remember where they came from. The red cord that springs from your marriage cord is your bloodline, which will continue even after the greater cord is severed.

You must now do the hardest deed of all, compared to which cutting a bond and merely walking away is an easy thing. You must destroy what your marriage created, without harming whom it also created. You must release your love for each other without disturbing your love for them. You must separate your lives but not lose touch with each other, for you will still need to work together to bring them into adulthood. You must be not wholly apart, yet not wholly together. It will be a hard place to balance in, yet you must do it, for their sakes. Will you swear to live in this space between together and separate and try your best to find what friendship you can to keep between you, out of love for those whom you brought into this world?

**partner a:** I do so swear.

**partner b:** I do so swear.

**officiant:** Take now the symbol of what your bond has created, and together destroy what was together made.

*Couple should now undo or unmake whatever item they have brought, snip photos, or whatever. Note: If a photo is cut in half, it should be one of only the adults involved and not the children. It is a very bad omen to cut the children's images away from the parents or cut them in half. The marriage object that is destroyed should also be something between the adults only and not related to the children or the family as a whole.*

**partner a:** It is undone.

**partner b:** It is undone.

**officiant:** Throughout life, there will always be deaths, as death is a part of life. In the name of the Goddess of Death and her dark consort, I ask you now to bow your head and mourn the marriage at whose funeral pyre we now stand. No matter how it ended, it began with love and hope and trust, and that is always worth mourning. With this death of one marriage, we rebirth two free people. Goddess, teach us to praise loss, death, and the passing of all things, for from this flux we know your blessings flow.

*Couple should bow their heads and make some attempt to mourn for what has been lost. If they wish, they can list the things that they will miss or that they mourn the loss of, but the officiant must be careful not to let it turn into a bitching session. Children can also speak, asking for reassurances, and the parents should give them at this time.*

**officiant:** With this blade and in the name of all gods of deaths and endings, I set you free. *(cuts the cord between the two knots; the ends of the cord separate but are still held together by the red cord, which the children are holding)* You are free, yet still bound, until your beloved children are all of age to care for themselves. Then, should you so desire, you may fully go your own ways. So mote it be.

**partner a:** So mote it be.

**partner b:** So mote it be.

**officiant:** Go in peace, but do not let one dimming of love's light dim your eyes to its radiant glory. There will be other loves in the future, if you do not close your eyes to it. May the earth support you; may the waters cleanse you; may the flames warm you; may the winds push you along to your new destination.

*With this last line, the officiant dismisses the elements and uncasts the circle, and the rite is over. The cord should be carefully rolled up and preferably should given to a trusted third party to hold onto, as it cannot reside in two households at once.*

*chapter 15*
# a note to pagan clergy

Neopagan clergy come in many stripes. No matter what your position—high priest or priestess, archdruid, grovekeeper or templekeeper, godhi, elder, legal with the government or not—sooner or later you will be asked to perform handfasting and/or marriage ceremonies. If you're legal clergy with a 501(c)3 church, you will have the additional burden of helping a couple get into a legally binding agreement from which they can only extract themselves with huge amounts of money, time, and effort. Even if you're not legal clergy and the union is only a trial marriage for a year and a day, you are asking the gods to bless a union and assisting them in making a public commitment. It's a big responsibility.

It's a special problem when a couple comes to you and asks for a marriage ceremony, and you really don't think they ought to be getting married at all. Maybe they just met two weeks ago at a Pagan gathering and are all starry-eyed and sure that their love will last "forever," while you suspect they'll be breaking up in two months. Maybe they've been having problems with their relationship and feel that some kind of a binding commitment will give their union strength and help keep them together, and you doubt it. Maybe one is Pagan and one is non-Pagan and they haven't really discussed exactly what that implies—including what complications this may entail for their ceremony—and you really feel that they need months of counseling before they should even think about weddings. Maybe one is gay or bisexual or polyamorous and is marrying someone who isn't, either to "cure" him- or herself of it or because he or she feels that love is worth throwing away personal needs, and you can almost see the inevitable explosion coming down the road.

It's a tricky situation. On the one hand, we've seen far too many starry-eyed we'll-be-together-forever couples who didn't even make it through a month, let alone a year and a day. We've seen couples marry with secret reservations or undiscussed issues on both parts, and spend years fighting before and after a nasty divorce. We've seen couples stay together in a bad marriage for the sake of the children or the principle of the thing, spending decades in misery and giving their kids the worst possible example of what a loving relationship should be. On the other hand, we also know people who we swore would never make it a year, and they're still together after many, many years and have managed to grow, stretch, learn and compromise. It's impossible to tell, in the end, whose relationship will be successful and whose won't.

It's also important to think about your definition of "successful." Over the years, we've come to believe that a successful relationship isn't necessarily one that stays married, but that stays positive. Raven has experienced this firsthand. There are wonderful people in his life with whom he is no longer a lover, but who are friends, sometimes very close friends. One is the co-parent of Raven's daughter; another is her goddessfather. While it wasn't appropriate for Raven and this person to stay in a committed romantic relationship, they did things in a different kind of positive situation. To us, these days a "successful" relationship is one where you have a lasting positive connection to someone. Successful relationships are relationships where you count them as dearest family, where you do not hate them for not being your life partner any more, nor they you, where you are still good friends, where their presence in your life has taught you and continues to teach you useful things. An unsuccessful relationship, by contrast, is one that ends in pain, anger, and suffering, and where the people involved wouldn't be upset if the other one dropped off the planet. Keep in mind that, okay, these people are likely to break up, but what kind of exes will they be? If you do this, you'll be less judgmental about who should and should not be handfasted.

There are many ways you can choose to handle unions that you are unsure about. Some Neopagan clergy simply won't handfast anyone whose relationship they have serious doubts about. Others feel that it isn't their place to judge and will handfast anyone. Some will only handfast Pagans; others will tackle mixed marriages. Some require a period of counseling with the clergy of that particular religious group in order to make sure the couple knows what they're getting into. Some will only handfast members of their church, congregation, coven, or grove; others will take on any sincere people who call and ask. Some will do a year-and-a-day nonlegal ceremony for anyone, but require proof of a good relationship for anything legal or long-term. As a clergyperson, you should what you're comfortable with. Set what boundaries feel right for you, although for courtesy's sake you may want to keep a list of alternate clergy with different guidelines—e.g., "I don't do legal weddings for people outside my group and tradition, but Firefly Meriweather will; here's her number," or "It sounds like you want a Norse ceremony, and I'm not familiar with that, but you might want to talk to Godhi Spindelbogen in Goatwagon Kindred," and so forth.

Tannin's personal solution for when a couple asks her for a handfasting and she's uncertain about their fitness for marriage is to ask them, "Are you asking me to perform a service for you as a service provider, or are you asking for my aid as a priestess?" Most will simply admit that they want someone to perform a service, which puts her in the position of a sort of Pagan justice of the peace, and it implies that all responsibility for their fitness to marry is on them, and she is only the bureaucrat needed to sign the paperwork. If they choose this option, she'll marry them regardless, because she believes that everyone should have the legal right to make his or her own mistakes about marriage.

On the other hand, if they ask for her aid as a priestess, that puts things in a different light. She is no longer just the person who helps them have a nice ceremony and signs a paper for them; she is being required to ask for the blessing of the gods to be on them, and it's really hard (although not impossible) to do that when you have serious personal doubts about whether these people are doing the right thing. If they choose this option, she will interview them thoroughly about their relationship—how long it's gone on, what their major disagreements are, what this commitment means to them, etc.

If you intend to interview couples about their relationship before being willing to handfast them, it would be in your best interest to get some basic knowledge about marital counseling, perhaps through a few college courses. This doesn't mean that you have to be these people's marital counselor; indeed, if serious issues turn up in an interview, you should probably refer them to an actual therapist. It's just so you will know the right questions to ask, and know how to keep your own biases from getting in the way. Another option is to form a partnership with a Pagan who has counseling credentials and require that prospective couples have an interview with this person, after which a report will be given to you. Many mainstream religious churches do this kind of mandatory in-house referral, so it's not unheard of.

Another tricky issue is handfasting minors. Don't assume it'll never happen; it's better to be prepared first in case it does. Obviously, legal marriage for minors varies from state to state, and you'd better be current on your state's laws. The age range will vary, but in most states parental permission or at least notification is required. Frankly, unless you're dealing with emancipated minors, we strongly suggest that you get parental permission, and preferably involvement, regardless of your state's laws. If you are held liable for something by angry parents, it will be harder for you as a Pagan clergyperson to defend yourself in court than, say, a Catholic priest with all the lawyers of Rome behind him. If you're worried about legal ramifications, don't do it without the parents closely involved.

Nonlegal handfastings—simple commitment rituals—are a different thing. Because there's no legal liability, you should decide this based entirely on your personal intuition of the matter. Some clergy won't touch teens at all, figuring that they're just not mature enough for anything resembling a real commitment. In some cases, a "wedding" of any sort may subconsciously give teens the idea that it's now okay for them to do anything that adult married couples might do, including getting pregnant. If you must do teen handfastings, we suggest that, first, you only handfast them for a year and a day, telling them that they can renew later if they still want to; second, you include no language in the ritual that would suggest penalizing them for breaking it off early; and, finally, you include in the vows a commitment to defer their fertility and resist the urge to breed until they are of legal age and are financially, emotionally, and physically able to handle it. A sample vow for minors is included in the section on vows (page 72).

Above all, it's important to take minors seriously because they will act regardless of your approval. Raven's very first handfasting illustrates just how determined teens can be when it comes to love. "I performed my first handfasting ritual at the age of fifteen, during a party at a friend's house. I handfasted two tenth-grade would-be Pagans for a year and a day, waving glass cups of water and salt, a birthday cake candle, and a kitchen knife, all borrowed on the spur of the moment from the friend's kitchen." Raven can't remember whether they stayed together even into the next week, but the point is that Neopagan kids who want handfasting ceremonies will find someone to do it, even if it's one of their own. It's far better for minors to be able to talk to an adult who will take seriously both their (possibly transitory, but probably intense) love and the physical breeding risks involved (if they're heterosexual) and find a good compromise that satisfies them and doesn't just blow them off as "too young to understand."

Tannin has found that when she has been asked as a priest to perform a ceremony that she found unsettling, it was helpful to request a few days to consider the matter. Deep introspection, prayer, meditation, and advice of elders are helpful spiritual tools. (In Tannin's path, it is not considered breach of privacy to consult elders if no names are mentioned; if you are in moral doubt, be bold and ask permission on that one.) Sometimes divination can also add a helpful perspective.

She has also found it an effective exercise to find a quiet place, ground and center, and visualize performing the couple's vows. Pay attention to your feelings. If you have a satisfied feeling from the visualization, or even nothing at all, then it's probably all right. If you feel uneasy or sick, then perhaps you are not the officiant for the job. This is not the answer on whether or not the couple should be married; it's only about whether you're appropriate for their needs.

As we've said, it's not unethical to decline politely if you have reservations. It's also not necessary to tell them why, if you think that would create more discomfort than it would alleviate, especially if you can refer them on to other clergy. Whether the end answer to this quandary is yes or no, it is important to give the matter the thought and attention it deserves. If the couple is in too big of a hurry to allow you or themselves the time to mull the matter over thoroughly, perhaps you aren't the right person for the job after all.

# choosing your wedding date astrologically

This appendix is designed for those with at least a basic grounding in astrology, i.e., people who can recognize planets, signs, houses, aspects, know the rulers of each planet, and can read an ephemeris. If you are not that well versed in astrology and you want to pick the perfect date according to the cosmic currents, please consult a professional astrologer.

First, flip through the ephemeris and see what the planets are doing during the period where you intend to schedule your date. (The larger and more flexible the time period, the likelier you are to have a good match.) This may be limited by what days you can actually hold the wedding on; most people can only do weddings on weekends, so you may be limited to Friday nights, Saturdays, and Sundays. If you are using a computer program, you'll want to call up one chart for each schedule-appropriate day.

First, check to see if the Moon is void of course. If it is, skip that time period. (The Moon can be void of course for as little as two minutes to as long as two hours. If there is a void of course Moon for a few minutes on an otherwise perfect day, schedule the ceremony well before the void-of-course Moon, not after. The void-of-course Moon gives people bad emotional judgment, not something you want to have on the morning before your wedding. Get the vows over with well beforehand and be seriously into partying by the time it goes down.)

However, the main culprit you'll want to track is Venus, the planet of love. Look for the following placements, in order of importance:

1.  Venus with lots of trines and sextiles to other planets, especially Mars, Jupiter, the Sun, or the Moon.

2.  Venus without a lot of squares and oppositions to other planets.

3.  Venus in a sign that is well represented in the charts of one or both parties (e.g., it's their Sun, or Moon, or Venus, or rising sign, or they have a bunch of planets in that sign).

If you can find all three of these on one day that fits your schedule, great. The likelihood is, though, that you'll only be able to find one or two of them going on. You may have a number of potential days. If Venus is making an aspect to a slow-moving outer planet and it's going to be going on for some time, and you have a choice of dates within that time period, it's better to go early than late. An aspect is stronger when it's "applying," or coming up to exact, than when it's "separating," or getting further away.

Now that you've isolated Venus, look for other factors.

1.  Are there any major terrible messes of squares and oppositions going on with the other planets in the sky on that day? The severity of this problem may vary from couple to couple. Raven and Bella both have grand crosses in their chart (trine to each other) and their composite has a T-square, so the fact that their wedding date also had a T-square didn't faze them in the least. In fact, it felt familiar. But it's your own judgment; some planetary aspects are worse than others.

2. Are there planets positively aspecting (conjuncting, trining, or sextiling) major planets in the charts of the couple? Are there any planets in their seventh houses? If so, great.

3. What planet is ruling Venus? (As an example, Neptune rules Pisces, so a Venus in Pisces would be temporarily ruled by Neptune.) Is it well aspected? Is it at least not poorly aspected?

This should help narrow the field, as it were. Once you've found the day that looks right, or at least innocuous, you need to figure out the right time. Cast horoscopes for every hour of the day from about 10 A.M. (we wouldn't get married any earlier than that!) to about 9 P.M., which is about as late as you can push a wedding, unless you're doing a late-night gothic-theme wedding or something of that sort.

You want the sign of the ascendant to harmonize with Venus. Obviously, Taurus or Libra is good. Also, the ruler of any planet that Venus is in good aspect to can comfortably rule the ascendant—for example, if Venus is trine the Sun, a Leo rising would be all right. Also, anything that puts Venus on or just over the descendant (the seventh-house cusp, which rules marriage), is decent. What the ruler of the ascendant *should not* be is a sign ruled by a different planet which is enduring a major terrible mess of bad aspects.

The final thing to look for, again, is general complementarity to both charts of the people involved. Planets and signs that look like these charts are a plus; so are major configurations (like a grand trine) that are present in one or both charts.

The likelihood is that you won't be able to find the perfect day, unless you have three years to look and none of your friends mind coming to a wedding at 5 A.M. on a Wednesday. What you'll be looking for is close enough. If there are enough of these good aspects and not too many bad ones, that's good enough. In the end, the best wedding-day chart can't keep together two people who aren't really right for each other; nor can the worst possible wedding day split up two who are destined to grow old together. It's just like a little boost in the right direction, not a fate-changing binding. But if nothing else, it may help the actual wedding go off with fewer hitches and more happy hearts.

*appendix B*

# symbols of marriage and union

Every culture has some sort of marriage rite, and every culture has its own symbolism for the joining of people's hearts in a public forum. The emblems in this chapter come from a variety of civilizations and traditions, and some of them are used differently, depending on era and area. Still, you ought to be able to find something special in here . . . perhaps to put on your invitations, your wedding announcements, your decorations, your favors, or even on the costumes themselves. Couples should closely discuss any of these symbols that one of them is drawn to: Is it something that the other partner would be comfortable with, or does it mean nothing to them—or worse, makes them vaguely uncomfortable?

We suggest that when you are introduced to any new symbol that you wish to utilize for a magical purpose (including your wedding) that you do a little research before making a final decision. In our observance, many symbols that are found in New Age/occult/Pagan supply catalogs are often "sweetened up" or overgeneralized to appeal to a less specific audience. For instance, Tannin has seen many sexual fertility symbols marketed as "unity" or "true-love" talismans. We would also recommend doing research into any deity that you want to invoke for your wedding—or whose personal symbol you want to use—that you aren't intimately familiar with. For example, symbols such as Voudoun VeVes are very beautiful and mysterious, and at the time of this book's writing, they have begun to be mass marketed in cheap pewter jewelry without adequate description of their true symbolism. Like many deities around the world, these have many names to reflect their different aspects, but manufacturers will often pick the version that is easiest to reproduce, and then match it with the most appealing epithet for that deity, even if it is incorrect. In our experience, many "love" deities are also in charge of things like virility, war, prostitution, and death. It would not be a good idea to accidentally invoke the destructive aspect of such a deity by using the wrong symbol.

Some couples have used symbols that we haven't listed here because they aren't culturally linked to love or marriage, but they had great meaning to the couple in question. For example, the theme of Bella and Raven's wedding was ivy and grapevines, put everywhere. This was partially out of respect to Bella, who is a priestess of Dionysus, but in addition the twining vines symbolized interdependence to them. The link to the Green Man also had deep meaning for Raven. You may end up picking your wedding symbol out of some activity that the two of you do together, or a deity you are both attached to, or a particular fairy tale or myth that you feel reflects some quality of your relationship. Communicate, and discover!

# material items

## cup

As well as being a symbol of water (and thus emotions) and of the womb (and thus womanhood), the cup is also the venue by which two people are ceremonially made kin. When filled with wine, which is the blood of the Earth and thus a substitution for human blood, two people can drink of the same cup and become symbolically "of the same blood" and thus bound by kinship bonds. A "loving cup" is traditional in many handfasting rites; if the couple dislikes wine, fruit juice can be substituted.

## ring

Rings are the circle of infinity, as said repeatedly in chapter 8, Words of Spirit. One sort of wedding ring is shaped like a serpent with its tail in its mouth, reminiscent of the Midgard serpent Jormungand who surrounded the entire Earth. Queen Victoria received one of these as an engagement ring from Prince Albert and thus popularized the style. Another Pagan style of ring has a carved hand wrapped around one side of it. This derives from an old Norse custom of pledge-making; one would hold up a large ring of woven grass to the sky and make one's oath, and the idea was that the gods were holding the other side. The clasped hands of the claddaugh ring are another popular ring symbol; see below.

## hands

Joined hands are another classic symbol, and the favorite is the claddaugh ring with two hands clutching a heart. Any two joined hands can be seen as both a sign of friendship and/or of love. Two joined hands with a ribbon binding them is a more obvious handfasting symbol.

## knot

Knotted cord, ribbon, or rope alludes both to the handfasting cord and to the knot spell, that primally basic magic where one ties a number of knots in a string to bind events to one's will. In a very real sense, the handfasting cord ritual is a consenting knot spell, and, in some handfastings, actual knot spells are used for the bindings. In ancient Egypt, the knotted-cord hieroglyph was the belt of Isis and was considered a powerful magical symbol.

## heart

Well, yeah, of course. Usually used in conjunction with some other symbol such as hands or a love-knot, so as not to look too much like a Valentine's Day theme. Some research we have seen on this very old symbol claims that the heart may not have originally been meant to reflect the blood-pumping organ at all. According to this theory, the graceful curved shape of the top of the symbol may actually have been intended to reflect the sweep of a prized lover's backside.

## fountain

Fountains are often found on the reception tables of upscale weddings, more for the spectacle of it than for any ancient symbolism, but the fountain can symbolize overflowing love whether the unwitting brides and bridegrooms are aware of it or not. If you have a fountain decoration, you may want to include a small goddess, mermaid, or naiad figurine in order to invoke the powers of the Sea Goddess or River Goddess, who is in charge of love in many cultures.

## wreath

The wreath of flowers represents the vulva of the Goddess, which is why it crowns the Maypole. Phalluses were a common ancient wedding symbol, including a phallus-shaped staff planted in the earth—like a miniature Maypole—which the bridegroom straddled while the bride placed a wreath of flowers atop its head. Today, many female members of weddings parties wear wreaths, thus inadvertently invoking the Goddess' blessing.

## shoe

The shoe, for obvious although rather curious reasons, has long connoted female sexuality and has been associated with weddings in many places and cultures. Brides carry a penny in their shoes for luck, and shoes are dragged behind the wedding barge. Long ago, brides would hand over their shoes to their bridegrooms, or the bridegroom would tap the bride on the head with his own shoe in order to symbolize his new sexual access to her. Irish kings had a shoe thrown over their heads to indicate their marriage to the land.

## threshold

Doors in general are sometimes a marriage symbol, as marriage is a doorway into a new life, but the threshold of the door is the particular part most involved symbolically, which is why brides are carried over it into their new home. The morning of a wedding, any threshold the couple will pass through should be quietly anointed with sacred oil for good fortune.

## peacock

Sacred to Hera/Juno, goddess of marriage, peacock feathers can be incorporated into a ritual as a smudge fan, a purificatory fan, or in bouquets.

## dove

Usually associated with peace, the dove is Aphrodite's bird and thus also represents love. Dove's blood ink is a magical ink generally used for love-oriented spells; it could be used for invitations or inscribing love sigils for the ceremony.

## apple

Cut sideways, the apple reveals five seeds in a pentacle shape and symbolizes love. Couples often cut the apple like this and ate half each as a symbol of union.

## nuts

Nuts are also seeds and can be planted to grow, but they are a strong fertility symbol often found in wedding iconography. Two different kinds of nuts can be used to represent the couple in table displays.

# abstract symbols

### infinity sign

The traditional position of two couples about to be bound with the handfasting cord was to stand facing each other, with right hands and left hands clasping, their arms crossing, thus making a figure-eight with their bodies when viewed from above. This mimicked the eternity sign—the figure-eight turned on its side—and symbolized their oaths lasting for eternity.

### gyfu

The Norse/Saxon rune Gyfu, or Gebu, meaning gift, is shaped like an X. It is an appropriate symbol for a wedding—and not just for the gifts that are given but for the gift of love that the couple gives each other. It has a collateral meaning of partnership, and its symbol is a crossroads, where two paths meet. It is also, should you need such a thing, a wonderfully unobtrusive mark.

### mannaz

Another appropriate rune for a wedding is Mannaz, or Mann, the rune of humanity. Its symbol looks like two people holding hands with their arms crossed, in the infinity sign mentioned above, thus indicating the union of a couple from which all humanity springs.

### yin-yang

The Taoist yin-yang sign symbolizes the meeting of opposites. While yin and yang have a whole list of adjectives attached to them—light/dark, wet/dry, hard/soft, hot/cold, etc.—people commonly associate yin with the female and yang with the male. This is too simple, though, and we discourage it. Femaleness and maleness are much larger, more complicated categories with many subgroups within them, and there are many yang women and yin men. If a couple chooses to use this symbol, they should think long and hard about which is yin or yang, and in which way. This sign is best used by a couple openly celebrating differences rather than one focusing on affinities.

*wotan's cross*

This symbol is a circle with a cross in it. Unlike the Celtic cross, which is actually a sun symbol, the arms of Wotan's Cross do not extend past the boundary of the circle. Among other things, it symbolizes the union of male (cross) and female (circle).

*double circle*

Two circles overlapping have long been a symbol of marriage. They are echoed as the basis of the Mars-Venus joining symbol, the double Mars, and the double Venus. In genealogical charts, the overlapping double circles indicate marriage between two people.

*mars/venus, double mars, double venus*

The Mars and Venus generally symbolize a heterosexual union of male and female, while the double Mars is a union of two men and the double Venus is a union of two women.

*double curve*

Among the Nsibidi people of Africa, the double curve—composed of the common part of the two joined circles—is used to indicate a married couple.

*nsibidi love charms*

These two ideograms from Africa both refer to marital love. One is the two-triangle hexagram, similar to the Star of David but on its side, with an eight-pointed star in the center. The second is four tree roots branching out in all directions.

*eight-pointed star*

The eight-pointed star traditionally means hope in western European symbolism, but in Nordic traditions it is associated with Venus, Freya, love, and fertility. Even as a metaphor for hope, though, it is not inappropriate.

*nine-pointed star*

The enneagram, or nine-pointed star, has been used in Christian symbolism to mean the nine gifts of the spirit: love, happiness, peace, patience, loyalty, benevolence, trustworthiness, gentleness, and temperance.

*appendix C*
# flowers of love

hanks to Allyson Chaple of Ritual Fantastique Theme Weddings for this exhaustive list of appropriate flowers for wedding bouquets around the theme of love. It is important to note that flowers may have different meanings in different sourcebooks. Just as tarot cards have positive and negative meanings depending on whether they are reversed or upright, flowers may also have dark and light meanings. These meanings were altered depending on how the flowers were ordered in a bouquet. In Victorian times, these elaborate meanings were pop culture jargon, and everyone knew them.

Some flowers have also changed their meanings over the years. For instance, to the Victorians the aloe plant meant grief and bitterness; today it symbolizes healing. Of course, a flower might have a meaning that is special to you—perhaps it was your favorite late grandmother's flower, for instance—and its traditional meaning may not matter to you. In this case, go with your personal interpretation of the flower. It is as important that you carry things you love as that you carry things that have traditional meaning.

### *planetary herbs (for flower arrangements for the astrological wedding)*

**Sun:** Heliotrope

**Moon:** Iris

**Mercury:** Fir

**Venus:** Aster

**Mars:** Wormwood

**Jupiter:** Fig

**Saturn:** Monkshood (which is poisonous; don't handle with bare hands, and if it is to be carried by bridesmaids, place it in the center of a bouquet where they don't have to handle it)

### *flowers that symbolize marriage itself*

**American Linden:** Matrimony

**Ivy Geranium:** Favored by the bride

**Orange Flowers:** Bridal festivities

**Pea:** Happy marriage

**Peony:** Happy marriage and virility (in Japan)

**Safflower:** Marriage, welcome

**Stephanotis:** Weddings

### *flowers that symbolize love*

**Ambrosia:** Love returned

**Anthurium (Flamingo Flower):** The heart

**Azalea:** Love, romance

**Bugle/Ajuga:** Most loveable

**Cabbage Rose:** Ambassador of love

**Coreopsis:** Love at first sight

Forget-Me-Not: True love

Myrtle: Love

Philodendron: Loving tree

Pink Carnation: Woman's love

Purple Lilac: First love

Red Catchfly: Youthful love

Red Chrysanthemum: "I love"

Red Tulip: Declaration of love

Rose: Love in all its forms. Sacred to all the love goddesses. Red, deep pink, and yellow roses are for passion, and are sacred to Aphrodite, Venus, and Oshun respectively. White or blue-lavender roses are to honor elders and are traditionally given to grandmothers. Light pink or (especially) peach-colored roses are used to honor mothers.

Rosehips: The fruits of love

## flowers that symbolize burning passion

Columbine, red: Anxious and trembling

Chorchorus: Impatient of absence

Elder: Zealousness

Fleur de Lis: A flame, "I burn"

Iris, red: A flame, "I burn"

Iris, yellow: Flame of love

Jonquil: Desire

Larkspur: Ardent attachment

Peach blossom: "I am your captive"

Statice: Dauntless

Syrian Mallow: Consumed by love

## flowers that symbolize fidelity

Arbor Vitae: Unchanging friendship, "Live for me"

Azalea: "I will always be true"

Baby's Breath: Everlasting love

Bamboo: Loyalty, steadfastness

**Bay Leaf:** "I change but in death"

**Bleeding Heart:** Fidelity

**Bluebell:** Constancy

**Camellia:** Steadfast love, "My destiny is in your hands"

**Canterbury Bells:** Constancy

**Caraway:** Infidelity prevented

**Cedar:** Incorruptible

**Clematis:** Unchanged for eternity

**Convolvulus:** Bonds

**Dahlia:** Forever thine

**Four-Leafed Clover:** "Be mine"

**Germander:** Faithfulness

**Globe Amaranth:** Immortality, unfading love

**Green Locust Tree:** Affection beyond the grave

**Heliotrope:** Devotion, faithfulness

**Honeysuckle (Wild Woodbine):** Generous and devoted affection

**Hosta:** Devotion

**Hyacinth, blue:** Constancy

**Hydrangea:** Devotion

**Indian Jasmine:** Attachment, "I attach myself to you"

**Ivy:** Fidelity in marriage

**Lavender:** Loyalty

**Lemon Blossom:** Fidelity in love

**Plum Blossom:** Keep your promise

**Salvia, red:** Forever yours

**Shepherd's Purse:** "I offer you my all"

**Strawberry:** Future promise

**Violet, blue:** Loyalty, faithfulness, sweetness

**Virginia Creeper:** "I cling to you"

**Water Lily:** Purity of heart

**Weigelia:** "Accept a faithful heart"

**Wisteria:** "I cling to you"

## flowers for happiness

**Buds:** Promise of good things to come
**Burnet:** Joy
**Buttercup:** Childishness, cheerfulness
**Caladium:** Great joy and delight
**Calendula:** Joy
**Everlasting Pea:** Lasting pleasure
**Gardenia:** Transport of joy, ecstacy
**Hops:** Mirth
**Lesser Celandine:** Joys to come
**Mugwort:** Happiness
**Oregano:** Joy and happiness
**Parsley:** Festivity
**Saffron Crocus:** Mirth
**Sweet Cicely:** Gladness
**Sweet Pea:** Lasting pleasure

## flowers that symbolize bewitchment by the beloved

**Almond:** Lover's charm
**Apple:** Temptation
**Bergamot:** "Your wiles are irresistible"
**Catnip:** Intoxication with love
**Circaea:** Spell
**Dill:** Irresistible
**Fern:** Fascination, magic
**Lemon Verbena:** Enchantment, "You have bewitched me"
**Pink:** Fascination
**Quince:** Temptation
**Vervain:** Enchantment
**Vine:** Intoxication

*flowers for affection*

**Gilly Flower:** Bonds of affection
**Gorse:** Enduring affection
**Milkvetch:** "You comfort me"
**Pear:** Affection
**Pear Tree:** Comfort
**Viburnum:** Token of affection

*flowers for hope, peace, unity, and faith*

**Angelica:** "Your love is my guiding star"
**Bind Weed:** "Let us unite"
**Canna (Flowering Reed):** Confidence in the heavens
**Cherry Blossoms:** Spiritual beauty
**Flowering Almond:** Hope
**Garden Anemone:** Faith, belief
**Hawthorn:** Hope
**Olive:** Peace
**Passion Flower:** Faith
**Phlox:** Unanimity
**Queen Anne's Lace:** Haven

*flowers that symbolize beauty*

**Amaryllis:** Splendid beauty
**Calla:** Magnificent beauty
**Cowslip:** Winning grace
**Daylily:** Beauty
**Magnolia:** Magnificence
**Orchid:** Beauty
**Poppy, scarlet:** Fantastic extravagance
**Sweet Alyssum:** Worth beyond beauty

## *flowers that symbolize remembrance of those absent*

**Artemisia, Silver King:** Sentimental recollections

**Blue Salvia:** "I think of you"

**Fuschia:** Confiding love, "Your charms are engraven on my heart"

**Heartsease, yellow and purple (Johnny Jump Up):** Happy thoughts (known as the Valentine herb)

**Heartsease, purple:** "You occupy my thoughts"

**Lemon Balm (Melissa):** Memories, pleasant company of friends

**Pansy:** Remembrance, thoughts

**Pussy Toes:** Never-ceasing remembrance

**Rosemary:** Remembrance

**Statice, sea:** Remembrance

**Zinnia:** Thoughts of you

## *flowers that symbolize adoration and admiration*

**Fennel:** Worthy of all praise

**Heather:** Admiration

**Iris:** Compliments

**Pineapple:** "You are perfect"

**Sea Holly:** Attraction

**Sunflower:** Adoration

**Sunflower, Dwarf:** Adoration

## *flowers that symbolize innocence and other old-fashioned virtues*

**Camellia:** Innocence

**Cherry:** Sweetness of character derived from good works

**Comfrey:** Home sweet home

**Freesia:** Innocence

**Grapes:** Prosperity and plenty, domestic happiness

**Lilac, white:** Youthful innocence

**Marjoram:** Blushes

**Sage:** Domestic Virtue

**Violet, white:** Innocence, modesty, candor

*flowers that symbolize other virtues*

**American Starwort:** Cheerfulness in old age

**Anemone:** Truth, sincerity

**Angelica:** Inspiration

**Basil:** Best wishes

**Bayberry:** Good luck

**Borage:** Courage, directness, "Speak your mind"

**Broom:** Humility

**Chamomile:** Energy in adversity

**Coneflower:** Life, conviviality

**Dog Rose:** Pleasure and pain

**Elderflower:** Compassion

**Evergreen Thorn:** Solace in adversity

**Flowering Cherry:** Nobility, chivalry

**Forsythia:** Good nature

**Garden Chervil:** Sincerity

**Gladiolas:** Strengthening of character

**Gloxinia:** A proud spirit

**Hazel:** Inspiration

**Hollyhock:** Fruitfulness and fecundity

**Honesty:** Sincerity, honesty

**Iris, blue:** Messenger

**Lamb's Ears:** Gentleness, support

**Loosestrife:** Wishes granted

**Lupine:** Imagination

**Maple:** Native American symbol of success and abundance

**Pine Cone:** Fertility, life, the testes

**Pomegranate:** Fertility

**Sedum:** Tranquility

**Spanish Jasmine:** Sensuality

**Stonecrop:** Tranquility

**Tarragon:** Unselfishness

**Wisteria:** Mutual trust

**Zephyr Flower:** Expectation

## flowers that symbolize useful phrases

**Aster, double:** "I share your sentiments"

**Chestnut tree:** "Do me justice"

**Euonymous/Spindle Tree:** "Your image is engraven on my heart"

**Feverfew:** "I reciprocate your affection," "You light up my life"

**Mistletoe:** "I surmount difficulties"

**Mountain Ash:** "With me you are safe"

**Thyme, Lemon:** "My time with you is a pleasure"

**Vernal Grass:** "We may be poor, but we will always be happy"

# suggested reading

*flower books*

*Language of Flowers.* Kate Greenaway; Avenel Books, 1884.
> *A wonderful reference. The original printing is hard to come by but it has been reprinted numerous times, most recently by Dover in 1993.*

*The Language of Flowers.* Margaret Pickston; Michael Joseph Ltd., London, 1968.

*Flora's Dictionary.* Kathleen Gips; TM Publications, 1990.

*The Language of Flowers.* Edited by Gregory Aaron; Running Press, 1991.

*The Language of Herbs.* Sheila Pickles; Pavilion Books Ltd., 1996.

*The Language of Flowers.* Marthe Seguin-Fontes; Sterling Publishing Co., 2001.

*Souvenirs de Fleurs.* Louise Kellenbaum; Chronicle Books, 1998.

*Tussie-Mussies.* Geraldine Adamich-Laufer; Workman Publishing, 1993.

*Gardening with the Goddess.* Patricia Telesco; New Page Books, 2001.

*Green Witchcraft.* Anne Moura; Llewellyn, 2001.

*A Floral Grimoire.* Patricia Telesco; Citadel Press, 2001.

*The Herbal Arts.* Patricia Telesco; Citadel Press, 1998.

*The Enchanted Garden.* Clara Rush; Gramercy Books, 2000.

*A Victorian Grimoire.* Patricia Telesco; Llewellyn, 1996.

*Tree Medicine, Tree Magic.* Ellen Evert Hopman; Phoenix Publishing, 1991.

*A Druid's Herbal.* Ellen Evert Hopman; Destiny Books, 1995.

*The Victorian Flower Oracle.* Patricia Telesco; Llewellyn, 1994.

*Garden Spells: The Magic of Herbs, Trees, and Flowers.* Claire Nahmad; Grammercy, 1999.
> *An excellent further reference for language-of-flowers information.*

## wedding books

*The Wedding Source Book*, second edition. Madeline Barillo; Lowell House, 1996.

*The Bride Did What?! Etiquette for the Wedding Impaired.* Martha A. Woodham; Longstreet Press, Inc., 1995.
> *Very funny—helps when you need to maintain your sense of humor.*

*The Complete Book of Wedding Flowers.* Shirley Monckton; Cassell & Co., London, 1993.
> *Beautiful pictures & good instructions and diagrams.*

*Miss Manners On (Painfully Proper) Weddings.* Judith Martin; Crown Publishers, 1995.
> *Common sense etiquette advice, with humor.*

*How to Have an Elegant Wedding for $5000 or Less.* Joan Wilson & Beth Wilson Hickman; Prima Publishing, 1999.

*How to Have an Elegant Wedding in Six Months or Less.* Sharon Naylor; Prima Publishing, 2000.

*Bouquets: A Year of Flowers for the Bride.* Marsha Heckman; Stewart, Tabori & Chang, 2000.

*A Bride's Book of Wedding Traditions.* Arlene Hamilton Stewart; Hearst Books, 1995.

*Wylundt's Book of Incense.* Steven Smith; Weiser Press, 1996.
*Incense for all occasions!*

*The First Love Stories: from Isis and Osiris to Tristan and Iseult,* Diane Wolkstein; HarperCollins, 1992.
*In case you want more inspiration for lover's myths.*

## ethnic traditions

*Handfasted and Heartjoined: Rituals for Uniting a Couple's Hearts and Lives.* Lady Maeve Rhea. Citadel Press, Kensington Publishing Corp, 2001.
*Good vignettes.*

*1001 Ways to Save Money and Still Have a Dazzling Wedding.* Sharon Naylor. Contemporary Books, 2002.

*Renaissance Magazine's* various Wedding Special Editions & *Martha Stewart Wedding Magazine.*

*Timeless Traditions: A Couple's Guide to Wedding Customs Around the World.* Lisl M. Spangenberg; Universe Publications, 2001.

*Wedding Ceremonies: Ethnic Symbols, Costume, and Rituals.* Gianni and Tiziana Baldizzoni; Flammarion Press, 2002.

*Teutonic Religion: Folk Beliefs and Practices of the Northern Tradition.* Kvedulf Gundarsson; Llewellyn, 1993.
*Asatru lore and rituals, including wedding ceremonies.*

*True Hearth: A Practical Guide to Traditional Householding.* James Allen Chrisholm. Rûna-Raven Press, 1994.

*History of the Gipsies: with specimens of the Gipsy Language.* Walter Simson; Sampson, Low, Son, and Marston, Inc., London, 1865.
*Old and extremely rare, this is one of the classic "Romany Rye" books, written by non-Roma who had nothing better to do than trail about after Roma and interview them. Several excellent descriptions of*

*English Roma wedding ceremonies of the period. You have the best chance of finding this book in large research and university libraries. University libraries that do not have the actual book may have a 1991 microfiche edition.*

*Sexual Life in Ancient Rome.* Otto Kiefer; Kessinger, 2003.
*This reprint of a mid-twentieth-century classic is a good reference for Roman mating customs.*

*Skymates: The Astrology of Love, Sex, and Intimacy.* Steven and Jodie Forrest, Seven Paws Press, 2002.
*A really great book to go through with your significant other, if you're interested in astrology, and learn via simple steps how to cast comparison and composite charts, and learn about yoru astrological compatibility. For learning the basics of astrology, check out their first book* The Inner Sky: How to Make Wiser Choices for a More Fulfilling Life.

*Magick Without Tears.* Aleister Crowley; Thelema Media, 1991.
*Magick: In Theory and Practice.* Aleister Crowley; Castle Books, 1992.
*Both of these are good for additions to or further studies in Thelemic ritual.*

*The Encyclopedia of Jewish Symbols.* Ellen Frankel and Betsy Platkin Teutsch; Aronson, 1992.
*The sourcebook on the Judaic symbols used for the Judeo-Pagan rite.*

# index

# GET MORE AT LLEWELLYN.COM

Visit us online to browse hundreds of our books and decks, plus sign up to receive our e-newsletters and exclusive online offers.

- Free tarot readings • Spell-a-Day • Moon phases
- Recipes, spells, and tips • Blogs • Encyclopedia
- Author interviews, articles, and upcoming events

# GET SOCIAL WITH LLEWELLYN

## Find us on [f]   [y] @LlewellynBooks

www.Facebook.com/LlewellynBooks

# GET BOOKS AT LLEWELLYN

## LLEWELLYN ORDERING INFORMATION

**Order online:** Visit our website at www.llewellyn.com to select your books and place an order on our secure server.

**Order by phone:**
- Call toll free within the US at 1-877-NEW-WRLD (1-877-639-9753)
- We accept VISA, MasterCard, American Express, and Discover.

**Order by mail:**
Send the full price of your order (MN residents add 6.875% sales tax) in US funds plus postage and handling to: Llewellyn Worldwide, 2143 Wooddale Drive, Woodbury, MN 55125-2989

**POSTAGE AND HANDLING**

STANDARD (US):(Please allow 12 business days)
$30.00 and under, add $6.00.
$30.01 and over, FREE SHIPPING.

CANADA:
We cannot ship to Canada. Please shop your local bookstore or Amazon Canada.

INTERNATIONAL:
Customers pay the actual shipping cost to the final destination, which includes tracking information.

Visit us online for more shipping options. Prices subject to change.

## FREE CATALOG!

To order, call 1-877-NEW-WRLD ext. 8236 or visit our website

## to write to the authors